PHANTOM FAST

PHANTOM FAST
A STORY OF LOVE, WAR, AND FAITH

ROBERT & LAURA PAYNE

phantomfast2003@gmail.com

XULON PRESS

Xulon Press
2301 Lucien Way #415
Maitland, FL 32751
407.339.4217
www.xulonpress.com

© 2023 by Robert & Laura Payne

All rights reserved solely by the author. The author guarantees all contents are original and do not infringe upon the legal rights of any other person or work. No part of this book may be reproduced in any form without the permission of the author.

Due to the changing nature of the Internet, if there are any web addresses, links, or URLs included in this manuscript, these may have been altered and may no longer be accessible. The views and opinions shared in this book belong solely to the author and do not necessarily reflect those of the publisher. The publisher therefore disclaims responsibility for the views or opinions expressed within the work.

The views expressed herein are those of the author(s) and do not necessarily reflect the official policy or position of the Department of the Army, Department of Defense, or the U.S. Government.

The public release clearance of this publication by the Department of Defense does not imply the Department of Defense endorsement or factual accuracy of the material.

Cleared for open publication on May 16, 2023, by the Department of Defense – Office of Prepublication and Security Review – reference 23-SB-0082.

Unless otherwise indicated, Scripture quotations taken from the Holy Bible, New International Version (NIV). Copyright © 1973, 1978, 1984, 2011 by Biblica, Inc.™. Used by permission. All rights reserved.

Paperback ISBN-13: 978-1-66288-298-2

Ebook ISBN-13: 978-1-66288-299-9

COL Robert and Laura Payne met while he was stationed at Fort Hood, TX and she was living in Austin, TX, initially connected by their Texas A&M friends in 2000. Robert left active duty in 2003 after the Iraq War but currently serves in the US Army Reserve while managing a career in the FBI. Laura and Robert have four beautiful children and have lived all over the US. Robert and Laura have been married for 20 years and started marriage with war and this is their story. Robert was a young Army Captain assigned to the 126th Forward Surgical Team "Phantom FaST" and deployed during the 2003 Iraq invasion. Laura and Robert married on January 2, 2003, at a Justice of the Peace just months before Robert left for the war on February 1, 2003. Letters were the only way to stay connected and this is their way to share our experience with friends, family, veterans, and others.

Dedication

John 15:13 "Greater love hath no man than this, that he lay down his life for his friends"

This story is a tribute to all veterans who have served in war, understanding the service and sacrifice – for all the soldiers, marines, airmen, seaman, coasties, DoD contractors, their families, and ultimately those veterans who lost their lives in service to our great nation.

Also, I dedicate this story to my fellow 3D Infantry Division 'Rock of the Marne' warriors and all my battle buddies of the 126th Forward Surgical Team

'Phantom FaST' of the 2003 Iraq Invasion. Although time has past I will never forget the combat experience with each of you that shaped our nation.

Most importantly, this story is dedicated to my wife and soulmate, Laura, and all she has endured to love and support us since we began our marriage journey over 20 years ago. Military service is a sacrifice, and those spouses and children sacrifice with us. This story is also for our children and all our future grandchildren and great-grandchildren and so on, to know and understand that sacrifice for love and faith.

A special thank you to Xulon Press and Dr. Larry Keefauver and his team for assisting in the compilation of the book while serving as trusted advisors throughout the process of how to tell our story of love, war, and faith.

Table of Contents

Introduction: Ready for **War**?........................xiii

Chapter 1: Deployment to **War** 1

Chapter 2: **Faith** and Persecution 5

Chapter 3: Rock of the Marne 9

Chapter 4: Reality of **War** 13

Chapter 5: Separation and **War** 23

Chapter 6: Anxiety of Waiting for War 27

Chapter 7: 40 Days and 40 Nights in the Desert 33

Chapter 8: Foundation for **Love** & **Faith** 39

Chapter 9: As We Prepare for **War**..................... 49

Chapter 10: Fear of the Unknown 57

Chapter 11: Road to Exhaustion 63

Chapter 12: First Causalities of **War** 69

Chapter 13: 12 Personal Observations 77

Chapter 14: Apprehension in the Combat Zone – Locked
& Loaded 81

Chapter 15: Near Death & Near God 87

Chapter 16: BIAP–Just Helping & Surviving 93

Chapter 17: Settling into War 105

Chapter 18: Our **Love** Will Endure 119

Chapter 19: What More Is Left to Do? 129

Chapter 20: Our Purpose Driven Life 153

Chapter 21: Dealing with Uncertainty 165

Chapter 22: Transforming Our Minds 207

Chapter 23: God's Timing 217

Chapter 24: Walking the Steady and Patient Road 229

Chapter 25: Commitment, Passion, and **Love** 237

Chapter 26: What Will Our Life Look Like? 243

Chapter 27: Heading Home 249

Prologue

Robert –

The attacks on September 11, 2001, changed our lives forever. Laura and I were seriously dating, and I was in a highly deployable 1st Cavalry Infantry Unit – 2nd Battalion 7th Cavalry 'Garryowen'. Before that day we had been existing as a country and military in a sense of calm peace. After the Al Qaeda terrorist attack, the sense of peace was no more. I had no idea of what was to come but everyone serving at that time knew the war was in the future. Ironically, the largest bulk of warfare did not begin for another two years in Iraq. This book is about that story. "Phantom FaST" was the motto of our Army unit and FaST is a reference to the Forward Surgical Teams (FST) which were created after the Vietnam War era to push surgical assets as close to the combat fighting as possible. Our unit was the 126th FST and supported the 3D Infantry Division, 1st Brigade during the 2003 invasion of Iraq, known as Operation Iraqi Freedom.

This book is a compilation of all war letters between a man and a woman, so in love, as they began their marriage amidst a deployment into war. In the New International Version of the Holy Bible **Deuteronomy verse 5 states, "If a man has recently married, he must not be sent to war or have any other duty laid on him. For one year he has to be free to stay at home**

and bring happiness to the wife he has married." Clearly, this verse is not Department of Army policy since so many service members have begun their marriages amidst war, especially since 2003. Some marriages survive and some do not. War can take a toll on a person in many ways–mentally, physically, and emotionally. The spouse (and family) one comes home to has to endure that with their veteran and all too often is not a simple process.

Our story is not new or significantly different than many other war veterans who have similar letters. But it is unique to me and Laura and our journey. On our tenth anniversary, I compiled these letters in one document as a gift to Laura and later a friend suggested it should be an actual book. Several years later I spoke with a publisher and a ghost writer (Dr. Keefauver) and here we are, Phantom FaST: A Story of Love, War, and Faith. I did this so we have a legacy of our story to share with our children and all the future grandkids we may or may not meet one day. The **story** you will read in these letters speaks to **love** shared, the effects of **war**, and the **faith** needed to survive.

Introduction – Ready for War?

To My Dearest Laura,

Ecclesiastes 4:9-12 (NIV)

"Two are better than one,
because they have a good return for their labor:
If either of them falls down,
one can help the other up.
But pity anyone who falls
and has no one to help them up.
Also, if two lie down together, they will keep **war**m.
But how can one keep **war**m alone?
Though one may be overpowered,
two can defend themselves.
A cord of three strands is not quickly broken."

Love of your life, soulmate, and best friend forever,
Robert

[I clearly remember realizing our unit was getting alerted to deploy to **war**. It was after the holidays and Laura and I had driven to her home in Ft Worth, TX so I could attend a Drug Enforcement Administration (DEA) Special Agent presentation to get a job application. I had already set my sites on leaving active duty, becoming a federal agent, getting married to Laura in April 2003, and living happily ever after. After the DEA meeting, my cell phone rang and it was my Team Commander, MAJ Kirk, M.D. asking me what I was doing. I found it strange because he knew not only what I was doing but why I was doing it. He asked if I would be able to come back to Ft Hood that night for a meeting first thing in the morning with the 1st Medical Brigade Commander, COL Johnny Hightower. It was late already and driving back from Dallas, TX would be tough. He said if I was back before lunch, we would have the meeting then. I asked why but he couldn't say. I don't know why I asked because I already knew and the pit in my stomach also let me know what was about to unfold. Laura asked why we had to go back the next morning–I made up some story about why I needed to be back sooner until I knew the answer for sure. The next day COL Hightower notified me, MAJ Kirk, and SFC Smith, that we were one of the first units being alerted for deployment to Operation Iraqi Freedom in support of 3D Infantry Division from Ft. Stewart, GA. To this date, no Forward Surgical Team had ever been deployed into active combat and we would be the first.

By this point, the 126th Forward Surgical Team (FST) "Phantom FaST" of Fort Hood, TX, 1st Medical Brigade, 3rd Corps Support Command deployed as 20 team members (plus our transfers later in the deployment):

- 1 Team Commander (Lieutenant Colonel or Major) who is an Orthopedic Surgeon – MAJ Kirk, M.D., later LTC Miller, M.D.

Introduction – Ready for War?

- 3 General Surgeons (Majors) – MAJ Beverly, M.D., MAJ Vinca, M.D., MAJ Lim, M.D.

- 1 Executive Officer (1st Lieutenant…or newly promoted Captain like I was) – CPT Robert Payne

- 1 Chief Nurse (Major) – MAJ Kuhns

- 2 Intensive Care Unit Nurses (Captains) – CPT Sanders and CPT Felix, plus two later replacements–CPT Holchek and CPT Keuhns

- 2 Certified Registered Nurse Anesthetists (Captains) – CPT Mercado and CPT Gegel

- 1 Detachment First Sergeant (Sergeant First Class) – SFC Smith

- 1 Intensive Care Unit Non-Commissioned Officer (Staff Sergeant) – SSG Kufro

- 1 Emergency Room Technician Non-Commissioned Officer (Sergeant) – SGT Molina

- 1 Operating Room Technician Non-Commissioned Officer (Sergeant) SGT Wilson

- 2 Operating Room Tech soldiers – SPC Lundy and SPC Garcia

- *3 Emergency Medical Technician soldiers – SPC Peppers, SPC Linn, and SPC Vasquez*

[We were a pretty tight team at this point because we had been through several field training exercises together and in November 2002 had been together for five weeks straight at the US Army Trauma Training Center (ATTC) at Ryder Trauma Center in Miami, FL. The Army Medical Department (AMEDD) knew what they were doing to prepare Forward Surgical Teams for **war** – send them to one of the largest US Level I Trauma facilities in the US. I will never forget that experience, not only as a young AMEDD officer but as a newly certified Emergency Medical Technician as well. The hours we pulled were grueling and the level of trauma tested us all from the Emergency Room, Operation Room, to the Intensive Care Unit Recovery. It was quite an experience that well prepared us for what was to come. Although I have lost contact with most everyone, they are all amazing warriors and will always have a special place in my heart and overall Army experience. If any member of the former 126th FST is reading this right now, thankyou for everything you did during Iraqi Freedom and your service to the nation.]

January 16, 2003–Defending Proudly – mass email to family–Notification of Deployment for Operation Iraqi Freedom (OIF I – the Iraq invasion)

Robert: *I am proud to have the opportunity to go and serve my country. Our way of life should never be jeopardized. I am deployed as the Executive Officer (XO) of the 126th Forward Surgical Team (FST). We were recently trained at the Ryder Trauma Center in Miami, FL, so we are trained and ready to do our job. By the end of January, there are supposed to be 100,000 soldiers deployed, and by mid-February 250,000. I just read that off the CNN news like you guys. It is amazing how much the news gets a hold of. Heck, if you do the research maybe you can tell me when and where I am going. They leave us in the dark until right before we go.*

February 2 Deployment Day 2 – Valentine's Day Card to be opened after I depart

Robert: *By now I have had to say goodbye, unfortunately. But what is most important is everything we must look forward to upon my return. New city, new home, new jobs, our new life together. Finally, we'll be together soon. This time will pass quicker than you know it. Every time I am away and you think 'I wish Robert were here,' write it down, and as soon as I'm back we can attempt to make up for as many of those instances as possible. After that write me a letter and again and again. Don't let me out of the loop of your life.*

*Just hold to the **faith** that this separation and my going to fight a possible **war** with Iraq is part of **God's plan**. He knows what we can handle and wouldn't subject us to it if we couldn't handle it.*

*He knows our **love** will only grow stronger every day we're apart. My days may be long, but I can make it through, no matter how long I am gone, knowing you'll be here ready to begin our life together when I get back. I am so blessed you have come into my life and are now my wife, Laura Payne. Whoa! That sounds great [our wedding was postponed due to the deployment, so we married at the Bell County, TX Justice of the Peace on January 3, 2003]. Never forget I **love** you more than anything in this world and I will always **love** you…now…while I'm gone…and forever. Don't hesitate to rely on family and friendships while I am away, but most importantly rely on the **love** in your heart and your **faith** in God. You are my world and I'll be home as soon as I can. I **love** you with all my heart, Robert.*

February 6 Deployment Day 6

Laura: *I got your new address and am sad that you may not get my*
first two letters. Please know that I did write. You never know, those letters might find you months from now.
*I feel so fortunate to have heard from you. I **love** your voice! Debbie [the Team Commander's spouse and Family Readiness Group leader] told me that she heard through a friend that e-mail and phone won't be so accessible these days. I'm preparing myself for this, but I look forward to receiving any letter you can write.*

February 8 Deployment Day 8

Robert: *We are now on our way to **war**. I am sitting next to SGT Wilson as she is talking to her kids. Man, it is so sad to hear. They don't understand why their mom is away.*

Introduction – Ready for War?

The talk of the actual combat plans is increasing. We now must develop our plans to medically support this Brigade [1st Brigade Combat Team (BCT) of the 3rd Infantry Division (3ID)]. Let's just say, when this finally kicks off, it will be very fast-moving. Haven't received any definitive movement orders. I hope that everything kicks off within the month and lasts no more than a week. I think the quicker this all happens the better.

CHAPTER 1
DEPLOYMENT TO WAR

February 9 Deployment Day 9

Robert: I did a 3.5-mile run and am now doing a Bible study. I read 1 John 4:18 which says, "There is no fear in **love**. Perfect **love** drives out fear because fear has to do with punishment. The one who fears is not made perfect in **love**." Makes me truly realize how God's **love** and the **love** God has provided me through you will last me through anything that's placed before me. There is nothing, I mean nothing more important than this **love**. The **love** from God and the **love** we share. I feel so much more fulfilled and stronger every time I rely on thoughts of you and our **faith** together. I hope this same strength finds you as you progress through our time apart. I get excited and caught up in my Bible study thinking about the **faith** derived from the **love** we share. It is perfect **love** if we allow it to be.

[**War** Mission] We are coming up with some great plans for our mission here because we will likely be moving very swiftly across the desert, not stopping for long periods of time. We have developed a version of the FST called QRST which means Quick Response Surgical Team. There is a QRST A Team and a B Team we have developed in case we can't set up the whole FST and we must break up our assets. Won't go into the details of why, but it is a good plan that I contributed to. Today we had some good training and I let the medics stick me with an IV. Actually, the first IV I have ever really had. I survived.

Laura: *Paul Carrozza, founder of RunTex spoke at church about perseverance and how you need to discover the race God wants you to participate in by reading the Bible, knowing your talents, and your spiritual gifts. Mac [our Lakehills Church pastor who performed our wedding ceremony in 2004 in Austin, TX] said his #1 race is his marriage because if that isn't working, nothing else matters. Every day gets harder and more upsetting, though, that we have to be apart. I am asking God to please show us why.*

February 11 Deployment Day 11

Robert: *Today, we had an open house where we invited medical units to come through our setup so we could educate them on FST and how it functions. Tomorrow, Dr. Kirk and I will leave the camp [Camp Pennsylvania, Kuwait] for the 1st time since we arrived. We are going to make some visits to other medical units at other camps and hopefully track down the Division medical planners to get some intel. Just use our time until we get orders to do something.*

I appreciate having Dr. Kirk [FST Commander–MAJ Michael Kirk, M.D. – Orthopedic Surgeon] to talk with and share Christian values. We have a few guys who aren't Christians and it's amazing how it shows through in people.

February 12 Deployment Day 12

Laura: *I pray for a peaceful resolution and am praying for you every day. You are in my thoughts and dreams every day. I can't even describe how much I miss you…The stress is hard for me to control, but I'm trying. Yoga is calling my name. Prayer and meditation* can help, but I might be praying all day. Please don't worry, things will be fine.

LOVE

"There is no fear in **love**.
Perfect **love** drives out fear because
fear has to do with punishment.
The one who fears is not made perfect in **love**."
(1 John 4:18 NIV)

WAR

"Blessed be the Lord my Rock,
Who trains my hands for **war**,
And my fingers for battle —
My lovingkindness and my fortress,
My high tower and my deliverer,
My shield and the One in whom I take refuge,
Who subdues my people under me.
(Psalm 144:1-2 NKJV)

FAITH

"Commit everything you do to the Lord.
Trust him, and he will help you."
(Psalm 37:5 NLT)

CHAPTER 2
FAITH AND PERSECUTION

February 13 Deployment Day 13

Robert: *Just finished listening to Cranberries' "Dreaming My Dreams" and it makes me want to break down and cry because I am not with you. But I am finding God is providing me comfort in my separation from you. Each time I have felt the most hurt, I'll open my Daily Bread Study Guide and the Bible, and I continue to find words that provide comfort. Romans 8:28-39 has some comforting words about how no one can be against us if God is for us. We can overcome and conquer anything with His **love**. Through God's **love** and our **love** for each other, we can make it and look to the wonderful day I am with you again.*

At 3 p.m., Major Kirk and I went to the battalion meeting. Then, we had our FST meeting. Recently, I started reading a brief selection from Daily Bread during the meeting and have met with some opposition. I prayed and felt strongly that I should not stop. Those who are opposed are non-believers whom I hope to reach in some way, so I am willing to risk ridicule and offense to say the words that are right and just.

February 17 Deployment Day 17

Robert: *The more I delve into the Scriptures and pray, the more I feel God weighing on my heart the true fulfillment of the **love** He has given us. We are so lucky to truly have found one another and we did it while growing in our **faith** together. My last phone conversation with you was lengthy and I needed to hear your voice that long. Sorry, I woke you up so early, but I had to talk to you. After talking with you, I felt reenergized but also sad at the same time. This experience will only make us stronger and so thankful for the time we have together. Every day, I grow to **love** you more and more.*

Today, I went to church with Dr. Lim [MAJ Robert Lim, M.D., General Surgeon] and the message was Psalm 91 ["Whoever dwells in the shelter of the Most High will rest in the shadow of the Almighty. I will say of the Lord, 'He is my refuge and my fortress, my God, in whom I trust'" (NIV)] and was applicable to being out here. Then this evening, Dr. Kirk and I held our first Bible Study and we had three attendees. We talked about prayer requests and our walk with God, and read some verses in the Bible. Not too involved. A lot of focus on prayer requests. Mine was for you being at home without me. I pray that God gives you peace and comfort.

*Since we have had two weeks here, you have started to see people's true colors. Strange that the Christian thing is shown in many actions or lack thereof. Get this, there have been a few guys who walked out of the tent when I read the Daily Bread **faith** message for the day! Makes me sad, but I'll continue to share good words and pray for them. I am trying to remain upbeat, but maybe some are getting annoyed with me, I don't know.*

February 18 Deployment Day 18

Robert: *I have been trying for several days to get through to you, but it always comes up busy or the line is down…So if I can't talk to your sweet voice, I keep trying periodically and I'll write. Hopefully, you won't mind if I call you late at night because that might be the only time the phone lines are clear [while in Camp Pennsylvania we had access to an old TA-1035 Digital Non-secure Voice Terminal (DNVT) to make phone calls through Ft Hood switchboard, but lines kept getting cut as we got closer to crossing into Iraq]. So, not much is new because no orders have been given, but if I had to guess it will come soon. I don't anticipate just sitting here much longer, but who knows? Sadly enough, I haven't received anything other than one letter.*

Those few guys who have been walking out when I read Daily Bread at our meeting have tried to take it higher up saying I am singling them out, but Major Kirk just told them they have the option to leave for the two minutes it takes for me to read it. Then a problem arose last night when they walked out and did not come back for the rest of the meeting. They said they would not be back unless we moved the reading to the end of the meeting so they could leave while it was being read. Dr. Kirk told them to talk to the battalion equal opportunity representative. One of the guys claimed he went to legal about it. They even went to the Chaplain to complain, believe it or not.

However, Dr. Kirk is firm in not changing when I say it or stopping me from reading it. The funniest thing about it is that it isn't even preaching or overtly Christian-focused, I have intentionally found daily words that just relate to a story of good moral lessons. There are only minor references to passages of God and Jesus. And these guys want to push this to this level. Dr. Kirk is *standing very firm on this and I am so thankful because I didn't want to budge. I spoke up the second day I did it and made the statement that anyone feeling uncomfortable can leave, but I hope you understand the message's intent not the focus on God. I guess people have forgotten we are "One Nation Under God" and that is why we are here defending. To me, it is not negotiable. I just feel sorry for them and pray for them to come to know God. There are several people I need you to pray in this capacity [for their salvation]. Their actions are not reflective of God's will. I cannot imagine being in health care without **faith**.*

CHAPTER 3
ROCK OF THE MARNE

February 20 Deployment Day 20

Laura: *I met a girl through Army training [Ft. Hood Army spouse training course] and her husband is in the 4th Infantry Division. They still don't know when or where they are going. Turkey wants something like 30 billion dollars to allow our troops there [the initial **war** plan was to have the 4th Infantry Division (4th ID) assault from the North through Turkey, but that never happened, 3D Infantry Division (3rd ID) did the assault alone with assistance from 1st Marine Expeditionary Force (1st MEF)]. I hate not being able to talk and share everything with my best friend. I miss you and talk to you every day.*

Robert: *Things aren't convenient here. We try to be as comfortable as we can, but when everything you touch is caked in sand, it gets old. We are still awaiting orders, but there is talk of a tentative movement date. Until a written order is published, it is all hearsay. The base fact is it all comes from political decisions. From what you tell me from the news reports you are hearing, it sounds like the UN doesn't want to support this **war**. One thing that scares me about that is how long will they leave us here while continuing to weigh the political options. Your guess is as good* as mine, but I highly doubt this many soldiers would be deployed and nothing happens.

We are now attached to the 3rd Infantry Division [1st Brigade Combat Team under COL Grimsley]. We had a visit yesterday from the Assistant Division Commander. His many references to Aggie football led me to realize he was an Aggie...Whoop! Everyone likes to rag on A&M football and the Aggies. But no one understands the experiences we are afforded by having attended Texas A&M. It just excites me to think of my life with you knowing we both possess the **love** for Texas A&M and the difference it made in our lives. Being an Aggie is just part of our identity and who we are. I know it **war**ms my heart to no end to think of holding your hand as we walk around campus, after we retire, making our way to our season seats.

As far as the positive message of the day that has drawn controversy from sad souls, no new changes other than the Chaplain and I talked about it. He recommended we put the message at the end of the meeting so they can leave and not have to come back, but I believe Dr. Kirk doesn't want to budge on it. Who knows? I'm just trying to share a positive message, that's all.

Please continue to have **faith** in God's plan for us and everything will work out. We are both for God and we know He will provide for us. He is already putting in my heart more **love** for Him and you every day that goes by we are apart.

February 22 Deployment Day 22

Robert: *Sadly, enough I still can't get through on any of the phones. I never thought I would have to go this long without talking to you, but I guess it might be this way. What sucks even* worse is I have only gotten two letters and I don't even know if you have gotten my letters.

Today, Major Kirk had to visit some other medical units, so I had to attend the 3rd Infantry Division (3ID) Commander's Meeting with the 3ID Commanding 2-star general. He shook my hand. Then, he gave us some good insights on things, but not much I can discuss.

This is all frustrating, but God is reminding me how much I **love** you every day. I just must pray for understanding and patience. God will see us through.

February 23 Deployment Day 23

Robert: *Thought it would be interesting to write a whole letter in cursive. Strange but we learn to write this in elementary school, but somehow revert to the manuscript. Enough of this...cursive takes too long. Having not been able to talk with you since a week ago was breaking my heart. Especially since the last time we talked, I had no idea that the phone system would have such problems and I wouldn't be able to talk with you again for days. At least now I have the comfort of mind that you know why I can't call and that our written correspondence will take precedence. Also, please understand, that once the mission begins, I may not be able to call or write because of operational security. They may halt mail outgoing out of the theater but may let mail into the theater. Unfortunately, I haven't received any mail since letters two and three from you. I hope to see more soon, and I hope you see my letters soon, too.*

*I have never felt such a weight on my heart as this **love** I have for you. As hard as it is, it also makes me thankful to God that He has allowed me to have found you in my life and **love** you this* *way. Man, what a powerful feeling and emotion that I don't think many couples find, but thankfully we do! I truly feel our **love** is so true and strong because of what we have endured and how our relationship grew together with our relationship with God.*

Folks know of our FST out here. We have gotten a lot of support and appreciation I guess because they know if the crap hits the fan, we become really important! I understand the other FSTs out here aren't getting taken care of as well as we are by our battalion.

*Not a day goes by I am not getting more excited about God's Word and that our marriage, **love**, and future family will be based on our Christian values and beliefs. Very powerful indeed. After the service, we went outside to watch almost twenty folks get Baptized! Amen. They opened a big old water bag to do it in. It was refreshing to see so many others come to Christ. I need some rest now because we get some mission information tomorrow morning.*

CHAPTER 4
REALITY OF WAR

February 24 Deployment Day 24

Laura: *I can't wait for the day that you call and say you're coming home. I'll probably pee my pants I'll be so excited. I wish you had better access to the news. I'd fill in for you, but I've stopped watching and reading the news. It makes me anxious to watch it. I'm looking forward to hearing what your days are like. That will help me imagine what you are doing. I'm always looking at the clock and calculating what time it is in Kuwait and then trying to imagine what you might be doing.*

February 26 Deployment Day 26

Laura: *I found out the Kuwaiti mail people may open the packages we send. Isn't that cool?! They want no pork products or nude pictures entering their country. So, to make sure you get everything, I sent two packages. The first package has snacks and a stopwatch in it. The second package has film, eight packs of batteries, and walkie-talkies [on a phone call I asked Laura to mail us these for our FST to use since not all our vehicles were mounted* with Army radios]. I am afraid the Kuwaiti mail people may want to take these items.

I still can't wait to get your first letter. That will be an exciting day. What will it be like when you can't call? I will cry a lot for sure. Robert, I'm trying to be strong, but I just must cry sometimes because my heart aches from missing you. Things keep going, but my thoughts are filled with you. I can't let you go out of my thoughts because I want to remain close to you, and that is the only way I can. I want our relationship to be just as strong, if not stronger when you get home. I have **faith** that it will be that way. We have so many prayers out there for us that God will hear this prayer. Speaking of prayers, I entered your name into the Presidential Prayer Team list. Some lucky person will get your name and pray for you.

Robert (1230 hours / 12:30 am): *I just finished watching When Harry Met Sally and I miss you so much. Granted it is about a divorced guy finding his true* **love** *later in life, having met her twelve years before. The point is, it is a sweet story about finding* **love**, *but my story is even better because mine is when Robert met Laura. He knew right away he was intrigued by her, but the interest evolved. As soon as he opened his heart to this sweet and beautiful girl, he was in* **love** *forever. Within ten months he knew he couldn't imagine his life without Laura and soon he asked her to be his forever. Then he whisked her away to Disney World and they lived happily ever after [Robert made an elaborate proposal in Austin & Hye, TX on their year dating anniversary and before taking her on a surprise week vacation to Disney World]… things got tough over time because they had to endure a lot of time apart, but it made their* **love** *even stronger. Sounds like an amazing story, huh? Well, guess we are living it.*

Up right now pulling [night] guard duty with EMT Non-commissioned officer in charge (NCOIC) to watch all of our secured [surgical and weapons] items. Most of our stuff is packed away now, but the little we have left can't just be left out. Also, we have had an officer and an NCO up every night in case something surgical happened to alert the crew.

*Tonight, I walked outside and looked up at the stars and thought about you looking at them as well. Laura, don't forget for a minute how much I am missing you and how incredibly in **love** I am with you. I thank God for you every day. Write soon.*

Robert (2200 hours 11:00 pm): *I think I already wrote you a letter for this day, but alas, I **love** you so much that I have to write you again. I am still so happy for having the opportunity to talk with you so much the past two days. Hopefully, I will be able to call once or twice before I lose phone access for a while.*

*Anyway, I slept for about three hours and awoke at 6 a.m. for some breakfast. Same ol' breakfast I have had for the last 26 days: eggs, bacon, potatoes, French toast, rice krispies, and an orange. See, I told you when I go to the field, I do some massive eating... why? Because it's there. Don't worry, I won't get fat. I'll still be the same studly-looking guy as when I left. So, after breakfast [my driver and I] finished loading our vehicle, "Laura," which is FST 04 [my driver and I were both married to ladies named Laura, so we named our **war** Humvee M1045A2 (HMMVW)–Laura 4]. We are carrying one of our Deployable Rapid Assemble Shelters (DRASH), the Meals Ready to Eat (MREs), water, and entertainment boxes (games, TV, movies, etc.). So, after MAJ Kirk did a little walk-through inspection, we loaded some of our bags. After that, we filled some sandbags to place on the floorboard for precaution against landmines. Don't worry, though, we are always **war**ned and avoid those areas. Precautionary only.*

The Battalion meeting was boring. However, I do have respect for the unit (3D Forward Support Battalion–FSB) because they have looked out for us and their meetings are fairly brief [the 126th FST was from Ft Hood, TX, and attached to 3D ID, 3rd FSB, 1st BCT from Ft Stewart, GA once we arrived in Kuwait and the 126th FST was one of three FSTs supporting the 3D ID invasion into Iraq]. Their Battalion Commander is a really good guy [LTC Bobby Towery, one of the greatest leaders I have ever worked for who sadly passed away in late 2019 after several years post-Army retirement].

So, after the BN meeting, we had our team meeting and, of course, I read the word of the day. Did I tell you MAJ Kirk compromised and moved it [Daily Bread message] to the end of the meeting and now everyone stays to hear my reading from the Daily Bread? I tell you prayer works because I certainly have prayed to reach everyone through word and deed. I hope and pray I can make a difference in some way to get them to know our amazing God.

February 27 (2133 hours / 9:33 pm) Deployment Day 27

Robert: *This is no longer training!* Today, consisted of a very long meeting at the new med building. The stuff we talked about is real. It is strange sometimes when I remind myself this is not a training exercise. No more scrimmage games, we are at the super bowl, in the locker room about to go out on the field. As apprehensive as I can get sometimes, I do feel as if I am now a part of something that will make a difference in our way of life and the security we have as Americans, and a difference in the lives of those oppressed in a country where they have nowhere to turn. Most importantly, I can push aside my concern apprehension, and *fear because I have **faith** in Jesus Christ as my Savior. My sins have been forgiven and I know this is all in God's plan. This is His plan for both of us as well. He has already impressed upon my heart the overwhelming importance of your **love** in my life. It is so strong and passionate, and I feel more and more in **love** with you and God every day. I was reminded of our bond earlier when I looked again to the skies to see the stars and we both look upon them from our locations across the world. Another aspect that is important in what we are doing here is the honor of those who have served before me. The sacrifices others have made before me so we can live as we do in the greatest country in the world, where a goofy-looking guy like me can marry a beautiful, sweet, caring, loving, funny, sexy woman like yourself.*

Not sure when the phone will be available again, but I hope these letters will reach you soon.

March 1 Deployment Day 29

Laura (and her best friends): *Happy Mardi Gras! We are sitting here on St. Charles Street waiting for the Endymion parade to start. We have all thought about you and wish so much that you were here. Mardi Gras isn't the same without you. It was two years ago that our awesome relationship began here. I enjoyed walking with you at the parade that year. We shared so many laughs together that day. Okay, our friends want to say something to you…*

Seth & Michelle: (Seth) *I woke up on St. Charles Street in my urine. Confused I remembered the night, the goats, and the pack of commanches. I realized at that moment you are a big piece of !!%?+-!. Robert, I hope all is well my friend. I miss you and wish* *you were here.* **(Michelle)** *Seth and I miss you. He is now laying in the street by himself, weeping. Come home soon and safe.*

Rina: *When the Saints Go Marching In. It's Rina! That's what the band is playing that's marching behind us. Mardi Gras weekend. Missing you Robert! I'm sending letters from my 7th graders soon. Feel free to share them with your team…We saw a float that made us think of you-everyone on it had velvet lunge outfits on. Well, take care, we* **love** *you and I'm praying for you and Laura every day.*

Jason & Kim: (Jason) *We're at the parade. You are in the desert. Too bad. Glad you are marrying Laura again. We'll get drunk and forget who you are. Then we'll remember you in the morning.* **(Kim)** *Jason left me at Harrah's casino on Thursday night until 7 a.m. I wasn't very happy. Kim.*

Marna: *I had so much fun with Laura here in New Orleans and Austin last weekend. We all miss you, though, and we wish you were here with us (Laura especially, of course). You're here in spirit, that's for sure. Everyone's been taking pictures and asking questions (they asked one of the cab drivers what the craziest thing was that's happened in his cab) in your honor. Take care of yourself and know that we are all thinking of you and you are always in my prayers. We're taking care of Laura until you get back. We* **love** *and miss you.* **Love** *Marna.*

Laura: *Robert, it's me again. I wanted to be the last to write to tell you how much I miss you. You are my knight in shining armor…I* **love** *you so much and wish you were here so badly! Please come home!*

Robert (0919 hours / 9:10 am): *So right now, I am sitting in FST "Laura 04" in a huge convoy of probably 100+ vehicles outside the gate. Essentially, we have been evicted from our camp and told to set up a place outside another camp. Not just the FST* but a whole lot of folks. Seems as if another unit is moving into the camp we were in [the 101st Airborne Division, light infantry arrived in Kuwait and had to assemble in Camp Pennsylvania while awaiting all of their equipment, so 3D ID moved to the border of Kuwait awaiting the movement order]. But that's okay because the more fighting units out here, the better as far as I am concerned. So, onto another location to sit and wait. Sounds like diplomacy and politics are dragging this out longer and longer while we sit here. Part of me wishes they would issue the order to go in so we could just do it and be done with it. Seems as if Saddam Hussein is playing the media piece by challenging Bush to a debate, conducting an interview with Dan Rather, and agreeing to destroy the long-range missiles Hans Blix's UN crew found. However, I have the ultimate **faith** in God's plan.

The "Laura Josie Pussycat & Robert Master G" picture [taken at 2002 Halloween] is taped up in the corner of the window of the HMMWV I sit in. Makes me smile. Also, we took a marker and wrote a big Laura 4 on the inside of the vehicle. Gotta go to a movement rehearsal.

Robert (2204 hours / 10:04 pm): *Long day of driving for us, the actual location we moved to couldn't have been more than 10 miles away, but it took 4 ½ hours to get there because of a large number of vehicles going into our area. The area we will fall into is next to a medical company in a Brigade Support Area called a BSA. It is where all the support elements are based out of for the infantry battalions – food, water, supplies, parts, fuel, and medical care based here and push down to the line units like 2-7 CAV [when I met Laura in 2001, I was still assigned to 1st Cavalry Division, 3rd Brigade Greywolf, 2nd Battalion 7th Cavalry (2-7 CAV) 'GarryOwen' at Ft Hood, TX]. So now we are in the BSA, which is managed and run by a Forward Support Battalion*

(FSB) and that is who we are attached to now, a medical company in the 3rd FSB [of 1st Brigade, 3D ID].

I **love** these marriage pics from today's box. Makes me wonder if we should have taken the justice of the peace thing more seriously since now we are legally married and all. I mean I took it seriously, of course, but you know, a nice dinner alone [after our Justice of the Peace wedding on January 3, 2003, Laura and I went to Outback steakhouse in Killeen, TX with my roommate 1LT Sergio Flores]. Maybe a weekend away, etc. I guess I'm just rambling, the real wedding will be great, wonderful, fun, and memorable when I get back [the actual wedding in Austin, TX was postponed due to the deployment, luckily we didn't lose any major deposits, all the vendors were very understanding]. I'll probably consider the wedding in my uniform a little more now. If you want the military wedding thing with an arch and all, I can look into it. We could use the 126th FST soldiers and I could locate some sabers or I could just ask the RV [Texas A&M Corps of Cadets Ross Volunteers – the State of Texas Governor's Honor Guard, I was a member of my junior and senior year of the Corps of Cadets at Texas A&M].

Anyway, we got here and set up two DRASHs to sleep in and will finish setting up tomorrow the 3rd DRASH for potential surgeries...

So how long will we be in the new location? Hopefully not be too long because the desert sucks. Windstorms suck out here. I guess we will be hanging out as long as politics and diplomacy are an issue. I want something to be decided soon, so I can get back home to Laura and our new life to build together. Time for sleep. I **love** you, Laura, Robert.

Chapters 1-4 Personal Observations

I would never actually have imagined when I signed my Army ROTC scholarship in 1995, I would have been sitting in Kuwait in 2003 getting ready to go to **war** having just been married at the Justice of Peace. It was almost as if the aftereffects of September 11, 2001, made me realize I am grown up and life is serious. Many join the US military for a variety of different reasons, and we all know the possible reality of **war**, but until you are there, and it is happening, it just seems like a distant reality. I was so in **love** with Laura and enjoying our young life in Killeen and Austin. We were so happy traveling, being young professionals, and having fun with our friends.

We were excited to be engaged and plan our wedding in Austin. I was going to separate from the US Army and become a clinical psychologist or federal agent. **War** altered this reality a bit. We had to grow up fast and make plans for what would happen if I didn't come home, never thinking about what would happen when I came home and processing the effects of **war** like so many of us must do. I remember after we were married at the Bell County Justice of Peace, the next day we had to go on base and enroll Laura into the military system for spouse benefits and name her as the primary beneficiary on my Service Group Life Insurance plan [$400,000 policy provided to a beneficiary when a soldier is killed].

Ironically, as we were waiting to enter the personnel office, we were outside with a young soldier. Then a huge caravan of black suburbans and limousines drove past us. Remembering President George W Bush was speaking that day at Ft Hood, I realized it was the President's caravan. I popped to attention and told the soldier to do the same. As the caravan slowed in front of us, the window of one limo lowered just enough to see President George W Bush return our salute. The soldier even asked me, "Who was that?" to me, to which I replied, "Soldier, you were just saluted by your Commander in Chief." That was when I knew it was real. Why else would the Commander in Chief make a special impromptu visit to the largest US military installation in the world? We were now planning for **war**.

CHAPTER 5
SEPARATION AND WAR

March 2 Deployment Day 30

Robert: *I am not concerned about the Army, jobs, family, friends, money, etc. I just need you, Laura, completely – physically, emotionally, spiritually. Praise God He has placed you as my wife – I have so much* **love** *to give you forever. Your happiness…our happiness together means the world to me. How I pray this will be resolved soon so I can come home to you…but I know you are my soulmate, Laura. The way I feel having been separated from you cannot be explained in any other way. I feel a void in myself that is only complete when you are near.*

I want to start some sort of **faith** *sharing with you by giving you a verse for us to read and pray about together. I am pulling them from the men's retreat Bible study information I have. Just something to know we are sharing the same focus on God in the same way. I feel that our* **faith** *has grown together and has blessed us with this strong* **love** *in our relationship. Here is the first one: Matthew 22:37-38. Jesus replied,* **"Love** *the Lord your God with all your heart and with all your soul and with all your mind. This is the first and greatest commandment."*

Wow! What more can we say to that? Sometimes I certainly fall short at times. Life moves so fast that we forget to stop and **love** *God. If we would remember this our lives would probably be a lot easier. It is through this* **love** *for God that you and I can have the* **love** *we have for one another. Tell me your thoughts on this verse. Not much else to say about today, we set up our 3rd DRASH [tent] with all the surgical equipment and sat around the rest of the day. I foresee the days seeming longer and longer.*

March 3 Deployment Day 31

Laura: *Happy 2nd anniversary! We have been "dating" for 2 years. I am so lucky to have you in my life. These have been the best years of my life. And I know that being with you, there will be many more. Well, in my last letter, I told you there was more to tell about Mardi Gras…I don't think I was emotionally ready to party hard at Mardi Gras. I wanted you there more than you'll ever know.*

I got your first three letters today. I enjoyed reading them. Now I understand what your day is like. I hated how our conversation on Sunday was cut off. The phone was completely sucking [as we sat in Kuwait nearing the start of the Iraq invasion the lines on the DNVT phone kept getting cut and the calls were continuously dropped].

I'm so happy to hear that you have been turning to God for guidance and sharing His word with others. I don't like that some are opposing but admire you for persevering. I am inspired by your letters to turn to the Bible for more daily guidance. You seem so busy, honey. I guess it helps time to pass. I can't believe we hit the month mark for being apart. It sucks! Five or eleven more months to go, who knows?!

Robert: *It's now 10:10 p.m. and I'm in my bunk to get some rest, which I don't need because we haven't been doing all that much, Back at the other camp [Pennsylvania] towards the end before we left, I was stretching it to find things to put on the schedule for training purposes. Now, over a month later, I am tapped out of ideas for a schedule and what to do. I see the result of idleness and boredom beginning to set in for us.*

Tonight, I walked outside for a little while to look at the stars, beautiful night here in Kuwait to think of you. Pray to God that He knows what is best for us and He is comforting you in this time. I truly **love** *you with every ounce of my heart. When I return, I anxiously await beginning our life without any reservations or worries, just full of my* **love** *for you. It might be somewhat difficult for us initially as I try and exit the Army and leave Killeen [home of Ft Hood, TX], but it will just merely be details compared to having the ability to reach out and hold you.*

So, what's in store for us tomorrow…I have no idea. I have no idea how long we will be out here in the desert. But they are moving the port-o-potties, the laundry, and the showers in, so I guess we will be here for a while. I suppose we are going to be sitting here with our thumbs up our ass until politics and diplomacy work this out. I know I must have patience for God's plan.

The verse for today is Proverbs 3:5 "Trust in the Lord will all your heart. Never rely on what you think you know" [This was also the verse my older brother David, who was also in the Army, gave me on a small card I carried in the top pocket of my uniform throughout the deployment]. I certainly second this because I know nothing and this is all God's plan…for our country, for Iraq, for all the soldiers, families, and ultimately, Robert and Laura.

March 4 Deployment Day 32

Robert: *Still sitting here doing absolutely nothing…I don't know when I will talk to you again because I am hearing that all state-side contact is on hold right now. Not sure why?*

It looks like about 60,000 more are coming in from the 101st Airborne Division [this unit from Ft Campbell, KY pushed 3ID from Camp Pennsylvania to the desert at the Kuwait/Iraq border and would attack behind 3ID, who is the main effort] and 70,000 from 1st Cavalry Division who just got their deployment orders [this unit from Ft Hood, TX did not come into the initial invasion so 3ID and 1st Marine Expeditionary Force (1st MEF) were left to conduct the Iraq Invasion alone]. I read this on CNN news that the Battalion TOC [Tactical Operations Center] printed out. Just check out CNN.com to keep up, but nothing was mentioned about any dates for us over here going in to kick some ass yet. Maybe soon.

*Things are getting slow here I pray you continue to write me as often as possible, I need your words to know what is happening in your life. Today's verse is 1 Peter 4:8, "Above all, **love** each other deeply, because **love** covers a multitude of sins." Well, we must praise God because we have abundant **love** and many sins to ask forgiveness for. Sometimes I still feel like a hypocrite claiming my Christian beliefs when I know I have and still drink, curse, have impure thoughts, have sex, pornography, judge others, etc. But I have come to understand that I am a sinner and only Jesus' salvation can save me.*

CHAPTER 6
ANXIETY OF WAITING FOR WAR

March 5 Deployment Day 33

Laura: *I'm getting sad about leaving Austin because we made a lot of memories there. Our relationship began there. I hope we return there one day. To be honest, I'm a little nervous about living at home. It will probably be stressful! No privacy! Please come back home soon. We are going to have so much fun living together [we were married at the Bell County Justice of the Peace on January 3, 2003, but had never lived together]. I wish you were here so much. I can't wait to get your next batch of letters. It's been too long since I've heard your voice. I miss it so much.*

March 6 Deployment Day 34

Robert: *Nerves are growing shorter. 36 days with all 20 of us living and working together 24-7 can get grating. I continually try to maintain optimism and be helpful, but you always have those who insist on worrying about their little world and do not understand the concept of not rocking the boat. But we have to accommodate all. I am certainly beginning to see how over time* you can lose your edge if you choose not to act…meaning we were at our peak probably a week ago. But the longer we are left here in uncertainty the more detrimental is it to the American soldier. Yet, we will follow orders and hold our positions until we are told to execute. The US military will then kick ass no matter what, but idleness can wear anyone down.

Today MAJ Kirk, MAJ Kuhns, and I were all talking about having kids and their ages when they had their kids. I have to tell you how it **war**med my heart just to think about the amazing family we will have one day and how I can't even put into words how great of a mother I know you are going to be for our kids. I **love** you so much and the idea of our family. I can now only pray for the day when I am by your side putting you and our kids as my ultimate priority through God's grace. I will be a great husband and loving father, I promise. [17 years later the Payne family consists of a daughter and three sons].

So, Mardi Gras wasn't a huge bucket of fun? Honestly, I didn't expect that it would be for you. You and your friends are at such different points in your lives and yours has certainly accelerated at a level they could not comprehend. We must pray for them as they do not all have what you and I have found. Our **love** is so powerful, passionate, and unconditional that they cannot understand where you and I are coming from or the pain in our hearts at being separated.

You know something else I have thought about is our wedding [Due to the deployment, we had to postpone the actual wedding we had scheduled in Austin, TX]. April 5th would have been awesome, but it is going to mean so much more to us now. It will be truly romantic, your combat veteran honey returning home to begin his life with you. Something certainly to look forward to.

*Not too much new here except the one CBPS we got [Chemical Biological Protective Shelter System, which was a newly fielded item to Forward Surgical Teams that produce an over-pressured shelter system off the end of an HMMWV allowing medical treatment and surgery to occur in an potential chemical environment. They didn't fare so well in actual combat and were never fielded to any other units to my knowledge]. We also plan on briefing the other [Forward Support Battalion] Medical Officers and Battalion Staff on our recent trauma rotation [one month before the deployment order our FST was pushed to the Army Trauma Training Center rotation at the Ryder Trauma hospital for Miami-Dade County, a Level I trauma center]. I should also make a trip this Saturday with SFC Smith [FST First Sergeant] to a base area near Kuwait City, called Camp Doha to get some missing parts of the CBPS and try and collect some DCU [Desert Camouflage Uniforms, when we arrive at 3ID, our FST was the only unit on all of Camp Pennsylvania to be in green woodland camouflage uniforms because Ft Hood ran out before our deployment…the running joke was once the 126th FST gets finds some DCUs, we could start the **war**]. Yes, we are still green in a sea of desert camo.*

March 7 Deployment Day 35

Laura: *Yesterday, I ran in my parent's neighborhood. I'm always aware of my environment when I'm running. There was a man in a white van that worried me so I kept an eye on him. He pulled into a driveway in front of me, so I started walking. He backed up and started driving towards me. Then a lady started calling me, so I walked to her. She explained that her neighbor had been accosted by a man in a white van in her garage. I looked back and he stopped again in the middle of the street. She waited by* the street while I ran home. I was scared and felt like throwing up. My dad and I went to look for the van and get a better description but weren't sure if the van we saw was the same one. I need my favorite running buddy to come home and keep me safe. [Laura was training for her first marathon while fundraising for the Leukemia and Lymphoma Society through Team in Training].

March 8 Deployment Day 36

Laura: *Bush spoke* [https://georgewbush-whitehouse.archives.gov/news/releases/2003/03/20030306-8.html] *Thurs night to the press and answered their questions about Iraq. He said when he took his oath with his hand on the Bible, he promised to uphold the constitution, so that is what he is going to do. He thanked people for their prayers for him and his family. Lots of people are protesting against* **war** *here at home. Dad and I discussed the protestors and he made a good point They probably feel that they have the things they have because of the government and not because of the people who fought for our freedom.*

We saw a 60 Minutes story on B Co, 4ID [4th Infantry Division, Ft Hood, TX]. They are overtrained and ready to go. It was interesting to see the different views of soldiers. One young soldier said he felt the US at times is a bully, but he is ready to do his job and cries every time the flag is raised. They said the days are now boring and they keep doing the same things to train because there is nothing else to do. [4ID was initially ordered to deploy in January 2003 before the **war** began but did not arrive in Kuwait until late March. The delay was caused by the inability of the US and Turkey to reach an agreement over using Turkish military bases to gain access to northern Iraq, where the division was originally planned to be located. 4ID began crossing into Iraq on April

12, 2003 and was first sent to Baghdad to take over security duties from the 1st MEF. It later took over command of the area north of Baghdad, including the cities of Kirkuk and Tikrit.]

March 9 Deployment Day 37

Robert: *The verse for this letter is I Corinthians 7:3-5 & 10-11 which is God's decree on marriage and divorce is not allowed so you are stuck with me now forever! Hahahaha! Praise God I am with you until we leave this earth because you are my soulmate and God's gift to me. Until I write you again…I* **Love** *you.*

March 10 Deployment Day 38

Robert: *The U.S. Military is not trying to hide much. The few "secrets" and I do mean few, things I have been told I see days later in letters or on our CNN newsprint outs or in the newspaper. I pray the US Air Force does a good enough job that we just drive across the desert and occupy Saddam's palace with no problem. That would be great, wouldn't it? Then we don't have to do our [medical] job here at the FST. It would bring some comfort to my heart to know that since things will probably heat up here soon. I'm sure you have read the papers or heard the news but looks like things are getting closer to moving us across. You will probably know when I do since there is so much media coverage of this whole thing.* [Before the start of the Iraq Invasion, media outlets from across the nation were allowed to be embedded within the forward-moving combat units. The Savannah Morning News was embedded with the 3rd FSB, 3ID, so they covered numerous stories on our movements].

CHAPTER 7
40 Days & 40 Nights in the Desert

March 11 Deployment Day 39

Laura: *I'm feeling lonely today. People have called to check on me, but I hate talking on the phone, so I haven't called them back. People also invite me to do things, but I haven't felt like doing anything. This is just how I deal with things. I feel like they don't understand that I just want to be left alone sometimes. I want to get this letter in the mail before the mailman comes, so you can have a letter from me almost every day. I just want to say thank you for defending our country and freedom. I'm so proud of you! I admire you for keeping your spirits so high even during this time of uncertainty and waiting.*

March 12 Deployment Day 40

Robert: *Well, still here sitting in the desert 40 days since I have seen you last. The stress levels are getting high here and it affects everyone. Even Dr. Kirk went off on CPT Mercado right before a briefing we were about to give [on possible movement]. He intentionally was sharp shooting our briefing for no good* reason. He seems to like holding others to technicalities and rules but not abiding by them himself. He was a former E-4 Specialist [before becoming a Nurse CPT], but often still behaves like an E-4. I am trying to help however I can. So, I ask for your prayers for them. They certainly need it. Then you have SSG Molina, the former Ranger Battalion medic, who seems to think he has all the answers. CPT Felix [ICU Nurse] asks a lot of questions lacks an understanding of her surroundings and is often difficult to work with. Sadly, I would say the two people causing the most issues, CPT Mercado and SSG Molina, are probably the two furthest from any relationship with God. I have encouraged Dr. Kirk we don't have to accept their unnecessary non-productive opinions; we can ignore them and drive on. Fortunately, the US Army is not a democracy, we must defend it.

What does help the team is I am a Captain now, so I attend the [Battalion & Division Medical] operational briefings. It has been good to stay in the operational loop. Being a Captain has made it a little easier because most think I am a commander, even though I am the Executive Officer of the FST. Things keep changing daily as far as our timelines. I attribute that to the UN diplomacy crap. Time to poop or get off the pot if you ask ol CPT Payne…but they won't so it doesn't matter.

I talked to David about how hard it is to be without you and how lucky I truly am to have our **love** for a lifetime. Distance apart has certainly made not only my heart grow fonder, but bigger for our **love**. I wrote in a letter to my family how important it is to me to know where each of them stands in their **faith** [based on knowing I may not make it back home]. I wanted and needed to know for ease of my conscience and heart if they have asked for their salvation from Jesus…it is certainly harder to talk to someone in person about their **faith**, so maybe letters will be easier.

*Remember Proverbs 3:5-6 which says, "Trust in the Lord with all your heart and lean not on your own understanding; in all your ways acknowledge Him and He will make your paths straight." I hope these words can offer you some comfort, but **faith** in your heart can carry you through day-to-day when things get hard. I have found my comfort in prayer and in studying the Bible. Just finished reading about David and Goliath in 1 Samuel 17. Different than this **war**, but a **war** nonetheless.*

March 13 Deployment Day 41

Robert: *Guess what? We finally got two sets of Desert Camo Uniforms (DCUs). We have to rip off our green patches and use them but at least we will more easily blend in now. We had all voted a few days ago to just give up on them but the good Lord always provides. As the timeline is drawing near, the temperatures in the desert are rising. In May and June, it will be over 100 degrees here daily.*

Today was the aftermath of or cooldown of Dr. Kirk blowing up at CPT Mercado. Things are cool now, the potential movement brief has been given to all, and several of us have talked with CPT Mercado, including me. Everything now seems hunkey dorey. I let Dr. Kirk bounce a lot of stuff off of me last night and today, mainly as a Christian friend rather than an XO. He works himself up to balance being a Commander and a Christian. But I assured him he is good at both and to not let the actions of a few bring him (or us) down. I just want as much peace and harmony among the team because of the mission that lies before us. We are waiting for something to happen because it does seem as if the timeline is drawing near. Starting to see the temperature rising in the afternoons, which is not good because, by May or June, it will easily be over 100 degrees every day.

Funny but since I have been here, I tend to hang out with the surgeons more than others, partly because I am around Dr. Kirk a lot. But also, because I find it hard to fit in with the Nurse Captains and I don't have any close connection with the NCOs. I certainly can't relate to the soldiers even though they are closest to my age. MAJ (Dr) Lim and I are fairly close in age and similar situations [had to go to the Justice of the Peace and postpone our weddings].

March 14 Deployment Day 42

Robert: We played an hour or two of volleyball today. We brought a net and strung it up between two vehicles. Nice break and helped me to be active. I haven't gotten a nice workout or run since we got to the new location [border of Kuwait and Iraq in the desert]. I have done some pushups and sit-ups a few times but not enough. Playing volleyball was like one of those **war** movies. We had music with Clearance Clearwater Revival playing, soldiers in boots, pants, and t-shirts hitting the old volleyball.

We have some newspaper reporters and cameramen from Savannah Morning News who came over to cover the "Soldier's Real Story." What they won't cover is that the soldiers are tired of waiting because our country leaders are so wrapped up in the bureaucracy. I wonder where I will be on April 21st for Aggie Muster? I have only met 2 Aggies in this Brigade Combat Team (BCT) so far. We listened to the news a little while ago and it sounds like they are trying to delay the UN vote another week. Not sure where this extra support will come from since France, Russia, and China have said no to any conflict. Don't think the inspectors *are helping any either because they are claiming that Iraq is cooperating. Again, only time will tell and only the Good Lord knows.*

Laura: *I cried last night when they showed me the sandstorm in Kuwait. I cry every time I see military stuff on TV. I saw an interview with Tommy Franks last night. He's a tough man who seems to have been through a lot. At first, his speech made me scared, but then his confidence started growing on me.*

CHAPTER 8
FOUNDATION FOR LOVE & FAITH

March 15 Deployment Day 43

Robert: *Today I read Matthew 7:7-8 which says, "Ask and it will be given to you, seek and you will find, knock and the door will be opened to you. For everyone who asks receives. He who seeks finds, and to him who knocks, the door will be opened." This tells me He is there for us and our every need. We can ask for His grace to open or close doors for us as we see fit. It's like answering or not answering our prayers to give us guidance. Lord knows we need it now.*

Heard on the news Bush would further consider diplomacy to resolve this. On one hand, I would like to resolve it peacefully, but that might keep us out here for a long time waiting. On the other hand, going to **war** *might get us home sooner but soldiers' lives are at risk. Damned if you do, damned if you don't, right?*

Remember I told you about the media here from Savannah Georgia? They are here taking pictures and writing stories about the 3rd Forward Support Battalion (FSB) to whom we are attached. They print stuff daily and you can find it on their website www.savannahNOW.com. I think the paper is the

Savannah Morning News and you can access the Kuwait link or the reporter archives under Noelle 2003. Maybe it will give some insight into what it is like out here. Although I hope I have been saying enough for you to understand somewhat. If I send this box back you can get the five rolls of film developed to see what has been going on.

Some people will never understand that **love** *is not a conditional decision based on emotion. It is not emotion-based. The bottom line, we have the kind of* **love** *many search for a lifetime but never find. Somehow God has blessed us.*

March 16 Deployment Day 44

Robert: *I have been trying to get an extra RT-1523 ASIP radio. The only radio we have assigned is in MAJ Kirk's vehicle [of 10 FST vehicles] but I have been working with an NCO to hook my vehicle (Laura 4) up with a radio. That way MAJ Kirk is in the front of our convoy, and I can go in the rear of the convoy with a radio. Luckily, thanks to an amazing woman we will have handheld radios for every vehicle. You don't know how much you helped our communication situation. Those handheld radios are worth their weight in gold.* [Our lack of communication assets was significant, and the little Motorola handheld radios were sent to us by Laura, who purchased them at home and mailed them to us. Troops not having everything they needed in the early part of the Iraq **War** was accurate.]

1730: Just got back from an afternoon briefing and guess what? I met a Civilian Affairs Army Reservist who is a Drug Enforcement Administration (DEA) Special Agent in his civilian career. I talked with him after the meeting for ½ hour or so. He told me the risk of getting shot is more minimal than people think. Most DEA raids are done by full-time local police SWAT teams, so they don't typically do as much grunt work as you would think. Of course, in the first several years as a new agent, you pay your dues but is often dependent on where you are assigned and what you are assigned to work. It is all in God's plan. He might still have me head to grad school or maybe work in a corporation. As long as I lay all my cards on the table and pray about it, I will wait for Him to make our 'paths straight' [Proverbs 3:5 reference.] If you could please do some research on the internet for federal agent positions in the homeland security agency. Not sure where to start, but you could try the search engine or maybe the new TSA airport guys. Most of the questions I had answered so far on the secret service were lost when my computer crashed so I have to begin again. When I am finally finished, I'll be sending it all back to you to help me type up my applications and get them submitted for me. [I intended to apply to numerous three-letter agencies after I returned home]. He did mention the divorce rate being high among new agents because of the long hours, other agents pulling them out for social stuff, etc. He mentioned there is little to no extended time away from home like in the military. Typically, he goes in around 8 or 9 and is home by 5 or 6 unless involved in a major case. But I know there will never be a time divorce would ever be a thought because you will always be my priority and are supportive of Team Payne, we will always persevere!

[This is all ironic reading so many years later. Once I returned from Iraq, I considered a corporate job which I landed with Proctor & Gamble but ultimately turned it down after an Army Reserve mobilization stateside, ended up backing out of graduate school applications for Clinical Psychology, and finally accepted a position with the DEA as a Special Agent. After Quantico, I *was assigned to Tucson, AZ working Southwest Border narcotics. The funny thing was the hours were significant and many of the operations were high-risk and not done by SWAT teams. Not to mention, it may not be the best career choice regarding less stress after coming home from **war**. Laura and I were on the brink of divorce numerous times as I never acknowledged the effects of Post Traumatic Stress Disorder from combat and the challenges of a new marriage started after leaving for **war** and a DEA academy at Quantico, VA. But through **faith** and **love**, we persevered. Did the stress lessen then? That would probably be another book!]*

2225: I feel the Lord growing stronger and stronger in my life. My heart is so full of **love** and **faith** in Jesus; more than I have ever felt before or known. I just pray to Him you will be touched by this same desire. Being away from you is hard, but He is filling the void because He is everything. Through Him, you and I can make it. We can do anything. I feel very empowered because today in our **faith** group meeting CPT Felix [ICU Nurse on the FST] showed up and boy can she talk. I do believe she knows Jesus but is missing some of the mark as she spoke of her concern for these Iraqis in foreign lands that won't be reached and how those who do good deeds aren't necessarily condemned to hell. As tactfully as I could, I corrected her and began to describe how infinite and forgiving Jesus' **love** is, there is only one true path- Jesus Christ. I referred her to John 3:16 and 14:6-7. It made me feel as if Jesus was progressing through my life in so many ways. I felt as if I was gaining an understanding of how to reach others with God's **love** and message. Also, 2 Timothy 2:23-26 made it very clear to me what we are to do as Christians.

*Not a day goes by that I don't feel more in **love** with our Savior and in turn, my **love** for you beats even deeper in my heart. It makes me so excited at the wonderful blessing that you and I must begin our marriage as Christians and not have to figure it out years later. It is going to make our marriage and life together so much richer and more amazing. I cannot wait to return home and **love** as Christ **love**d His church. I will respect you forever, put you on a pedestal, and make you feel like the most beautiful angel in the world sent down for me. I have legally and emotionally pledged my life to you, but I so look forward to our "official" wedding when we bond for life spiritually. Our life together will be blessed no matter what lies before us. If things have been difficult for you as we have been separated, begin rejoicing in the things that I speak of and turn towards God. Through Him and Him only can we find comfort and answers. Laura, I know when I return that our lives will be so much better for us. It will be like a renewed spirit that you and I will get to share and never allow one another to let go of. Laura, our **love** is enriched through Christ.*

*Ephesians 5:25 says, "Husbands, **love** your wives just as Christ **love**d the church and gave Himself up for her…" In Him, we can find in each other someone who will forever **love** to forget the worst and bring out the best. I know with that being true, nothing will ever separate us. I know these things I have written are powerful, but I feel that I have to express these words and feelings to you, and hope this reaches you as soon as possible. I have all the **faith** in the world in God that you know this and feel it in your heart, too. I have to know it, please tell me in your own words. Pray in your heart for it.*

I am so glad I wrote my contract to you that I will have to revise throughout our marriage to remind me how to be the best husband to you. How I long to see you and have my arms around you, but I will continue to pray God has the ultimate plan that will lead us back together again in His time. We have so much through Christ to look forward to in our marriage and I can't wait. I **love** you very much. Thank you, God, for sending me, Laura. I must praise God for our two years together because of the amazing evolution of our **love** through Him and our growing **faith**. One of the greatest times we have had was our profession of **love** and we were baptized together under Christ our Lord.

March 17 Deployment Day 45

Laura: We watched President Bush speak last night. I am worried because the future is so uncertain. I want you to come home now. I don't want you in harm's way. Every night I pray that you will be safe and come home soon and know that I **love** you. It is really hard to look at photos of us. That is what prompted me to be sad, then listening to Bush, then our phone conversation was cut off. It sucks so much when that happens. I just want to talk. It didn't feel like I was even able to say I **love** you. But please know that I do miss you so much. I hope that this happens quickly, so you and all the other soldiers can get back home. I'm assuming this was our last call for a while and that is what scares me. [This was the last phone call we made before our lines of communication ended which was a very empty feeling to know it was possible, we may never speak again if I didn't make it home.]

March 18 Deployment Day 46

Robert: *How happy and sad can I be within one minute? Well, I just got through on the phone and as you were giving me your address we got cut off. I tried and tried again. But I am so glad I got to tell you I **love** you and miss you, which is the most important thing you can know. This is our 'Happy Marriage' card since I can't be there on April 5th I hope this card and the flowers reach you. [We were to have our wedding on April 5th, so I had a very close friend bring Laura flowers and this card on April 5th.]*

*Readiness has become our focus. The President addressed the nation and gave Saddam Hussein and his regime 48 hours to flee into exile or face military support. I think everyone in Kuwait knows he will not go into exile, so we are within 48 hours of going into Iraq. What can I say at a time like this that I haven't already said? Laura, through Jesus Christ, you are my world and my life. I **love** you unconditionally and promise to **love** you forever. I cannot imagine my life without you. With the utmost sincerity, I know you are my life soulmate because you are God's gift to me.*

*When I got cut off talking to you, MAJ Kirk said, "Well, at least you got to say I **love** you." Capt. Felix said, "I'm sure you don't even have to say that because she already knows that without a doubt." People outside of us even know how strong our **love** is. What I need you to do is turn to God every day and continue to pray for me and everyone here. Pray that you and I will soon be reunited in God's plan. I trust in Him that He will protect us all. With His strength, we can handle it all.*

Chapters 5-8 Personal Observations

I never imagined during a **war** in 2003, we would have to shift to old-school letter writing like veterans of WWII. Not to mention trying to make calls with an old-school DNVT [military wired] phone that would eventually get cut off for security purposes. There was minimal to no internet access except for the tactical operations center (TOC). Shortly before our unit was to cross the border to start the **war**, I was handed an Iridium satellite cell phone to help manage patient evacuations, but we were admonished no personal calls, Army business only. So, the reality of communications had truly set in during this period. I honestly had accepted if I were to be killed in combat, I was thankful for the **love** I had found with Laura. I could not fathom anyone preparing for **war** with no reliance on **faith**. It was only through **faith** and **love** I was going to endure this experience.

It was during this period the reality and stressors of preparing for **war** were setting in for us all on the 126th FST, and the rest of the soldiers I presume. 3ID had a unique challenge when we were all pushed into the desert at the Kuwait – Iraq border so the 101st Airborne could come into Camp Pennsylvania. 4th ID was to come from the North through Turkey but that didn't happen. The 2003 Iraq Invasion was initially handled by 3ID, 1st Marine Expeditionary Force, and the 173rd Airborne Brigade to my memory. I do not believe that was the initial tactical plan and deviating from that without the amount of resources to provide governance and fully occupy would be a tragic error the US military handled for over a decade.

I remember a funny story briefed at a Battalion Operations meeting when 3ID moved to the border some of the front-line Iraqi units began surrendering because they thought the **war** had started. Our military force was overwhelming against the Iraqi military. The Iraqi military had no idea what was about to come….'shock and awe' of the US military!

CHAPTER 9
AS WE PREPARE FOR WAR

March 19–Pre-War Day 1

Robert: *Please remember the security of all of this info is not to be discussed. By now you are probably seriously worried. Since our mail service will be limited for a while you probably won't get this until the whole mess is over. I'll write anyway so you know what I was thinking and feeling during this. The key to the whole thing and my coming home safely is the Lord. Pray to our God to make this go according to His plan. Last night, a few of us who have been meeting for this **faith** group met and prayed for every individual on the team and our families. So now I am sitting in my HMMWV listening to the Army radio on my little stereo. I lost reception to the one American station, but I found a Kuwait station that occasionally plays American songs.*

*I can't say I am not a little apprehensive, but I have **faith** in all the prayers. I just hope you're okay. Know that I think of you all the time and miss you so much. I sent a letter off before the **war** began talking about how fortunate life will be as we begin as a Christian couple.*

*I never thought I would be sitting in my HMMWV with everyone lined up near a border prepared to go to **war**. Hopefully, once the air strikes begin our job will be minimal. I hope no one needs our FST* services. From what the media has said, the airstrikes will be ten times more than Desert Storm in a third of the time. That's a lot of destruction. I certainly pray for those Iraqis who want to leave but can't. If I'm a little scared, I can't imagine what they think as they are about to face the largest, most powerful armed forces in the world. God bless us all. I know I have to continue to thank God for all that I have, even here. So, I relate to this verse for today, Ephesians 5:20 which is: "Always giving thanks to God the Father for everything, in the name of our Lord Jesus Christ."

We are waiting on the President's call and for the air strikes to begin. Maybe our prayers will get Saddam into exile to avoid all of this.

March 20 – Pre-War Day 2

Laura: *I'm wondering and concerned about how you are doing. Are you scared? I hope your **faith** will remove any fear you may have. You will be safe because God is on your side and He knows you have so much to come home to. Robert, you are an amazing person. I've never known anyone as special as you. You live life like we all should, to its fullest. You have this natural charisma that attracts people along with a heart filled with so much **love** for people. I'm so lucky to be able to spend my life with you.*

*So, do you know what your role will be in establishing peace there after the **war**? I wonder if you will work in a hospital or what. I just can't help thinking about what you do every day. I look forward to hearing all about your experience. It will be an experience that most of us will never know. I'm going to be here with an ear to listen and a heart to care. This is what I can offer for a lifetime. You know, even though we are apart and can't talk much I still feel so close to you… my best friend, husband, and soulmate. I **love** you so much and can't wait for you to come home.*

Operation Iraqi Freedom

For Immediate Release
Office of the Press Secretary
March 19, 2003

President Bush Addresses the Nation

The Oval Office
https://georgewbush-whitehouse.archives.gov/news/releases/2003/03/20030319-17.html

10:16 P.M. EST

THE PRESIDENT: My fellow citizens, at this hour, American and coalition forces are in the early stages of military operations to disarm Iraq, to free its people and to defend the world from grave danger.

On my orders, coalition forces have begun striking selected targets of military importance to undermine Saddam Hussein's ability to wage war. These are the opening stages of what will be a broad and concerted campaign. More than 35 countries are giving crucial support — from the use of naval and air bases, to help with intelligence and logistics, to the deployment of combat units. Every nation in this coalition has chosen to bear the duty and share the honor of serving in our common defense.

To all the men and women of the United States Armed Forces now in the Middle East, the peace of a troubled world and the hopes of an oppressed people now depend on you. That trust is well placed.

The enemies you confront will come to know your skill and bravery. The people you liberate will witness the honorable and decent spirit of the American military. In this conflict, America faces an enemy who has no regard for conventions of war or rules of morality. Saddam Hussein has placed Iraqi troops and equipment in civilian areas, attempting to use innocent men, women and children as shields for his own military — a final atrocity against his people.

I want Americans and all the world to know that coalition forces will make every effort to spare innocent civilians from harm. A campaign on the harsh terrain of a nation as large as California could be longer and more difficult than some predict. And helping Iraqis achieve a united, stable and free country will require our sustained commitment.

We come to Iraq with respect for its citizens, for their great civilization and for the religious faiths they practice. We have no ambition in Iraq, except to remove a threat and restore control of that country to its own people.

I know that the families of our military are praying that all those who serve will return safely and soon. Millions of Americans are praying with you for the safety of your loved ones and for the protection of the innocent. For your sacrifice, you have the gratitude and respect of the American people. And you can know that our forces will be coming home as soon as their work is done.

Our nation enters this conflict reluctantly — yet, our purpose is sure. The people of the United States and our friends and allies will not live at the mercy of an outlaw regime that threatens the peace with weapons of mass murder. We will meet that threat now, with our Army, Air Force, Navy, Coast Guard and Marines, so that we do not have to meet it later with armies of fire fighters and police and doctors on the streets of our cities.

Now that conflict has come, the only way to limit its duration is to apply decisive force. And I assure you, this will not be a campaign of half measures, and we will accept no outcome but victory.

My fellow citizens, the dangers to our country and the world will be overcome. We will pass through this time of peril and carry on the work of peace. We will defend our freedom. We will bring freedom to others and we will prevail.

May God bless our country and all who defend her.

END 10:20 P.M. EST

March 20 – Iraq War Day 1 – declared at 0545

Robert: *Woke up today at 0400 and I have been fairly busy today getting grids for my map, digging a hole for trash burning, creating a way to poop between the vehicle and the trailer, then we*

watched a 2LT get promoted to 1LT. We heard bits and pieces of the President's speech as he announced we had begun our attack to remove Saddam. Sounded like 0545 our time, at dusk, the air strikes began which prevented me from believing the ground fight would begin 24 hours later. That means sometime tomorrow we should roll across the berm into Iraq. This all still feels so like training that I have to stop and remind myself this is the real thing. Had our first "real realization" today when it came over the net radio that a scud had been launched from Iraq. It was headed way south of us into Kuwait somewhere as we are close to Iraq. Luckily, it was intercepted, blown up, and never hit its target area. Thank God. But it means somebody wants to fight and that sucks.

Laura, you have come across my mind so many times today. I am praying for you, for your comfort and understanding during all of this. I know how hard this must be and I wish you didn't have to endure it, but you know I am here for all the right reasons: the future of our country, the future of our children who will grow up in the U.S., my friends, my family, you, and God. Because He has placed me here away from you, He has a plan, and it will lead me home to you soon. We have to continue to pray and have **faith** in His plan for us. That is what will get us both through and back into each other's arms.

You would not believe how many vehicles we are moving with! Three columns of 160 plus with over 500 vehicles are just the support unit for one brigade. There are many more out here. It's all very overwhelming moving on these convoys with so many people. But we must get there being outside Baghdad, about 300 plus miles away. It will take many long days and nights. I pray God keeps us all safe. But realization sets in when we realize we have real clips of ammo, the NBC antidote shots, and the real chemical gear.

I'll reflect on Psalm 27:1 for comfort, "The Lord is my light and my salvation whom shall I fear? The Lord is the stronghold of my life of whom shall I be afraid?"

CHAPTER 10
Fear of the Unknown

March 21 – Iraq War Day 2

Laura: *I've already moved to Ft Worth, but I came down to Austin tonight to wrap up. I miss it here and hate to leave the place where our memories together began. We will make memories wherever we go. I was so excited because I received four more of your letters today. You are so amazing with your words. Your letters made me so happy that I cried. And you know I'm not a 'happy crier'.*

*I can tell through your letters that your **faith** and relationship with God have grown even stronger. This is so wonderful. You are inspiring me with your words. I have been praying every day and reaching for God's Word for comfort. I think that is the way I can grow stronger with you. Becki once told me you should always be reaching up for the hand of a Christian stronger than you to help you grow. You are that person for me because you are stronger. I have also been watching 700 Club. The person speaking was an officer in combat in Somalia. He said that if it were his choice, he would have laid down his weapon and hidden it in a corner. He prayed to God and then remembered that it was His will and not ours. Then he was driving through the city and a Somalian* launched a shoulder rocket 10 feet from his vehicle, it flew over the hood and hit the wall. He couldn't believe it! He shared Christ with his fellow men that day. Now he's a chaplain in the Army.

I was saddened in your letter from day 23 that you hadn't received any letters except 2 & 3. It makes me cry to hear that because I have written almost every day.

I can't wait to have a family with you. You are going to be the best dad ever, I know. Our kids will be so lucky! I was thinking about this the other day – do you think many people talk about issues like how to raise children, money, debt, etc. before they get married? I just don't see how one couldn't. I'm so fortunate to have such an open husband who talks through issues before they arise. That is going to help us so much in our marriage. On our marriage, I can't wait to be together again.

This is the first day that my emotions have been filled with sadness and fear. You guys are kicking ass out there. I can't imagine being there and watching the bombs drop in Bagdad. I keep watching TV, flipping through the news hoping to get a glimpse of you. The pictures we got this week helped so much. I look forward to the day I hear your voice again.

Robert: Today, we crossed into Iraq, probably somewhere around noon or 1 p.m. It was fairly clear where it was because of the triple fencing and barbed wire that had been breached. We have been sitting in an "attack position" holding area awaiting move-out orders to another attack position about ten miles shy of a major highway we'll be on. Then we will be a quarter of the way to Baghdad. Tonight, we will be driving at night which always complicates matters, but we'll have our lights on. I pray for all our safety. We had to get into our chemical suit last night for precaution, but man does it make things hotter and make you feel like a doughboy.

Fear of the Unknown

Last night about midnight, I had the crap scared out of me. I was sleeping and was awakened by some extremely large and loud rockets in the sky from us into Iraq. Man, they lit up the sky like nothing I've ever seen before. At first, though, I didn't know where they were coming from. Very shocking to be woken up that way from a deep sleep. We woke up at 0400, prepped vehicles, went to a meeting, and moved out a few hours later. We had lunch sitting in Iraq eating a black bean and rice burrito with Tostito salsa someone else had. Pretty good. It's the small things that keep one happy.

We are moving three columns of 160 vehicles marked with circles, squares, or diamonds [marked on the rear bumpers] and made up of everything in the BDE Support area. We are in the middle column with 10 vehicles and 8 trailers. We were able to borrow two High Mobility Multipurpose Wheeled Vehicles (HUMMWV), not being used, and acquire the two CBPS systems giving us a total of ten vehicles. More than enough room so everyone is either driving or sitting in the shotgun seat. I am in the trail vehicle with Dr. Kirk up front. I was able to acquire an Army radio, so I hear all the command traffic. It is a great idea to always have a military radio in the front and back of any convoy. Thus far, I believe there has been little confrontation which is a good thing. The Marines have seized a port and the British forces have secured some oil fields. The Army forces have control of an airfield and continue moving toward Baghdad. Once we are close to the city, we anticipate there may be activity. I pray it doesn't.

*I continue to pray for your comfort of mind. Colossians 4:2 says, "Devote yourselves to prayer, be watchful and thankful. That is everything that it takes." I miss you and **love** you.*

March 23 – Iraq War Day 4

Robert @ 0545: *It has been a long few days, working about 36 hours with only 2-3 hours of sleep and that wasn't great. Most of our time has been spent driving or sitting in our vehicles. Just now listened to a whole conversation that involved an accident at the rear of our convoy. Sounds like a Marine HMMWV C3/2nd Marines ran into the back of a towed 5-ton truck. Dr. Kirk and Dr. Beverly went back with the C 3rd FSB medics and I stayed on the radio in the middle of the column with the FST to get the Quick Reaction Surgical Team ready if we are needed. Well, we didn't need to go back there. A call MAJ Kirk made said they were waiting on a MEDEVAC (medical evacuation) [mark of ink in the original writing where I fell asleep at this point writing the letter as exhaustion was already setting in]. Sadly, one of the four people in the wreck died. So sad because he was just moving out like everyone else and an accident took his life. So far there have been two helicopter accidents and this one happened an hour ago. The total missing or dead is twenty and I believe those are all accidents and not combat-related. Goes to show how dangerous things can get. We have been on a major highway sitting for several hours waiting to move forward. You would not believe the immense number of vehicles trying to move north toward Baghdad. You probably have seen or heard about it on TV.*

Robert @ 0807: *Dr. Kirk came back and I saw pictures of the accident. 3 of the 4 guys were asleep and then the driver fell asleep sideswiping three vehicles before hitting head-on into the towed truck. I think the driver must have died from blunt-force trauma. The others had various facial traumas. I pray for them all.*

So, we are all still waiting on the side of the highway…those Marines are in front of us. [Chris Chase is one of my best friends *from Texas A&M Corps of Cadets and a Marine officer deployed into the same **war**, but we never crossed paths while deployed]. I wonder if he is out here and where he is. It would be great to randomly run into him out here.*

Heard that they have been bombing the crap out of Baghdad. We haven't heard this far back, but the more havoc we cause now hopefully the less painful this will be later. We have only made it a little over a quarter of our way. The last three quarters will be the main concern because we will be just outside Baghdad, but God is with us so we cannot fail.

CHAPTER 11
Road to Exhaustion

March 24–Iraq War Day 5

Robert @ 1725: *It has been about 48 hours now with three hours of sleep. The movement and sitting in the vehicles have been nonstop. When we do move, it is so painfully slow you just want to shoot something. What we saw yesterday driving on the outskirts of Al Nasiriyah was the impoverished citizens of Iraq. Felt like I was watching a Sally Strothers commercial. All they wanted from us was MREs and water. They were mainly children, but we were told not to give them any food. Kept having to shoo away people from the vehicles. I think they were supportive of us being here or they just didn't care. The only thing I did was trade a US dollar for two Iraqi (dollars) with Saddam Hussein's picture on it.*

We are wondering if they killed Saddam yet. We are not getting any updates out here except what one of the guy's shortwave radio reports from the British news. Sounds like mainly accidents have taken soldiers' lives thus far except for some crazy enemy soldier who threw some grenades and fired into a command TOC. Don't know the details.

[Ironically, this incident mentioned above was a terrorist attack by an Islamic extremist within the US Army that I have

recently used in my briefings on Military Extremism, which was my 2020 US Army **War** College strategic research project/topic. What happened days before the US invasion of Iraq, on March 23, 2003, Hasan Akbar threw hand grenades and shot at soldiers of the 101st Airborne, killing two officers and wounding 12 others. When asked why he did it, Akbar calmly stated, "You guys are coming into our countries, and you're going to rape our women and kill our children." Akbar was a US Army Sergeant at the time of the attack. (Bart E. Womack, Embedded Enemy: The Insider Threat, (Irving, TX: Inspire On Purpose Publishing, 2013), 111. When I was with 3D ID in 2003, we were pushed from Camp Pennsylvania to the Kuwaiti border awaiting the go-to **war** order, 101st Airborne took possession of Camp Pennsylvania. Days after that occurred, SGT Hasan Akbar attacked his fellow soldiers at Camp Pennsylvania before 101st was to begin the Iraq **War**. It was a devastating and horrible terrorist attack, yet the efforts of this military extremist did not stop the **war**. The US military still served and executed its primary objective of warfighting for a political purpose. Naturally, the DoD addressing military extremism as a priority has been challenging through two decades of fighting wars. Radicalization within our ranks and military extremism has existed as a US national security threat for far too long and now is the time for action. In 2020, after the US Capitol riots on January 6th, the Secretary of Defense, Lloyd J. Austin III, made the issue of military extremists a priority. The topic was my strategic research project for my time at US Army War College in the Academic Year 2020 and allowed me to stay on as a research fellow and present over 25+ different engagements on military extremism].

    Today was a blur other than driving across the desert this morning. It was a nice sunrise, but then the sands came. They were horrid, barely able to see in front of your vehicle. I had to break off with Major Beverly in a convoy to let him do a neuro check on a soldier who had fallen off a fuel truck and hit his head. Turned out to be a concussion. Then during the sandstorm, two vehicles turned over with only minor injuries although they did air evac. Now I'm in the HUMMWV Laura 4 again waiting at the refueling point before another several-hour drive to a location that is maybe halfway there. It will be 48 plus hours without sufficient sleep. Can't say I have been 'driven' as hard as this before. Last night, one of the drivers almost flipped a CBPS when he slid off the side of a small ravine, but you know how he fixed it? Laura 4's wench! We used your wench to pull it free. So glad it worked rather than flipping [ironic because I was almost killed when a HUMMVW flipped over the night we assaulted into Baghdad]. I am just continuing to pray we do not have any American casualties, and that this is all over soon. Would be nice to think the closer to Baghdad the closer I am to home and you. Every time I have needed an energy boost or pick me up, I look at a picture of you and your smile. This has certainly been an adventure. Everyone is looking worn, but we are at least getting to sleep while we move because one vehicle stopped working so we are towing it.

Laura: *Hanging with friends has been a good distraction from the incessant coverage of the* **war**. *It has been such a trying week. I just worry about your safety. I don't want to live life without you. I can't even imagine my life without you. God is on your side and He will protect you. I check the news, and e-mail, and read the reports from the Savannah Now (reporter) team that is with you to get a sense of what you are experiencing. The day we were supposed to marry is fast approaching. I wish we were here, living the life we had, but this time has made me feel closer to you. It's* strange how we've had little communication, but I feel that God has strengthened our relationship even more.

March 25 – Iraq War Day 6 (Deployment Day 53)

Robert @ 1656: *Everything is blending so it's hard to realize what has happened because it was all a blur thus far. Last night, our movement took us to a large refueling area where it took well over four hours to finally refuel the Brigade Support Area (BSA). One part of the whole BSA got split up and went ahead to our next assembly area while the large majority had to find everyone, police broken vehicles, get fuel, deal with rollover accidents, etc. So, after refueling the 3D FSB Battalion Executive Officer (the Battalion Commander was with the forward units) made a great leadership decision to let everyone sleep for 4 hours in a holding area and move out at daylight. [I distinctly remember this night amongst all the vehicles refueling and myself and MAJ Kirk going to talk with the Battalion XO about our planned movement. He was getting pressure from the Battalion Commander, LTC Bobby Towery, to keep moving our logistical train and medical units to catch up. But MAJ Kirk and I pled with him to delay the movement or more soldiers would needlessly die that evening due to exhaustion in more vehicle accidents. I think this advice coming from his Forward Surgical Team leaders did the trick and he agreed to a four-hour pause where we all rested and rotated security. I still think that rest saved people's lives before we moved out again.]*

We then moved through a large encampment incline, went way out in the desert, stopped next to some small village, moved again, and now we are set. It has been almost 200 plus miles in 5 days, and it is rough. Wearing all this gear and the chemical suit doesn't help anything because it is getting hot during the day. We are now all sitting in the HMMWV to get out of the worst sandstorm ever. You literally cannot see 5 feet in front of you. It is 4 p.m. but so dark because of the sandstorm and it is turning the sky into a swarming band of orange. It is a weather phenomenon I have never witnessed. It is really kind of scary when we hear artillery rounds going off near us and our forces returning fire.

*Right now, we are awaiting some inbound enemy prisoner-of-**war** causalities. Not sure of the nature of their injuries, but the FST might have to operate if needed. The problem is going over to set up with the Charlie company in this weather [sandstorm]. I know God will see us through this. I am glad we haven't seen any American soldiers yet, but we are ¾ of the way now, 5 days into the **war** and about to move to assault Baghdad, so it could start happening soon. I pray it doesn't though.*

*There was a solemn moment today when the Battalion commander was briefing us that twelve American soldiers (3D ID) had been captured in Al Nasiriyah when they went the wrong way. [This is the highly covered media story about the convoy with Iraqi Freedom's first Prisoner of **War**, PVT Jessica Lynch, with the 507th Maintenance Company, within our convoy. PVT Lynch was later saved by Special Operations Forces on April 1, 2003, the first successful rescue of a POW since WWII and the first ever of a woman in combat. Their convoy simply made a wrong turn at some point and was ambushed near Nasiriyah, which was near the Euphrates River northwest of Basra, Iraq. Honestly, we all heard the radio traffic to go around the town and stay in line, so I don't truly know how that happened to their convoy. Of the 11 soldiers killed in the ambush, I recall one of them was from 3D FSB, our battalion.] He said they executed seven of them on TV. Dear Lord, how do I process that and manage to focus on their* *families and **love**d ones? It preceded more information on the small fighting Iraq contingents that probe areas in 2- or 3-man teams that fire indirect mortar rounds.*

*No one has been reported hurt yet. I just hope the airstrikes are successful, the safer it will be for American forces. This is surreal at times but certainly proves to be an apprehensive situation. The loss of any human life is a sad thing, but a soldier is tough to handle knowing they have a family back home waiting on them. Not to worry, my **faith** and prayers will bring me home to you soon. Sounds like the EPWs have arrived. Not enough info yet for us to react though. Gotta go, I'll write later.*

CHAPTER 12
First Casualties of War

March 27 – Iraq War Day 8

Robert: *This has probably been the first time I have slowed down since my last entry. The casualties have been steadily coming in. As the FST, we have operated on two abdominal injuries of Enemy Prisoners of* **War** *(EPW) and we checked out an American soldier who got shot in the neck/shoulder area. We could not operate because he needed more than we could do here, but he was breathing on his own. The adjacent medical unit has had several more, a few soldiers but about six or seven EPWs. I heard from our brigade S-1 that there are some 600 plus Iraqis that have been killed and some that probably haven't been found. The American numbers are undetermined, but no matter what, it is more than what it should be.*

The reports that seven Americans had been executed turned out to be Iraqi propaganda and not true, so I am told. I certainly pray that is true. This is something, seeing the real thing come in from direct fire conflicts from **war**. *We have also had a couple of injuries from head-on collision accidents.*

You wouldn't believe how painful 2 nights ago it was once we arrived in our most recent area. The first patients were five EPWs and we were not set up next to C Med yet because of a horrible sandstorm. This was the most difficult setup ever, very physically demanding. When we were less than 500 feet away trying to bring two more of our vehicles back, four of us had to hang on to one another and walk through the pitch black. Visibility was one foot in front of you, horrible sand blowing, trying to find our stuff. 30 minutes later, it was just as hard to find our way back. [This was a shamal sandstorm that stopped the **war**. I have never seen anything like it again in my life the sky turning from orange to black because of the sand. I remember wondering if this darkness would have been what the rapture would be like when Jesus would return to take Christians to heaven. It was surreal and a very difficult point for us in the initial phase of the **war**. I almost got lost in the shamal trying to find our vehicles to lead them back to the location where we were setting up the surgical tent. I found myself wondering how I would get back if I did get lost in the shamal. The only thing that saved me was a small Garmin GPS I bought at Best Buy before I left. Once we assembled the team and began offloading all the treatment and surgical equipment the hard work began. This is where I injured my rhomboid in my left shoulder which is a chronic injury that I deal with to this day. I am thankful for the VA and my service connection to help me treat it over the years, although I have accepted it will never get better.] The night finally ended with our 2nd CBPS up for surgery and several of us laid out, sprawled out, consuming water as quickly as possible [from physical exhaustion].

 The next morning, the sandstorm continued making the sky a very orange-colored day. Guess who led out two ambulances in it to drop off EPWs and pick up some blood? Yours truly! It was a bit apprehensive being we had five injured EPWs, about nine medics with M-16s, and two [non-medic soldiers] for security with machine guns, but no other [armed] escort. We made it there and back safely. [This was very scary, escorting 2 FLAs (Ambulances) to the next level of care the 212*th* M*A*S*H, which I still believe was the last known M*A*S*H in the US Army before it was later de-activated [https://www.stripes.com/branches/Army-s-last-mash-unit-stretched-to-its-limits-in-iraq-1.4194]. That little Garmin GPS truly was a lifesaver rolling through the middle of the desert because we had to alter course off a road after coming upon an infantry unit that had 10 or 12 Iraqi Republican Guard enemy soldiers prone at gunpoint. The Infantry unit NCOs **war**ned me not to go on the road we were on. I was the convoy commander and I recall staying confident and calm for all the soldiers/medics but I was scared shitless as well. Thankfully we made it to the 212*th* M*A*S*H, dropped off our patients, re-supplied, grabbed some MREs, and headed back before our convoy moved out towards Baghdad.]

It was surreal that at one point [last night], we had one American soldier and one EPW each on a litter five feet from each other that could have been shooting at each other just before they came in for medical care. Sometimes it is hard to decipher how the injuries have occurred, but we do the best we can. [I recall how ironic that moment was and nothing had ever prepared me for any training scenario where a US soldier and an enemy prisoner of **war** were lying near one another, we treated them both, and took the enemy in for surgery before the US soldier due to the severity of the injuries. It proved to me what medical professionals do when they swear an oath to provide care and what separates the US from our enemy countries.]

We have traveled ¾ of the way and are stationary for a few days before the next assault. We probably have one or two more jumps until our final destination, but I have finally gotten some rest. I continue to pray and count God's blessings. I hope and pray we do not see more wounded American soldiers. Here is my verse for today: "Cast your cares on the Lord and he will sustain you; He will never let the righteous fall" (Psalm 53). I believe we are the righteous.

Laura: *I've been keeping up with the Savannah Now reports. Today the article talked about treating the Iraqis. You guys were mentioned…also, Jessica told us that Randy jumped into Northern Iraq yesterday. [Laura is referring to one of my best friends from my Army days as a young Platoon Leader in 2/7 CAV. Randy Riker was a Captain with the 173rd Airborne from Vicenza, Italy who jumped to secure the oil fields of Northern Iraq. Randy served 20 years and deployed many times as an Infantry Officer. I still talk to Randy today and consider him a close personal friend. He retired in 2020 which made me start to feel like an old Army officer!] The media makes me so mad telling every move we are making. I feel like they should take the battle plans and just hand them over to Saddam. Your part of the 3rd ID doesn't get any TV coverage that I have seen. I'm glad they are being kept on the down low, maybe that will keep them safe…I **love** you with all my heart Robert. You are the most important person in my life. I pray that you are safe and that we will be back together soon.*

March 28 – Iraq War Day 9

Robert: *Had our fourth surgery patient last night. Only have done surgery on three of them and they were all EPWs (Enemy Prisoners of **War**). The last guy was pretty shot up. He had at least four gunshot wounds to the belly, femur, ankle, and arm. He was a young guy, perhaps an officer. They certainly expended some supplies fixing him up. Crazy isn't it? We have to fix what we break.*

I have been assisting in the evac process, ordering supplies, following vehicle maintenance, and helping where I can. Looks like we will be moving forward soon. Pray for continued safety for us and all our soldiers. We hear reports of Iraqis using civilians as shields or making them surrender with white flags to ambush us. They are certainly playing dirty.

*Sorry if I make you anxious but I am with a large support element, protected on all sides by mounted weapons, and the Lord is here helping us all. I read some good scripture on hope through **faith** as an example to others: I Peter 3:14-15, "through Him I have hope in all"…His plan for us, this **war**, my return home safely, my return home soon. I miss you so much….whoa, they just fired off some artillery and it scared the 'bejeezus' out of me. Anyway, getting used to it…it will be a transition when I return getting back into the groove of one another's company every day but a minor challenge I can't wait for. Just know that I will return the same old Robert that left, just one that **love**s you more every day.*

*[This is true, I do **love** my wife every day since I returned from the **war** in 2003 but I did not return the same Robert that left. Post Traumatic Stress Disorder is a real thing many veterans deal with because they are exposed to stressors and things you are not supposed to see, things you cannot unsee once it has happened, and the constant threat of death. I returned and chose to ignore it all. I had my life to live and move on. It wasn't until 2009, shortly before my first child was to be born that I went to the Veterans Affairs and sought help for my anger, my frustrations, and my anxiety. Those several years after my return and entering my Special Agent career with the Drug Enforcement Administration (DEA) working narcotics on the Southwest Border in Tucson, AZ was not ideal. I still thank God to this day I stayed married during*

those years. I had challenges that I didn't understand. I sought help and am thankful Laura stayed with me.]

*It sucks not knowing what you are doing, did you start the job, are you still looking, how is home, how is the marathon? Sorry had to stop writing, a call came over the net [radio] and I had to put on my [chemical protective] mask. So now I'm sitting here writing you in my mask. What a joy! Only a precaution though, nothing in this area. Man, I need to scratch my nose. I'm going to check on an incoming Enemy Prisoner of **War** (EPW) since I can't eat now.*

March 30 – Iraq War Day 10

Robert: *Well, this certainly isn't the 100-hour Persian Gulf **War**. It is now 10 days into the **war** and the end isn't on the horizon as far as I can see. [Ironically, I would have never guessed the Iraq **War** would have lasted 8 years from March 20, 2003, through December 15, 2011]. We still have to make the final push North to Baghdad. This will begin tomorrow, and it is a bit apprehensive because the Iraqis know we are coming and how we are coming. They are sending all the fighting forces in front of any support elements in hopes of decimating any defensive resistance. My fear is our [FST & C Med] protection as we travel with a smaller logistical element of the Brigade Support Area (BSA) called a Forward Logistical Element (FLE). [3D ID, 1ˢᵗ Brigade] wants their FST up as far forward as possible [hence Forward Surgical Team!]. I trust the leaders' decisions because I know they wouldn't put us at risk as we are such an asset. Nonetheless, all is in God's hands so no need to worry.*

So, the latest in-patient care. We had our 5ᵗʰ patient and 4ᵗʰ surgery. An EPW that had shrapnel and gunshot wounds all over. His whole right knee had been blown out and I witnessed Dr. Kirk amputate his leg. I got some pics but none I am sure you would like to see. [I will never forget standing outside with our Chief Nurse, MAJ Bill Kuhns, after the surgery, holding the amputated leg in a biohazard bag and discussing what we do with it. Something that was never discussed in the Army Medical Department Officer Basic Course. We ultimately decided to put it in the burn pit and move on with our operations. I will never forget Bill Kuhns, he was an amazing man, and his humor always lightened the moods amid chaos.]

So, I'm here in Iraq, middle of the desert, about 150 miles from Baghdad, helping out with patient treatment [as an EMT], air & ground evacuation, ordering medical supplies, and ordering maintenance supplies for the vehicles [the essence of an FST Executive Officer]. I am about to go to a Protestant service in an hour and will pray for His guidance, **love**, comfort, and protection in all of this mess.

How are the finances? I hope you are seeing the extra money [hazard duty pay, combat pay, and tax-free salary]. If not, I'll get back paid and we will have a lot of it come in at once. Not to worry, I trust you with all my money decisions. I don't care at this point, it's just money. I only care about returning to my life with you. I pray you are as happy as can be. I'm sure your heart aches as mine does. I guess this is the feeling when soulmates are pulled apart. I **love** you so much. God be with us both.

CHAPTER 13
12 Personal Observations

When thinking back to before the **war** started, I remember the two General Officers' 'go to **war**' speeches. The first one was from MG Blount, Commanding General of the 3D Infantry Division, to his line commanders. I was sent because I was a Captain even though I was not officially a commander at the time. Everyone just assumed I was because most did not realize Forward Surgical Teams were commanded by a Field Grade Officer Surgeon. He was very personable and honest. He told us he needed four good days from us, but I never expected that meant – I need you to cross the border into Iraq and go for four days straight without stopping to make it to Baghdad. That was essentially what happened, and it was rough. I have never been more scared, anxious, or exhausted in my life. The only time in my life I can equate those feelings, emotions, and physical exhaustion was after each one of my kids was born. The funny thing is I also remember MG Blount's fly was open as he spoke to us because I was on the front row, and he propped his knee up on a chair. It was so distracting, and I don't know how his aide didn't notice, or maybe he did and didn't know how to interrupt the Commanding General during a 'go to **war**' speech and say, 'Hey sir, your fly is open."

The other 'go to **war**' speech was also in Kuwait before we crossed into Iraq. It was from LTG William Wallace, V Corps Commander, to hundreds of 3ID Task Force. He was very motivating, but no one could get passed the fact his name was William Wallace from Braveheart. One young brave soldier screamed out a Braveheart movie line, "He's William Wallace and he's got fire coming from his arse!" But LTG Wallace didn't miss a beat and turned around, grabbed his cheeks, and showed us his butt (not dropping his pants of course), like in the movie. I was never able to confirm but he made an Aggie reference so he may have very well been a Texas A&M graduate. He made it clear the 'shock and awe' and 'road to Baghdad' was not going to be easy and we would lose some, and not everyone would come back home. Both humbling and scary to hear that in a speech. Nothing can truly prepare you for those anxious feelings no matter how much you have trained. But he also motivated us as well that we were part of an opportunity in history to liberate a nation from a dictator and protect America from an emerging threat. It was surreal, being motivated and scared in one, but it also felt like I was in a movie.

Ironically, I will say that the training I had experienced since entering the Army Medical Department Officer Basic Course and as a Platoon Leader in 2-7 CAV at Ft Hood, TX was not too far off from my experience in **war**. In the Army, we train as we fight for sure. The 2003 Iraqi invasion was the closest thing to true combat the US military had since the Persian Gulf **War**, but their forces never crossed into Iraq. When I went to the National Training Center in the Mojave Desert in November 2000 with the 1st CAV – 3rd Brigade, it prepared me well for the road to Baghdad. Our FST training at the Army Trauma Training Center (ATTC) at Ryder Trauma Center in Miami, FL in October 2002, prepared our team well to do our surgical mission. But nothing could have ever prepared me for how exhausting those four days pushing to Baghdad were and seeing up close and personal the graphic effects of **war**. Our team had to rely on and trust one another since the 126th FST was pushed so far forward within 3ID, 1st Brigade as the main effort of the fight. For that reason, I will never forget those team members. To this day, I would still presume the 126th FST was the furthest-Forward Surgical Team–ever deployed into an active combat operation. Our motto was 'Phantom FaST!'

CHAPTER 14
APPREHENSION IN THE COMBAT ZONE – LOCKED & LOADED

March 31 War Day 11

Robert: *Sitting here in a convoy waiting to move to a new location about 20 miles away for a few days until we move north for the final push. So, another move for 2-3 days then onward North...I don't know if there is an end in sight. I am not sure when this will all be over for us and I need to have you near me now. I met with our **faith** group last night and everyone is apprehensive and missing home. I have come to realize what it means to **love** you, my wife, as Christ **love**d the church. I **love** you with my whole being, with everything I have, and my life would be incomplete without you in it.*

It is very difficult to not get letters from you (or send them) much less get the chance to talk to you. The feelings and longing I have for you will only prove to be one of the greatest reuniting of two hearts of all time...I wish I knew what you are doing daily.

Things here are very austere. It has been 11-12 days since I bathed, we have only eaten MREs, and I use the bathroom [#2] sitting on an MRE box with a hole in it and a poncho over my head and will continue to wear the same MOPP [Mission Oriented Protective Posture] suit while we are out here. I change my socks, underwear, and T-shirt about every three days. Underneath my MOPP suit, I have only been wearing my boxers and brown t-shirt. Easy access for you, huh? Ohwa Ohwa (funky kinky noise insert here), I miss making you laugh. I miss falling asleep holding you to only awake in the middle of the night realizing we've turned away and I pull you in even closer to me...for now I have to go to a movement rehearsal. Your soulmate, Robert.

April 1 War Day 12

Robert: *Well, we aren't staying in one place very long. We got to a new location last evening, set up most of our stuff, and now have been told to tear down we are waiting to move to a point off the road and await an order to move forward. We have branched off from the BSA into a FLE (Forward Logistical Element) with about forty other vehicles to move forward in front of the BSA (Brigade Support Area). We'll stay a distance behind the fighting force for immediate surgical/medical attention.*

If I say I'm not worried or apprehensive, I would be lying. We are about to move closer to Baghdad through a controlled narrow passage and it could have Iraqi enemy throughout. Pray to God everything makes it safely without ever having to fire our weapons. I am riding with an M-16 in my lap just in case.

Laura: *It is hard to always remember God is in control, but I do know that it is His plan and not mine. I am so thankful and understand that God gave His only Son for us to be forgiven of our sins and that accepting Jesus as our savior is the only way home. I can tell by your letters that you are growing closer to God. Your* letters are inspiring me to dive into God's Word. That is a recognized absence in my life. It is something I need to devote time to. I do pray a lot and recognize that God is who you should look to for everything.

Your picture is on the Texas Aggie network page. It is the pic with the Aggie flag and people are starting to see it and pass it around. You're famous!

April 2 War Day 13

Robert: *Been moving with the FLE since late last night. Working on about 1 hour of sleep for 24 hours, but that's okay. I would certainly say I have been more apprehensive since we have been moving toward Baghdad. Where we set up last night off the road, we watched the initial onslaught of artillery into a town called Karbala which we traveled through today. It was a massive barrage of artillery. I pray for those it may have killed.*

Yesterday, a car full of women and children was killed when they would not stop approaching an American soldier convoy. It was a direct result of anxiety and fear caused by a car bombing that killed four soldiers in the 2-7.

Today, the initial advancement has begun and no causalities as of yet, thank God. So, we are awaiting word to continue moving forward. Not too much further to go. I hope we get to leave from somewhere out here rather than travel back down to Kuwait, that would be painful.

At this point, I certainly have felt the worry of being in a combat zone. Wearing and carrying all the right chemical protection (atropine injectors, etc.) and loaded magazines and weapons. We locked and loaded rounds into the 9mm and M16 as we moved today. Very surreal to have loaded ammo in a weapon with the intent to shoot another human being. Pray it never comes.

Sorry, I fell asleep again [in my writing I often had moments where my writing would fall to scribbling as I would fall asleep]. Boy, I'm pooped. So anyway, it is all in His plan and I'm just a passenger so it will be okay. Psalm 55:22 says, "Cast your cares on the Lord and He will sustain you, He will never let the righteous fall." I **love** you my sweet wife, Robert.

Laura: I just had to write my sweet loving husband tonight. I want to tell you that I **love** you and miss you so much. The world is just not as bright without you in it. We haven't talked in 2 ½ weeks which is an eternity to us! I miss your voice and I miss talking to you every day. Things feel weird right now with the realization of how long you might be gone. I'm trying to make the best of the situation by setting some goals and trying to stay focused. You are the one person I want near me and it is so sad sometimes to think that you aren't. My letters are probably so depressing to read, haha! I apologize I just want to let my feelings out and this is the best way. I am still so very proud of you for doing what you do. It's hard to imagine what you are seeing, how you are feeling, and how you are living. I look forward to hearing about your experience.

Can you believe that our wedding will be this Saturday and next week we would have been in Australia? [Ironically, we never made it to Australia, we settled on Nassau at the Sandals Royal Bahamian Resort for the honeymoon.] We would be in heaven and having so much fun, I'm sure! That is the stuff we can look forward to in the future. Lying on the beach in Australia top-less with you drooling wishing you could jump my bones right there. You never know what might be legal there! I am thinking of you always. I **love** you with all of my heart. Please be safe and come home soon.

April 3 War Day 14

Laura: Today, I received three letters from you. It was so great to hear from you. You had me laughing, smiling, and crying with your words. I **love** sitting on the couch or in my bed reading your amazing writing. Your thoughts just flow together so well.

You had some questions in some of these letters that I do not know if I answered. The Mardi Gras was pretty cool. Rina worked with one of the guys dressed up as Santa Claus. You know I would never share my thoughts with anyone else. They are all for you, my **love**. The move went well. Most things are in storage less than a mile from the house. My bed, desk, dresser, computer, TVs, clothes, and all the electronics are here at the house. They are safe with me. We have a lot of stuff in storage. It is going to be so much fun to move to our new place, whenever that might be. As for saving, we are going to do that. The entitlement kicked in on April 1, so they have some catching up to do. So, the money will start rolling in now and we are going to be in great shape. I bought the camcorder for us so that will be an added expense, but we will have fun with it.

I will do some research for you on the Homeland Security Department. They will probably all want you in their agency after this experience. Robert, I want you to do what makes you happy, but I am concerned about your safety in the fed agencies and the safety of our future family.

[I started with the DEA in 2004 and sadly, as I write this now, one of my fellow first office agents, SA Mike Garbo, was killed on October 4, 2021, in Tucson, AZ where we worked together, he was a fellow agent, neighbor, and friend who will be sadly missed by many. Laura was right, it is dangerous, but I **love** what God has allowed me to do as a Special Agent while continuing to serve others].

I trust your decision to pursue whatever you feel you want to do. I want you to be happy and enjoy what you do. You will make a difference in people's lives no matter what you do because you are so compassionate. [Interesting to read this now because after I came home, I was offered a job with Proctor & Gamble which I accepted. We were gearing up to move to Cincinnati, OH in early 2004, when Laura came to me and said she didn't want us to go because she knew my heart would not be into it, recognizing my continued desire to serve. Fortunately, an Army Reserve mobilization stateside bought me 6 more months until the DEA called me to Quantico and the rest is history].

I would like to find a gym that has a good aerobics program. The best bet seems like Gold's Gym. We are going to Shreveport on Saturday for my mom's birthday. I'm going to hopefully see your mom.

Can you believe our wedding will be this Saturday and next week we will be having so much fun in Australia? That's the stuff we can look forward to in the future.

Have I told you I can't wait for you to come home? I miss you! Will we be able to talk and figure out your homecoming? Do you want certain people to be there? You can let me know and I'll work out the details. All I know is that I want you alone, so I can work you over right!

always. I **love** you with all of my heart. Please be safe and come home soon.

April 3 War Day 14

    Laura: *Today, I received three letters from you. It was so great to hear from you. You had me laughing, smiling, and crying with your words. I* **love** *sitting on the couch or in my bed reading your amazing writing. Your thoughts just flow together so well.*
    You had some questions in some of these letters that I do not know if I answered. The Mardi Gras was pretty cool. Rina worked with one of the guys dressed up as Santa Claus. You know I would never share my thoughts with anyone else. They are all for you, my **love***. The move went well. Most things are in storage less than a mile from the house. My bed, desk, dresser, computer, TVs, clothes, and all the electronics are here at the house. They are safe with me. We have a lot of stuff in storage. It is going to be so much fun to move to our new place, whenever that might be. As for saving, we are going to do that. The entitlement kicked in on April 1, so they have some catching up to do. So, the money will start rolling in now and we are going to be in great shape. I bought the camcorder for us so that will be an added expense, but we will have fun with it.*
    I will do some research for you on the Homeland Security Department. They will probably all want you in their agency after this experience. Robert, I want you to do what makes you happy, but I am concerned about your safety in the fed agencies and the safety of our future family.
    [I started with the DEA in 2004 and sadly, as I write this now, one of my fellow first office agents, SA Mike Garbo, was killed on October 4, 2021, in Tucson, AZ where we worked together,

he was a fellow agent, neighbor, and friend who will be sadly missed by many. Laura was right, it is dangerous, but I **love** what God has allowed me to do as a Special Agent while continuing to serve others].

I trust your decision to pursue whatever you feel you want to do. I want you to be happy and enjoy what you do. You will make a difference in people's lives no matter what you do because you are so compassionate. [Interesting to read this now because after I came home, I was offered a job with Proctor & Gamble which I accepted. We were gearing up to move to Cincinnati, OH in early 2004, when Laura came to me and said she didn't want us to go because she knew my heart would not be into it, recognizing my continued desire to serve. Fortunately, an Army Reserve mobilization stateside bought me 6 more months until the DEA called me to Quantico and the rest is history].

I would like to find a gym that has a good aerobics program. The best bet seems like Gold's Gym. We are going to Shreveport on Saturday for my mom's birthday. I'm going to hopefully see your mom.

Can you believe our wedding will be this Saturday and next week we will be having so much fun in Australia? That's the stuff we can look forward to in the future.

Have I told you I can't wait for you to come home? I miss you! Will we be able to talk and figure out your homecoming? Do you want certain people to be there? You can let me know and I'll work out the details. All I know is that I want you alone, so I can work you over right!

CHAPTER 15

NEAR DEATH AND NEAR GOD

April 5 War Day 16

Robert: *My heart is now filled with joy and happiness. I have just finished my several phone calls with you. It also makes me somewhat sad, but I am so glad I got to hear your sweet voice. What a surprise you were in Shreveport with my family! Got to hear from Momma, too. What a blessing. I am the XO and probably took advantage of being primarily responsible for the iridium cell phone [satellite phone for our surgical team to call for medical evacuations from the battlefield but after my near-death experience described below, I asked Dr. Kirk if I could violate protocol and use the cell phone to contact Laura…not to mention it would have been our wedding day had I not deployed to Iraq]. Oh well, I got to talk to my beautiful bride on our tentative wedding day. Not sure when I'll be able to call again, but that will fill my heart for some time now. It was great to finally know the moving process was complete and that you have started working. Putting away my paycheck should save us some good money to begin things with, not to mention, ensure we have an awesome honeymoon. It warms my heart and makes me happy to know our families* (and you) are interacting even without me. I'm glad you and my mom could share the experience of hearing from me together for the first time since the war began. I hope you continue to support each other well (even through some tears). I hope they understand that I wish I could talk with everyone, but I had to talk to you.

We made it to our final destination as you guessed – Saddam / Baghdad International Airport (BIAP). We are set up in one of the hangars/bunkers off the runway. We had hoped to get the use of one of the terminals, but unfortunately, the 101st Airborne Division got it. But along with the 16 Medevac pilots that attached today and the FST, we cleaned out the bunker fairly well. I set up my little cot with all the things I have left, after last night.

Now we sit around all day waiting to get told to move forward to the airport. Only the FLE (Forward Logistical Element) of the BSA (Brigade Support Area) was going.

It was dusk when we finally got on the road so we lost all use of daylight. We were on a hardball road for about 2-3 miles until a turn onto a dirt trail for about 2 miles. This dirt trail was very narrow with ditches and trenches on either side.

The first problem we had was helping CPT Felix and SPC Garcia after they slid off the road. We had to get a more skilled driver down there with a wench to pull them out. 30 minutes later, we were finally done. We followed them now and made it maybe 500 feet until a curve where Peppers somehow allowed the driver's side wheel to slide off the edge of the path. Even though he was wearing night vision goggles, it was still tough to see and follow the guy in front of you.

So we are tilted on this embankment which I thought we could recover from quickly. We pulled the wench front our front and hooked it onto the rear of a big truck in front of us to pull it out. SPC Peppers froze up a bit as far as reacting because I

Near Death and Near God

think he couldn't believe he (a former diesel truck driver) had slid off the path.

I hopped on the driver's side and turned the engine on to turn the wheel and give it some gas while they pulled. At first, it was pulling me out, but then it started sliding more. I jumped into what I found was a 3–4-foot ditch/creek and yelled to stop but they didn't. As they kept pulling it, the tension and the angle flipped the HMMVV and trailer right in my direction. It was probably the most life-threatening situation I have ever been in. I saw the HMMVV rolling towards me in the water. By God's grace, I dove, ran, and jumped (whatever) to get out of the way. I fell into the creek with water up to my face and prayed the HMMVV wouldn't fall on me and pin me in or catch my legs. Somehow, it didn't! I finally came out of the water to swing around and hit my hand on the still-rolling wheel. The entire truck had missed coming on top of me by about 2 feet. Thanking God was all I could do. Just knowing He saved me so I could come home to you meant everything.

I called up to the embankment that I was okay, as I waved my green chem light that had been in my hand the whole time. Lucky light I'll say. After scrambling to the top, it was back down to the vehicle to recover sensitive items (radio, cell phone, map, laptop, GPS, and other personal gear we could find standing in the water. SPC Peppers and I searched and passed things up to others. Finally, when we couldn't get anything more out, we went back up the embankment with help and got in an equipment 5-ton truck and continued ... still praising God for my safety. SPC Peppers was worried and concerned about his stuff and what had happened. He kept referencing what we didn't get and what we were gonna do until I told him I didn't want to hear another word about material possessions when I almost had a truck crush me...

underwater. [This was a pivotal point in the deployment to experience a near-death experience during the chaos of war and indirect artillery in the distance on the little dirt ball road in the middle of the night. Thankfully we weren't receiving direct fire at that time. It was ironic that it happened to us after helping two other vehicles that had gone off the path and gotten stuck. After it happened everyone with a radio on the convoy knew it had happened and many thought I had been crushed because it took a few minutes for me to get someone's attention from the creek. After I took the ASIP radios from the mounts the one item I was still missing was the Iridium satellite cell phone. It was a big deal to have lost that, so I prayed at that moment, reached down into a couple of feet of water in the overturned part of the passenger's seat, and found it. A God moment yet again. Plus, the phone later worked after it dried out! I grabbed as many items as I could get but left non-sensitive equipment, my bags, and all the MREs behind to keep moving. After SPC Peppers and I climbed in the 5-ton truck he could not rationalize what had just happened to us and our vehicle. I had to raise my voice to him to realize how lucky we were to still be alive with the accident and the enemy in the distance with indirect artillery. By that point, I had so much adrenaline in my body that I passed out from exhaustion only to wake up several hours later at Baghdad International Airport (BIAP). We had made it safely into Baghdad. I'll never forget when we arrived it was daylight and as I hopped down from the back of the 5-ton truck MAJ Kirk was standing there. He gave me the biggest hug and said I had given him the biggest scare of his life because they thought for several minutes I had been killed.]

"I have the strength to face all conditions by the power that Christ gives me." (Philippians 4:13). [Insight: Christ is strong when we are weak. Lack of faith and love weakens us. Strength *comes to us when we fix our eyes on Jesus Christ, the Author and Finisher of our faith.] Ain't that the truth? Please continue to turn to Him in prayer whenever you become sad and angry. He will comfort your heart. I miss and* **love** *you, my beautiful wife.*

CHAPTER 16
BIAP – Just Helping & Surviving

April 7 War Day 18

Robert: *Well, we have gotten situated here at Baghdad International Airport (BIAP). We initially moved here with the FLE (Forward Logistical Element) with one treatment team from the medical company. The company commander of the C Med has been traveling with us as well. His name is Captain Dan Misigoy and would be my equivalent out here. Pretty nice guy. I have helped him and his XO, Lieutenant Cook, as much as I can. They seem to sometimes let things slide [because they would often get overwhelmed with patients and logistical issues] so I lend a hand [as a fellow Medical Service Corps Officer]. She (LT Cook) is a nice girl, who went to Notre Dame, so we have shared a few tradition stories.*

We are located in a jet bunker made of concrete. MAJ Kirk and I have set up our sleep areas here in the control room (or what is left of it). Looks like these things had been abandoned and bombed before we arrived. The rooms and outside bunker were burned out and had bird droppings, broken items, and plastic everywhere. We had to do some major sweeping and eventually, we had a cleaned-out bunker fit for living. It is kind of eerie though, sleeping in these rooms because they resemble confined cell rooms, coffin boxes, or maybe the steam showers at a concentration camp, but we are making do. We found some Iraqi rugs in a warehouse to make our "rooms" more homely. Pulled out the laptop with the media player cranking out some Harry Connick and Frank Sinatra and I'm making it home. I have the swirl thing going from the media player which makes me think of making **love** to you and you fall asleep in my arms. How I miss that more than anything.

We are still without hot showers, hot food, no mail, and no bathrooms. Although we rigged up a shower point with water bags and found a folding chair with a toilet seat on it which made it easier to use the restroom today.

We took our first onslaught of casualties after the first several hours here two days ago. I turned into the Medic XO and took care of an Enemy Prisoner of War (EPW). Started his IV, helped irrigate and bandage his shrapnel wounds, and took his vitals. He kept saying peace (with two fingers) and "Go USA" and "George Bush good"... Of course, after we shot him and then we took care of him.

Last night, the full medical company moved in with us and we had 11 casualties. 8 Americans and 2 EPWs. One soldier died before reaching us. Since there were so many, as Medic XO, I helped again by taking care of PFC Jared... something...from Oregon. He had gotten shot in the calve area, clean and straight through so I cleaned it up, bandaged him, took vitals, etc. All these casualties keep coming... mainly EPW now, but we can't evacuate them. The Medical Evacuation [Blackhawk] helicopters won't fly because of the low visibility we have been having. So it looks like a med surg ward here in the hangar. But again, it's our home now. Got word on our overturned 'Laura 4' HMMWV. It is busted up and some items are still in it, but some items have been stolen including both of my duffle bags. Can you believe that someone would go down into a ditch and steal my bags? It probably wasn't an enemy either sadly enough. Now it will take some paperwork to cover the losses and damage. If you could call the USAA Insurance/Renter's Insurance section and ask if I can claim my losses out here because of my accident? Otherwise, I might be out of pocket some money when I clear because of the Army equipment I have lost. Just let me know so I can work up a list with numbers and costs. Some of my civilian clothes and shoes as well. But I'm here and safe so no worries. Just material things.

Hopefully, the weather will be clear enough to evacuate all these patients. Need to snap 50 shots of our setup for you but I am almost out of film. Please send more Advantix. [Between the digital photos MAJ Vinca had taken and all the actual film pics I have there is a treasure trove of photos from the entire deployment, including an amazing scrapbook Laura made me after I got home]. The US forces are advancing into the city, so I pray the end is in sight. Know I think of you all the time. My heart is still on a high hearing your voice.

Laura: *Honey, I found "Our Daily Bread" online. I thought you might enjoy these to use for your daily study of God's Word. I pray you continue to find comfort in His Word. Your incredible* **faith** *shows through in your letters and is so inspirational to me. I'm so excited to be married to such a strong Christian man. Our family is going to be amazing because we share our Christian values. God has truly blessed us by bringing us together. I love you so much! You are the* **love** *of my life. My soulmate. I miss you!*

April 8 War Day 19

Robert: *Got a full night's rest last night. Quite refreshing, and this evening I took a shower. We set up a shower point between two trailers with a wooden pallet and two ponchos. It works, though. During the morning just took care of business, but the afternoon was quite an experience. SFC Smith and I followed the 3rd FSB HHC CO and 1SG to the Saddam Hussein Palace off the airport perimeter. We initially went to what I thought was the palace, but it was just another guest house I suppose. Everything on the property was green with palm trees and water. All the rooms were ornate, and all the bathroom and kitchen fixtures were gold-plated. Looked cheesy. Took home many comfort items like pillows, blankets, floor mats, pictures, silverware, plates, and saucers. Felt a bit guilty about taking stuff because it wasn't mine, but we got enough souvenir stuff for all the FST. Also, we had one of our mechanics hotwire a small Toyota 4-cylinder truck. I drove it into our medical area and immediately helped transport a small Iraqi family with children to a Medical Evacuation bird. [This was a very interesting adventure day in the war where a small handful of us went into the Saddam palace grounds that had recently been cleared by Special Forces. Although we knew it was cleared, we were still with our weapons and vigilant. But it was strange walking around these abandoned palace grounds that were so lavish. The best item I took was a pillow that I used the rest of my time in Iraq & Kuwait...it is the small comforts that make a difference].*

Laura: *Today was a pretty good day. I hope it was for you, too. Although there was a point tonight, I had to cry by myself because my heart aches for you. Some pictures helped to make things better. Seeing your smile makes me so happy. I found one* more roll in the bottom of your box. This roll had the most pictures of you in it. I laughed at you pretending to kiss the desert lizard. That lizard looks pretty scary. I can't believe people would touch them.

Well, living at home has been challenging. Please begin to pray my mom will find salvation and that she gains the inner strength to begin caring about her health. She has such a messed-up view of the world and lashes out at everything and everyone. She never said anything nice, so I confronted her twice. Both times she started crying and left the room telling me to stop talking. I've been feeling anxious being here. I just don't handle stress very well anymore. Let's pray for her.

Today, I studied some more for work and had lunch with my parents. Then, I studied some more and went to check out Gold's Gym in Arlington. They have a great new facility. I went kickboxing at a fitness center located on a hospital's "plot of land." It was fun to do that again. Fitness motivates me, so my goal is to pick another date to get my certification. I would love to work at Gold's Gym in Ft. Worth. The perfect opportunity would be to offer to teach 5:30 a.m. classes because they currently don't offer them. Also, it's a small gym compared to the others, so the classes won't be that big.

April 9 War Day 20

Robert: *Sorry I fell asleep writing last night. Guess the soothing dark control room with my little dome light and classical music playing lulled me to sleep. Now I eat some morning meals (not necessarily breakfast food with MREs) and burn a John Mayer CD into the laptop. Makes me think of you as I listen. I miss you so much.*

Finally got a new chemical protective mask to replace the one I lost in the accident. Been three days without one. Pray, I will never really have to use it. [During the rollover accident that was the most sensitive item I lost was my chemical protective mask which I needed due to the ongoing threat of chemical weapons being used on us. It was unnerving not having it for three days. 3rd FSB had to go back to Division to find me one but they did thankfully].

You wouldn't believe what the HHD company guys of 3rd FSB next door procured. Two fancy, gold-lined, velvet, Saddam Prince Carriages. Right out of a Robin Hood movie set-looking carriage. We took some digital photos with Dr. Kirk's camera. It is as gaudy as all the things I saw in his palace yesterday.

We went to several smaller palace buildings on the grounds as well as the big one. They all seemed as if no one stayed there ever. Some of the silverware I saw was still in saran wrap. Maybe I'll bring you home a whole set [which I didn't but the unit did as a war trophy we had to get approval to bring home]. In all of the buildings, he had pictures and paintings of himself. One, in particular, was very odd. It was a painting of him and a little girl standing in a living room of some sort looking out the window. Outside the window was some car on fire with three militant guys around it fighting (having thrown Molotov cocktails). No idea what it meant other than he was a lunatic. Not sure if our forces have killed him yet, but there are always unverified rumors. It was very surreal rummaging through the Iraqi president and his son's palace homes. This estate was only one of the many throughout Iraq while his country's people starved and lived in poverty.

The casualty inflow has slowed a bit, but we have even more medical assets on the ground and supposedly another FST has been ordered up here. Don't need them, but if they have to come oh well… the more the merrier.

If no casualties today, I will be focused on laundry, putting some medical crosses on the Toyota, and going through the palace stuff to give to the team. Probably need to sort through patient records as well. The first order of business is the laundry because I have nothing clean.

Rumors are the 21st Combat Support Hospital (CSH) might get pushed up here eventually [21st CSH was our higher unit that we reported to back at Fort Hood]. That would have to be a good sign for us. Sounds like we certainly have our presence in Baghdad now so maybe there is a small twinkle of the end in sight. I pray so. Need to be near you soon.

Laura: *I've been slacking this morning. There's studying to be done, but I feel distracted. My heart isn't into this work, yet, or it may not ever be. Only God knows at this point. At least I have some sense of independence with this job. It was pretty crazy to see our tanks in the center of Baghdad today. It's history in the making. Three times now they tried to kill Saddam based on human intelligence. Why can't we get him? Hopefully, the Lord will protect everyone from his evilness. I'm making another care package for you. There are several probably sitting in Kuwait. I hope you get them soon. I think you should receive 6-8 packages from me. I lost count. Hopefully, my letters and packages have made your days brighter there. I'm thinking about you all the time. I miss you a lot. I have to go get to studying, but I will write later today. I **love** you, Robert. I pray you come home soon so we can begin our life together as Team Payne.*

April 11 War Day 22

Robert: *I just re-read many of your letters to feel closer to you. I also took some gum and used it to put some pictures of you* on my wall. My little burnout control room is becoming quite my little home. Found two small shelves with a swing door for Dr. Kirk and me. Got a candle, pictures of my favorite person, my A&M flag, and of course, Army equipment everywhere. I'll certainly have to take a picture as soon as I get more film from you. I hope to get some care packages soon. I am all out of goodies. Oh, the shoe box thing is out the door. Send whatever size you want.

Today, I didn't do too much. Last night I started inputting all our surgeries into a patient database and finished it up this morning. Worked through some blood paperwork. We have used six units so far, but we still have to switch out our unused stuff because it expires. They (surgeons) are working on our 18th patient now. Nasty GSW or shrapnel wound to face and arm. There is another FST with us now from FT Bliss. 1st and 3rd BCT is who we support, and we are in this one area sharing space. Tomorrow they'll set their stuff up. Once they do, between two medical companies and two FSTs, we have three treatment teams, two patient holds, and four OR beds. We are almost the size of a supporting hospital or maybe closer to an M.A.S.H (Mobile Area Surgical Hospital–like on TV). [A little piece of history was on the ride up to Baghdad when we were evacuating to the 212th MASH which ended up being the last one in the US Army until de-activated in 2003 when they returned to Germany. The ironic part is now as a US Army Reserve Medical Brigade Commander I have overseen the recent conversions of Combat Support Hospitals to Hospital Centers that now have Field Hospitals which are essentially like the former MASH units but to my knowledge, we haven't deployed Field Hospitals into active combat to date].

The rest of the afternoon I spent with CPT Reed, CPT Gegel, and a mechanic driving around Saddam's palace grounds looking for a vehicle to steal for CPT Reed and his Special Forces medical unit. [CPT Reed had been a Nurse Anesthetist formerly assigned to the 126th FST. Because he was a former Special Forces member, he decided to go back to a team just before Iraq so when we saw him randomly at BIAP it was like a small reunion. He was well-liked amongst the team and was always good to me. He even let me intubate others and allowed me to try it during surgeries in the hospital, but I found it to be quite difficult. He was also very encouraging to me to separate from the Army and become a federal agent. I wish he knew how it worked out for me!]. Been trying to get through a movie called Black Sugar, which is proving to be good. About hip hop, love, and relationships. No word here on what is next. You probably know I appreciate how proud you are and the nice things you have written about me. So, as I continue to get settled in, know I am thinking of you.

Laura: *Hi! How is my sweet and loving husband doing? Everything is okay here. This week I've been studying all day, every day. I talked with Lanny today. Next week, I am going out into my territory and meeting surgeons. Some surgeries are coming up this month. It's like I'm just not feeling this job. I'm not enthusiastic about it. It seems like God has placed me here because Lanny has his priorities straight. 1. God. 2. Family.... Work (last). This is what I've always wanted. God has big plans for us I know, so I'll just follow His lead.*

Last night, Rina, Jen, and I went to Marna's to hang out. We had a nice time. I enjoy that kind of gathering right now. When you go out, you can't talk and quite frankly right now I don't like partying without you. You are the person I want there the most. For now, dinners, lunches, and just talking is what I need.

Wow, I just can't even describe how much I miss you. Looking at pictures of you helps though. Yesterday, I got your heart's package! It made my day! Ever since you told me about it, I have been praying for it to find me. Your hearts were wonderful. I was laughing and smiling looking through them.

I love how you appreciate the small things in our relationship, not just the big things. Like the one about me sitting next to you in the Jeep with the top down (which got a bath this week and looks good!). I love those things too and they all warm my heart so much. Your CD was awesome! I laughed, I cried, and I smiled through every song. Each one had such a vivid memory attached to it. The Harry Connick recipe song… I could just imagine you singing it and dancing. I love it when you sing! Also, with Superstition, I thought about your rap and how the first time you did that for me we were on our way to Shreveport! So many wonderful memories. When you get back home, we'll begin some more. I'm wrong this time apart I have memories. The special moments when I heard your voice!

This weekend I'm going to Austin to run fourteen miles with the team. It's probably going to hurt because the past two weeks, I've slacked on training. I pray that you can be at the marathon. But, if not I know you'll be there in my thoughts. Scotty G is running, too. Hopefully, we'll catch up while I'm there. I don't remember if I mentioned that I want to train for a triathlon with you. It's a big commitment because you are training for three things, but I think it would be so much fun to do it together. [We did our first triathlon together with Team in Training when we moved to Tucson in 2004…way harder than we thought]. I'm missing you so bad I have **faith** I will talk to you soon. I continue to pray for your protection and safe return home.

When I want to escape to a place where I know I'll be heard, where I can cry and it will be okay, where I can be myself, and that will be okay, too…

Laura: *I've already written today, but I wanted to include a letter with this care package I put together today. Hopefully, these packages can brighten your day. Know they are especially packed and sealed with my love. In this envelope, you will find a Cosmo tip sheet. I want you to read through the list and circle the ones you would most like to see happen. You can bring it home with you, and I will make these things you want to happen. Reading those articles was always so much fun. Thank you for buying it for me. Today has been uneventful. I've successfully blown off studying today. Steven and Cameron have baseball games tonight, so I am going to go watch. Then, it's off to Austin. I'm going to stay with a girl named Angie, who is doing Team in Training with me.*

CHAPTER 17
SETTLING INTO WAR

April 13 War Day 24

Robert: Not sure what I have been doing to pass the time. I know that I have been handling work-related stuff just not sure what. Everything and all the days are beginning to blend.

Took the time yesterday to take all your letters and put them in document protectors in date order. I know you think I'm anal, but that is one thing that makes you smile about me right? [Ironic yes, I then took it on our 10th wedding anniversary and made it into a chronological book of the actual copied letters and gave it to Laura in front of all our friends we invited to Austin to celebrate our 10th wedding anniversary. And here it is 10 more years later I have worked with a ghost-writing team and publisher to make it a book to share with you and all my future family members I may never meet one day. My goal was to have this made into an actual book you are reading by the 20th anniversary of the Iraq invasion in March 2023]. Also, I will put them with my letters to you and all the pics when I return... Ahhh when I return, who knows? They haven't given us a clue. If I were a betting man, it would be July, but that is just a guess from the idea they sent us out here for at least six months.

Every day away is a day too long apart from you. Since things have calmed down, I have started to think about what happens when I return. First and foremost, I will praise God because I will have you back in my arms and we will have our wedding. I'm a bit apprehensive about the job thing, though. I will have very little time before my Army service is over (Aug 15th) and I will possibly not have a job. And if you're not receiving a commission (over a base salary) yet, will we have enough money to live on? I don't expect you to know the answers to this. No matter what, God will lead us, and we'll have each other. We might have "broken" each other, but your love is all I need. God and Laura's love fill my heart, so how can I lose?

I figure by next January I will have applied to the schools in Texas and either I'll get into Grad School, or the Fed Agencies will have let me know something. It'll all be okay. [How true God had a plan for us!? I never fully applied to graduate school for several reasons, but I was eventually hired in 2004 as a federal agent and am still doing that to this date with no regrets. I love my chosen career to have had the opportunity to continue to serve, help others, and protect the nation in a much different way. Although I have stayed in the US Army Reserve, which I may have not done in hindsight because of all the extra time it has taken over the years. Yet, I haven't been able to walk away from the US Army for over 24 years because it has been such a part of my life.]

You said in your letters you're willing to go anywhere because you don't feel as confident about your sales job. I would say just make the best of it until I return then we can reassess the situation, but I know you will do great. You're personable, you know the folks, the territory, the products, so how can you lose? Also, helps that you're beautiful and have a hot body.

Sounds like the marathon training is coming along. It has been well over thirty days since I have worked out in any way, shape, or form. Need to at least get back into pushups and sit-ups. It's the longest I have gone since I can remember without working out. If I make it to the marathon somehow, I certainly will support you from the sidelines. Not much ability to run around the airstrip.

We have gotten pretty settled now and patient traffic is very minimal. We have started to go to battalion meetings and talk about awards, etc. Certainly, a good sign that things are settling down. Not sure who is moving to fight north, but hopefully not us. There are some forces still fighting supposedly.

More medical assets moved to the airport which is making this place certainly safe for patient care. Wish you could see my little burnout control room setup. The most important items now are Laura's pictures and the Texas A&M flag. It has two candles that make it nice as well. The pillow I grabbed from the palace makes my sleeping more comfortable. It is amazing the difference a pillow can make. About to go to a small Protestant service so I'll pray for us both.

Laura: *This card made me think of you. I feel like I am falling in love with you all over again. I didn't think I could fall any deeper in love with you, but I found it was possible. Through our letters and conversations, I feel closer to you. We are going to have such a great life together. I got so excited inside thinking about life with you. I'll get to wake up next to you every morning and fall asleep on your chest every night. I can imagine laughing with you and dancing with you.*

Angela, LeeAnne, (old mutual friends of ours from Texas A&M days) and I hung out for a little bit tonight. It was so good to see them. They said hi and that they are thinking about you. They are so happy that we are together. Things are going well for them both. LeeAnne is so funny. She was talking about her recent "adult moments." Mike and LeeAnne are looking for a house in Hurst. They all get together and cook out sometimes. So, we'll have some couples to hang out with. Also, Amy Collier is pregnant! That's so wonderful. Beth is due in May. It's baby fever around here! They're going to help with planning your welcome home party.

I want to talk to you about Church. I haven't visited any yet, but I want to wait and find one together. Jessica and Jonathan invited me to visit theirs. That's what I plan on doing, just visiting. I pray we find a church that we love and can be a part of. Lake Hills could have been a place like that for us if we both lived in Austin. I would love to be a group leader for fellowship and open up our home to people. We could be great at that. That's one of my goals to study this Bible and grow confident enough to lead a study with friends.

Wow, my family is being hard to live with. You are so lucky to have such a loving family. Everybody is angry here! Today I commented how I am so lucky to be with you because you aren't angry, and you are patient, kind, understanding, and loving. It's fun having a conversation with you. Your world isn't all gray and gloomy like everyone here. Oh, I hope if I am ever like that, you will kick me in the butt. Being with you brings out the best in me, though.

Not much else is going on. I ran with the Ft Worth Team in the Training Group. We ran thirteen miles and it hurt! I had slacked on training the past two weeks and I wasn't up to par. The run/walk program has helped my knee not hurt as badly. For each segment, I run eleven minutes and one minute. It slows the pace a bit but helps physically. This group was all on different mileage. Only three of us were running what was on the schedule. I brought up the rear! Someone has got to do it. I still need to raise $1500. There's another garage sale in my future.

I'm looking forward to the next time we get to talk. I'm thinking of you always. I miss you!

April 14 War Day 25

Robert: *It is still Sunday, but this letter will roll over into Monday. I have written so much that I had to go to my notepads. Good thing I bought them.*

I got another letter and a card from you. It is so great to hear all the loving, sweet words from you. I certainly think and feel as if Christ is a blessing and strengthening our relationship even as more days go by. I will only continue to **love** *you more every day that goes by. You are my beautiful gift from God, and I can't wait to* **love** *you as God* **loves** *His church, to put you high on a pedestal, satisfy all your desires, take care of you forever, and* **love** *you for a lifetime.*

I know through your letters you feel the same and it is amazing to share these feelings with my best friend and soulmate. You are my world and don't know what kind of man I would be without you. It makes me so energized and full of **faith** *to be loved by you. I don't deserve your complete devotion and unconditional commitment since we started dating, but you wanted to love me anyway. Thank you for never giving up on me. Bless those green cookies that made me start to realize how big your heart is and prepared to completely open for me. [Green cookie is a reference to when we were casually dating I was not ready for a relationship but my roommate Sergio Flores saw that Laura had made me some St Patrick's Day cookies and dropped them off. Sergio* essentially told me not to mess the relationship up with Laura and not to walk away from a good thing!]

We are made for one another, Laura. I can see it in everything we do... our smiles in our pictures, the way we hold each other, the way we laugh, the way we challenge each other to be better people, the way you look at me, the way you touch my neck, the way we even argue. I **love** you for everything you are good and bad, and I know you love me even though I might act stupid sometimes. I take such comfort and blessing in knowing you will always be there for me.

I'll write more tomorrow, I just wanted to say again how much I truly **love** you for everything you are and the man you make me. I am over here for you and our future family.

Robert 0725: Today is another glorious day because God is with us, and I still have your unconditional **love** for His. It put a smile on my face this morning just thinking about it.

I had a dream last night that had you and your mom in it. And don't be mad but for some reason, it had Colleen (my former long-term girlfriend from Texas A&M) in it. We were all at an amusement park. Somehow, I was separated from you and your mom and Colleen began following me around. Eventually, she confessed to me her marriage was horrible and she had made a mistake. All I wanted, I keep telling her to go away because I wanted my life with Laura. We walked for hours it seemed and I couldn't find you. Finally, I saw you at a distance and you saw me. That's when I told Colleen she must go, and you left where you were with your mom and I finally was able to embrace you. It felt so real as if I hadn't held you in months. It felt as if the world stopped for our embrace and hug and nothing (or no one else) mattered. It was just you and me and I had such a feeling of completeness and comfort.

I want that feeling so much. I can have it because I know spiritually and emotionally how much you love me, but to complete the circle of our love, I have to physically have you in my arms to truly feel oneness with you and the ability to protect you. That day will come soon I pray.

*I hope you are not bothered by my dream and her being there, but I had to share it with you because of the wonderful feelings and comfort it gave me to find you. I **love** you so much my heart hurts every day. I thought I knew what it meant to love another person, but the more I have become involved with God and prayed to Him, the stronger and more clearly, I see His purpose in our lives is to become one. I never knew love could feel this way and can only count the days to returning and beginning our life together with this focus and Christ's influence.*

Our future family will be so blessed because of our devotion to one another. This must be what God has put me here to show us. The difficulties and separation of the past year were to show us He will never give us something we cannot work through together. We can never give up on one another.

*He has placed me in this desert not only to help others and serve my country but to put in our hearts the ultimate understanding of what our **love** will mean in our marriage and life together. Think how lucky we are to know this before we begin our marriage! God's **love** will make everything different.*

*David sent me a book called "The Purpose Driven Life" by Rick Warren. It has 40 chapters addressing God's role in our life. If you can get the book and we can read it together, it would be great. The first chapter focuses on "It All Starts with God" and the verse focuses on **Colossians 1:16**:*

"For everything, absolutely everything, above and below, visible and invisible. Everything got started in him and finds its purpose in him."

The overall point of chapter one is focusing on ourselves will never reveal our life's purpose. That is such great news because the burden of responsibility in our lives for direction is with Him. We just have to praise Him and pray to Him and live it. Luckily, we get the great fortune to live ours as one. One house of Payne!

Enough of how much I **love** you (which I'm sure you don't get tired of hearing), but I hope your life is well. Is the job keeping you busy? Will it take six months before any commissions roll in? Is living at home bearable? Just try and have patience there. The money we are saving by you being at home will help us so much when I return. It means we can have a honeymoon and possibly buy a home that much sooner.

Hopefully from the wedding letter sent out before I left our families are taking advantage of this time to put money back (especially my dad). Need to take the time to write others. Haven't written anyone else since before the war began. Guess I need to let others know I am doing well.

Your aunt and uncle (Robert and Nancy) wrote me a nice card. I appreciated that. They welcomed me into the family. Speaking of family, how was the Shreveport trip? Are any Lubbock trips planned? I hope they are all doing well. How much have you been talking to your chicas, and have any of the boys been checking on you?

Is the additional money coming in? There is some confusion here on the actual stipends we should be receiving. I'll work my questions here when the finance team comes with my Leave & Earnings Statement (LES) if you can call and ask questions from your end. The days after I return are we going away or would you just prefer a few nights in HYE, Texas, or 7F Lodge? We have to make sure and tell them who we are and why we are coming. Maybe there might be some (military) discounts. Certainly, would appreciate and take advantage of all the benefits and perks of being a veteran that I can. Many sacrifices from my best friend and wife Laura Payne! Sounds so nice.

Well, I'm going to place this letter in the mail now and hope it finds you soon and brings a smile to your face and warmth to your heart. My beautiful angel. I **love** you with my whole being.

April 15 War Day 25

Robert 2150: *Lying here in my bunk, all clean after my shower, and thinking of you. Had another strange dream last night. Can't remember the details, but somehow, I was forced into marrying some woman so she could get into the US. But I was able to get a divorce. Then it happened again that I had to marry someone against my will, but I couldn't get out of this marriage, and I remember that painful, uncomfortable feeling because I knew I loved you and wanted to marry you, but I legally couldn't and I didn't know what to do. Guess it represents this deployment holding me back from you somehow. Another pretty bland day. Began the process of assessing the damage to Laura 4 after flipping over in the ditch. It isn't pretty, but it can be fixed [The entire frame was bent above the driver and passenger seats so they had to replace the top frame part on the back cover poles]. The trailer is okay as well. Like Laura, she never quits! I look at your pictures and miss your smile so much. It lights up a room.*

Tonight, I attended a memorial service for SGT Buggs who was killed in an ambush when his maintenance recovery vehicle went the wrong way. He was in 3rd FSB, B Company (I think).

Much like silver taps (Texas A&M tradition conducted each month on campus that honors those Aggies that have died) just sad. [This was one of the casualties associated with the infamous PVT Jessica Lynch maintenance company who was behind us on our move up to Baghdad, who essentially made a wrong turn– https://abcnews.go.com/GMA/story?id=125251&page=1]. A reference was made in the eulogy that he was a Christian, which is a blessing.

*Haven't read my book for today so let me do that now. Day three's message: thinking about my purpose and the reference verse is Isaiah 25:3 [Therefore strong people will glorify you, cities of ruthless nations will fear you.]. I hope people can see my Christian values in how I carry myself. The main purpose is accepting our salvation from Jesus, and it all falls into place. Getting sleepy so I'll finish the letter in the morning… wish you were here with me. I **love** you.*

April 16 War Day 26

Robert 1:10 pm: *Still here in the same location, but some rumors of movement elsewhere. So many rumors these days, it is hard to tell what is what. Oh well, I'm here, safe, and have food and water, shelter, and clothes. Can't complain. The only necessity of life I am missing is my soulmate, Laura to fill my heart with love. But I guess you can still do that thousands of miles away just by knowing you are there.*

I have been working on awards for everyone. The challenge and problem is everyone on the team deserves one, but when you are dealing with twenty people, it is noticed when five or six out of twenty don't get one. I have recommended to Dr. Kirk that we can't award something to someone who we feel doesn't deserve it just because they might feel bad. Try to look at the awards from the standpoint of who contributed above their job duty in some way. Essentially, we have two awards to give. Army Commendation Medal (ARCOM) or Bronze Star for Meritorious (BSM) service. They can be awarded a 'Valor' distinction but none of us committed any true valorous acts to be noted. A few guys are being submitted for Bronze Stars, most for ARCOMs and five guys get nothing.

Enough of the boring Army talk. Today's excitement centered around a casualty that was brought in and we were told he was a senior leader in the Ba'ath Party, maybe a four-star general. Details were scarce, but several folks were around after we operated and evacuated him. His wife came with him and his son, but she was unharmed. He and his son are not so lucky. They'll live but got shot up pretty well. Guess they shouldn't have shot at Americans when they came to get them. Hope they can get some good information from him.

The rest of the day I did awards and played, "You Don't Know Jack" with Dr. Kirk. Tonight, watched "Saving Silverman" with the docs. Looks like there is some talk of the change of command happening, but only hearsay at this point. Don't say anything to Debbie because no one knows for sure.

I hope Dr. Kirk can get back to his family as he planned to separate from the Army. If we are kept here too long and I have a way back, know that I will take it so I can come back to be with you and take care of us… Team Payne!!

I miss you so much, baby. I know this is hard and I pray for you every day. Please continue to ask for God's help and have patience. I'll be home before you know it and years down the road this will all be a distant memory. Please hang in there at home. I know it might be difficult sometimes, but it is probably the best thing for you and our finances right now.

I would just pray about it and love those kids [Laura's nephews] as much as I can. I'm sorry but growing up as they have and experiencing the things they have with their parents. During adolescence, they are likely going to struggle. We can only pray they come out all right. Rest assured since I am in the family, now, they'll never disrespect you or your mother in my presence without me saying something. Hopefully, I can serve as a positive role model because I am closer to their age. (Sorry for the spots I sprayed some bug juice on me).

What you said in your latest letter is right about our kids. They will be raised with discipline and respect for all adults, especially their mothers. I will never allow disrespect from our children to you. You are to be forever put on a pedestal and honored by our kids, and by me for that matter.

I hope my prior day's letter made some sense (about the dream and all), but I was about to fall asleep. I hope my letters continue to be comforting and convey my love for you. Words cannot convey my love for you and how much I miss you. I am so blessed to have you. I have to praise God every day for you. I miss you so much. Time for sleep so I'll finish in the morning and mail this off.

Laura: It has been two days since the last letter. This work week has been insane. Every morning I'm up at the crack of dawn. I've seen friends almost every night this week. I'm just soooo tired of driving. When can we have a normal stable life where we don't drive 100+ miles per day?

Chapters 13-16 Personal Observations

On March 31, 2003, I knew true fear for the first time in my life. Crossing into Iraq with loaded weapons and actual chemical protective gear with atropine was surreal. When I signed my Army scholarship at Texas A&M in 1995, I never thought I would have been at that point. As a nation in 1995, we were coming off a cold war and sat in a sense of false peace until September 11th, 2001, when terrorist attacks occurred. Then 2 years later we were in two different wars in Afghanistan and Iraq which would exist for almost the entirety of my Army career.

Once we crossed the berm, we were attached to the 1st Brigade of the 3D ID main effort behind the Forward Logistical Element (FLE), which put us very far forward to be closest to where the point of injury would occur to save soldiers. But it made for very fearful moments all the while the love of my life, my new wife was having to just live her life as before I left. Writing letters to stay connected was our only way to maintain contact. Shortly before the war began our lines were cut and there was no way to speak by phone. Letters were the only way but after we crossed, the letters didn't catch up with us for weeks. I just wrote and sent them back hoping they would make it to Laura.

War means no baths, no toilets, and only MREs. Luckily the JLIST Chemical suits we had on kept us warmer at night but during the day it would get really hot. The four-day journey into Iraq was hard as hell and many died on that journey due to accidents. The pace was overwhelming and most of us moving up in three columns were exhausted and operated on just a few hours of sleep. I have never been as sleep-deprived as that journey. That led to the issues we faced before getting to Baghdad. The night we moved into BAIP I almost died in the rollover accident. I still believe it was God's grace that saved me. How I was able to jump out of the way as it flipped, I will never know. To include none of the indirect fire that ever reached our FLE as we made our way to BIAP. Once we arrived the real work began as casualties caught up to us, both US and Iraqi civilians. The concrete bunker we set up gave us a fair amount of security. The coolest deviation while at BIAP was getting to the Saddam Palace grounds and taking the pillow for comfort after a long journey!

CHAPTER 18
OUR LOVE WILL ENDURE

April 17 War Day 27

Robert: *I love* my little organized book of your letters because I re-read them now so much more easily. It fills my heart with comfort to read your words. Your letters mean more to me than you'll ever know. It makes my day when I get one with that Andy Warhol stamp and my beautiful wife's name on it. I received all of Rina's class's letters. I truly appreciate it on Rina's behalf, and I'll certainly write her back. I am glad they all came to me because I would be embarrassed to hand them out. With a few exceptions, they mostly consisted of "What's up," "I'm bored," "I'm in whatever period chillin'" and many misspelled words. These kids must be of some lower education levels. Quite sad. A few were nice, and it was sweet that they said things to you. Our future is in trouble if these are the kids that will lead it. Illiteracy is alive and well in America! I truly appreciate Rina doing that. She did comment on her letter to me, she knows she can't relate to the emptiness and pain you must be enduring with my absence. At least that's honest. We're lucky… so lucky to understand and have these feelings because of what it means about the amazing love we share.

In a sense, we should embrace these feelings of heartache and loneliness knowing what they truly mean.

*I read chapter 4 today in the "Purpose Driven Life" and it was powerful. Rick Warren discusses eternity. He conveyed the idea of our lives as the dress rehearsal or only temporary in comparison to the eternity we will spend with Christ. He relates that if there was no eternity then we could indulge in self-centeredness and do whatever we want without repercussions. But death is not the end, it is our transition into eternity so there are eternal consequences to everything we do on earth. Although our brains cannot fathom how wonderful it will be. 1 Corinthians 2:9 says we should rest assured that as we are both Christians this will not be the end for our love, we will get to spend eternity together. How exciting! After we leave this earth, we eventually will reunite and have forever together. Point to ponder there is more to life than just here and now. The verse to read is 1 John 2:17. The question to answer is since I was made to last forever, what is the one thing I should stop doing now and the one thing I should start doing today? Pretty powerful stuff huh? Certainly, things to contemplate and embrace as we approach Easter. Studied the crucifixion versus our **faith** group (Luke 23, John 19, Mark 15, and Matthew 27).*

I haven't heard from any other people in a while. Are their hands broken from writing? Got a card from Lisa Prewitt and she is praying for us both. Wrote your aunt/uncle, mom/Joal/David, and family, and Val's class, but still need to write Seth, Lisa Prewitt now, and Rina. Try to write at least one letter to everyone who writes me. Oh, I also wrote Mawmaw | Marvin | Nanny. Did you get to see them on your visit?

Jamming to some Neil Diamond right now. Wish we could have seen his concert in San Antonio. I believe Justin and Mary went. Would love to make that Norah Jones concert with you.

Pray, I can make it for your birthday. Should be able to call you this weekend so I look forward to hearing your voice. Going to make some calls soon to inquire about my ETS. Not sure what to do if they can't get me home sooner than July or even August because then if it goes past 23 Aug 03, I won't be drawing a paycheck and I'll be without a job. God will see us through. I guess the more money we save the better.

Hope to finish up these awards today. Narrowed down the bronze star recommendations to MAJ Kuhns, SSG Kufro, MAJ Kirk, and me! Not sure if I deserve it, but MAJ Kirk was adamant about me getting a Bronze Star over an ARCOM. About eleven others are getting ARCOMs. [Assessing who got what combat awards was very difficult to process for MAJ Kirk, but not everyone performed in the same manner during the chaos of war. Rest assured everyone needed some level of recognition and we ultimately were able to get every member of the 126th FST awarded the Combat Medical Badge]. Again, please don't say anything to Debbie or other spouses because things can change.

Well, the 21st CSH and the 1st Medical Brigade are here with COL Bruckhart and COL Hightower [these were our higher command units we reported to at Fort Hood]. We have yet to see them. Certainly, means getting me replaced might be easier. Who knows? We'll see how it works out for Dr. Kirk. Things here are certainly quiet. Lots of folks are reading books, magazines, etc., listening to music, and writing letters. Whatever it takes to pass the time. I miss you so much. Please continue to write and send packages as often as you can.

Laura: *You know, I am sad right now because I long to have you home. This morning Debbie sent us your newsletter and part of it started my day wrong. The commander said you will be there for 6-8 weeks followed by a month in Kuwait. I can't wait* that long! I'm going to freak out! This living situation sucks, my job wears me out, and I feel like a big fat piece of poop because my workout schedule is sporadic. I keep expressing my desire for stability and that is still what I want. I don't like where I am now, don't know what is going to happen once you get back, and my job has me driving 100+ miles per day. Maybe I can start running to work, that way I'll be training for the marathon. Ha, ha! Here I am bitching again, two days in a row. I just don't feel like my happy self this week. I try so hard to look at the bright side, but I cannot find it this week. I miss you so much. I've been anxiously awaiting to hear your voice again because we got the word you can call once a week. Please call soon my heart hurts and I need to hear your voice.

Here's what I did this week:

Monday: Got up at 4:30 a.m., drove to Plano, drove back to FW, and back to Plano for dinner with Suzy and Susan.

Tuesday: Got up at 6:30 a.m., met Lanny, drove around FW

Wednesday: Got up at 6 a.m., drove to Dallas for surgery, back to FW, and then to Los Colins to ride with Marna to Freebirds in Dallas.

Thursday: Got up at 7 a.m., had surgery in FW drove to Denton for surgery until 7 p.m., and drove back to FW.

What am I going to do? You know how tired I get of driving. Okay, I have to stop bitching.

Brighter side...

I am so thankful the war has settled down drastically. The fear you guys are in great danger is beginning to subside. That is such good news. The best news was the release of the POWs which we have to praise God for because He answered our prayers. I am also thankful you could provide the care needed for soldiers and civilians wounded during the conflict. The Iraqi citizens will be able to live freely because of the job you guys accomplished. Thank you, Robert, for serving and protecting this country so we can live that wonderful life we both so desire together.

To update you on friends: JRyan and Nicki broke up (initiated by him). He was still having those feelings like before. I can't remember if I told you Amy Collier is pregnant. Anna and Mike D have a cute webpage for their wedding. Rina has a boyfriend named Jason. But Jason G's girlfriend Kim got her front teeth knocked out when his roommate Joe dropped her off of his back. Ouch!

*That's about it for now. I decided not to go to see your family for Easter. I just went two weeks ago, and frankly, I need a break from traveling. Our families are going to have to come to see us when we are finally together. I am so sorry my last two letters have probably not been the most uplifting. I'll try next time to be more positive-spirited. I miss you tons! I **love** you!*

April 17 War Day 27

Robert: *Please allow me to request some items before I write. Please send some cotton balls, clean and clear, Advantix film, boot socks, pens, baby powder, snacks, and some pics of your beautiful face. I miss it so much. Listening to Norah Jones and thinking of our beautiful love. Glad to hear in your last letter the work ball is rolling. Hope your poor car doesn't take a beating driving all* around Dallas/Ft Worth all the time. Sounded like you moved to Ft. Worth and then went back to Killeen. How come you didn't pick it all up in one swoop? I'm sure it all worked out. Thank you!

Heard word today that 1st CAV orders were deleted so maybe Sergio will get to school soon. So when is he moving out? Any money problems with the house? Going to miss the ole Glenoak Country Club. You're right we have lots of memories there. Cooking, pool, barbeque, watching movies on the couch, fun parties, and running around the neighborhood. You fill everything in my life and I'm just not complete without you.

I think there is a good chance we'll have to leave our nice little home we've made here. Not sure but becoming highly likely.

What are your Easter plans? Aggie Muster? I only know two guys from A&M around, but not sure if we'll be in the same area or not. Hope so.

Tried to call the Medical Service Corps branch manager to ask about my ETS [Army separation] but I had to leave a message. Guess I'll try another day. Never hurts to ask right?

April 18 War Day 29

Robert: *Greetings my beautiful wife. I have almost been getting a letter a day and that makes me so happy. Just got my first package – my CDs and hard drive.*

Have a feeling that at any moment we could lose this one we're using. Finally finished up the awards and am almost ready to turn them in.

Got a care package from an old fish in my DG named Gina. Haven't spoken with her in a long time. Very nice gesture to send me a package. Nothing compares to your letters though. Thanks for everything you have done so far if I haven't said it. Thanks for everything you did before I left, moving me, mailing me stuff, replying to my emails, and generally being so loving and supportive. I am lucky, so lucky, to have you.

Today was another experience like nothing else. Since we might move soon, the battalion conducted a leader's recon to the location in the city. [It was quite deflating for the battalion to be told we would be moving into the middle of Baghdad since we had such a nice setup at BIAP in the concrete bunkers]. There we are cruising through the middle of the city with traffic passing us, folks along the road, and kids waving from their windows. It was surreal and a bit frightening. Who knew what could happen and who would we shoot with so many Iraqis around? We drove by the Saddam statue they toppled when the coalition forces arrived. I took the door off the HMMWV (I was riding in the back) and had an M-16 at the ready. Strange having rounds chambered and little kids waving as we pass by.

Laura: *I hope you are feeling my **love** as much as I feel yours. I am comforted by your letters and pictures. Each letter has warmed my heart and confirmed I am the luckiest woman in the world to share my life with the one and only Robert Payne. I was thinking recently about how we have endured a lot in our relationship, dealing with the past, feelings and emotions, stresses of jobs, etc., and now prolonged separation. I hope these things show you I will never leave you, quit, or give up on us. I **love** you more than anything else (except God) and would never sacrifice the greatest thing in my life, the **love** I share with you. We have proven love endures all things.*

Now that the Iraq situation or conflict rather, is winding down, it is hard not to get anxious about your homecoming. I keep wondering what you are doing. The reporter leaving your group has stopped my knowledge of what is happening daily. It was wonderful to have the insider's perspective to read every day. It helped to connect with your situation. [Around this time is when the Savannah Morning News must have returned to the US after having covered our journey through the war – these articles are included within an appendix at the end of this book for your review]. Have you heard any details about coming home? I'm ready because I miss you tremendously.

This was my first-day making sales calls to surgeons. I pretty much just dropped off literature at three offices today. Lanny has a very laid-back approach where the key to the sale is "subtle persistence." The first visit is to drop off literature without seeing the doctor. Then, you write a follow-up letter and call to set up an appointment one week later. It's one product at a time. The key is that you continually have some form of contact, so they begin to see that you are reliable and steady. I know it is a perfect approach for me, but pressure sales would scare me. I know I don't like pressure sales, so I definitely wouldn't want to do it. All in all, it was a crazy work week.

I had a weird dream last night. You came back from Iraq and lots of people were around us who wanted to see you. I'm not sure who they were, but we didn't get to kiss or hug or anything. It was very sad. Then we were at home and all of these guys with "Air Force" glasses and buzz cuts came in to do something with you because you had been to war. It was all strange but left me feeling so disconnected from you in my dream. It was as if all I wanted was to be able to feel your lips against mine and it was an intense feeling that felt real. No more of those dreams, I hope. I like happy dreams better, a lot better!

Tomorrow is 15 miles of running. My dad is going to be part of the support group. This is a group of maybe three people who want to meet even though most of the group won't be there because of

Easter. It should be a good run. Hopefully, I'll remember to put on sunscreen and wear sunglasses. The sun was blazing in our eyes last time. The weather is starting to warm up making running a little more difficult. I can't believe you trained during the summer last year. You are brave!

CHAPTER 19
WHAT MORE IS LEFT TO DO?

April 19 War Day 30

Robert: *This paperwork crap is getting old. Awards, equipment losses, evaluations, etc. Guess I'm the admin guy, huh? Between you and me, I'm submitting an exception to the policy request to release me from the stop-loss to ETS on 23 Aug 03 like I'm supposed to. Could get me home sooner. You know I'll try my best but please still have patience. I love you and want everything to work out for us upon my return. But I know it is going to be difficult at first since you'll be in Dallas and I'll have to be in Killeen while I clear out of the Army. All in God's plans though. He'll work it out for us, I'm sure.*

Hopefully, I can fit in finding a job, and get married with a honeymoon in the 65 days of terminal leave I'll have built up. As soon as I get there, clear, and go on my terminal leave, I will be by your side as often as possible. You're going to have to say, "Robert, give me some breathing room" because I'll be all over you like white on rice!

The game plan when I know I can come home is to go ahead and get us a place for the next month (sign a 3- or 6-month lease). Unless you want me to go with you, but I don't want to stay with your parents when I get home. I'll need quality time alone with you for a while. We certainly won't have that unless we are in our place.

I think finding a job will be a challenge to tide me until grad school or the federal agencies call. I'll shoot for a job to last me at least until August 2004. That's when grad school could start for me.

Enough of that stuff. I have to continue to pray about being here and remaining safe. Our next move is a bit worrisome because it is through Baghdad. Everything seems fairly secure, but you never know. Never stop praying for me until I have you safely in my arms. Going to follow up on some business so I'll write later.

*You are my sunshine, my only sunshine, you make me happy when skies are gray, you'll never know dear how much I **love** you…*

Laura: Hey baby! My dad and I just got back from marathon training. He was our hero today because he provided the water breaks. Last night, I bought Gatorade, water, pretzels, Pringles, and Fig Newtons to snack on during the run. There were only three of us there from our group. We were so thankful to have breaks this time.

I've been walking some during the long runs. It helps relieve my left knee. But I tried today to run consistently and ended up walking for one minute here and there at the end especially because the muscles around my right knee were not feeling right. With a little rest and ice, I'll be fine. It's weird how you have a different twinge each week. Only five or six weeks until the big day. It will be a good time, but I so wish that you could be there.

San Diego would be a great place for us to visit sometime. I'll go anywhere as long as it's with you.

LeeAnne was telling me that she and Mike and another couple went hiking for a week and had a great time. If she can do it, so can I. It would be fun to go hiking with you. That reminds me of Enchanted Rock. How we had so much fun hiking and relaxing by the lake. We need to go back there soon to hang out for the day. I miss you, honey. I can't even explain the longing I have for you in my heart. I hope to talk with you soon!

April 19 War Day 30

Robert: *Your latest letter from the 5th of April almost made me cry. Your words and sincerity touch my heart. The power of prayer certainly was actualized when you told me of the night before my accident you prayed for angels to watch over me and they did. God certainly placed His hand on me that night and saved me. He must have a bigger purpose for me, one of which is to* **love** *you with all my heart for all our lives and be the best husband and father. Loving God and this will be my priority above everything. Laura, you are my everything and I am so happy when I think of all we have to look forward to. There is so much uncertainty, but we will always have each other from here on out to work through, discuss, plan, and pray together.*

I am so proud to hear about your 12-mile run alone. Remember 9 miles with me was your last feat? You've only got 8 or 9 more to go and you're ready. I certainly believe God will have me there to support you as you did when I ran my marathon. Not sure I could train quickly enough unless I got back really soon. Haven't run since I was in Camp Pennsylvania, which was over a month ago. I just started back working out.

For the past three days, I have been doing pushups, crunches, and dips. Also, I've started walking around the compound (bunkers) since we aren't authorized to run. The next location we are moving to has a track near so maybe I'll get to start back up. The only problem is I have no running shoes or PT gear. Guess I could run in boots. Certainly, can't let you run me down when I get back. I know I'll have to work up to your endurance, so you'll have to have patience. All I have been doing here is eating MREs, peanut butter and jelly, and getting fat. Well, maybe not fat.

Do you think you can still get Norah Jones tickets? I would say get them and if I'm not back take a girlfriend or something. But that would be so awesome if I were back in time and we could go.

Been meaning to ask you if Marna has heard from Chris. Wonder if he is out here? [One of my best friends Chris Chase was with the 1st Marine Expeditionary Force during the invasion as a logistician but we never connected, he ended up back home a month or so before I made it home]. *Saw some Marines when we went on our leaders' recon through Baghdad. Man, it was nerve-racking being so close to all those Iraqi people. Many of them gave us thumbs up. Not sure of the sincerity of the appreciation of our presence.*

Three American soldiers came in today with shrapnel wounds when they said a little girl had picked up a cluster bomb and brought it to them. Not sure if she maliciously threw it or just dropped it not knowing any better. Very sad. But all three guys will be okay. We worked on one guy's leg (compound fracture). Meanwhile, the fightin' XO was working on paperwork.

Looks like MAJ Kirk's replacement will be here shortly, maybe even before we move. He might be gone before the end of the month. Good for him I say. Had to talk to him the other night about not feeling guilty about going back early. Explained he has made his sacrifices many times over now and the people who matter the most (his family) shouldn't have to sacrifice anymore. Made him feel better, I think.

You know one day our kids are going to see all my pictures and read our letters and know what it was like when dad was away at war and how much we loved and missed one another. You are so amazingly beautiful and sexy. I am so lucky.

Everyone that has written talks about how great we are together. Lauren Faulkner wrote for the third time and I quote, "I truly hope that there is a quick resolution so that you can return home to start your life with your new wife. Both of you are so amazing and it is really powerful to see how you and Laura were brought together." See everyone knows we are the most amazing couple in the world. God has truly blessed us. Two caring and loving people like us deserve one another. I thank God daily. Tomorrow is Easter so praise the Lord because He has risen. It is so great to be a Christian and **love** *you. He has given me so much.*

April 20 (Easter) War Day 31

Laura: *Happy Easter! I wish you could have been with me today. It was good to hear from you by e-mail. It's good to know I may hear from you soon. It's hard to explain how badly I need to hear from you. Inside this package, you will find two CDs. One is a sermon given by Mac about the biblical reasons for war. It is a great sermon, so I purchased it for you to hear. Also, the other CD is a PowerPoint show that I had so much fun making for you. I wanted to do something to make your day a little brighter. It was so much fun to reminisce as I went through our pictures.*

There is a song with the show, I hope so much you can hear it. Also, it will go through the slides, so don't push the buttons.

Today, we had a lot of food to eat. You would have loved it. I didn't make it to church today, unfortunately. I did sleep which I needed to do. This week I have to go to Plano on Monday and Tuesday. Those will be early mornings.

How are you? I look forward to being able to ask you that and hear you say how you are doing. Last night, we watched the homecoming of the 1st CAV pilots to Ft Hood. It was such a relief to see them reunite with their families. Seeing them hugging their loved ones made me think about how it would feel to hug you for the first time. Just thinking about being in your arms makes me so happy.

I have to say I am so sorry my letters have not been very uplifting lately. I'm trying to keep my spirits up when I write. This time apart hasn't gotten easier. At first, time flew by but now the time has been creeping by. I pray you to come home soon. I'll continue to pray for your safety. I **love** you!

Happy Easter! One day we'll be enjoying Easter with our family watching little Robert hunt for Easter eggs. Such a happy thought. I'll be thinking of you on Easter and wishing we could share the day by going to church to honor God and then heading off to have a nice quiet picnic in the park. Reminds me of one of my favorite lunches with you in the Arboretum at the duck pond. I didn't want to leave that day. I just wanted to stay there at the duck pond with you all day. We have so many great memories to cherish for a lifetime. You have brightened my life emotionally, physically, and spiritually. The bond we have cannot be broken. I can't wait for you to come home to begin making more memories. I think about that day so often. I can just picture you and see you for the first time. I will not be able to control my happiness. Oh, *and that first kiss. How amazing it will be. I know that Dr. Kirk and a few others there have provided you with great fellowship. I pray you have the opportunity to have fellowship on this day! I **love** you so much!*

April 21 (Aggie Muster) War Day 32

Robert: [*Happy Aggie Muster! Today is a special day for all Texas A&M Graduates called Aggie Muster. It is one of the most special traditions where Aggies gather near and far to celebrate and remember those Aggies lost during the past year. As the Texas A&M Corps of Cadets campusology states Aggie Muster "Sir, On April 21st each year, on the anniversary of the Battle of San Jacinto, Aggies gather together, wherever they are to commemorate fellow Aggies who have died during the year. The tradition begun 21 April 1903, Sir!" The bond Laura and I share as fellow Texas Aggies is a strong one for the amazing experience our days in College Station made us the people we are and the people we hope to be. Aggieland is a special place that teaches you the values of tradition and caring for others. Below is the list of all the Texas Aggies who have died during the two decades of war. One of those was a good friend to me while at Texas A&M, CPT Ernie Blanco '98, and my own Aggie brother's old roommate was also killed, LTC Todd Clark '94. Ernie and I served on the Texas A&M Ross Volunteers together which was a selective junior and senior Texas A&M Corps of Cadets unit which served as the Texas Governor's Honor Guard. My older brother and I, COL (RET) David W Payne Jr., Aggie, and Army bond is quite special and often connects us beyond just family. Makes it even more special that our younger brothers, Chris & Nick Payne, served as NCOs in the US Air Force and US Army. Texas*

A&M commissions more officers than anywhere in the nation other than the service academies. In WWII, Texas A&M had more Aggies serving in combat than even West Point. Because the University was founded in 1876 as a military college it has a rich tradition and connection to military service. The Corps of Cadets is still central to the heart of Texas A&M University to this day even with a student body growing to almost 70,000 students.]

IN MEMORIAM–HTTPS://WWW.AGGIENETWORK.COM/HEROES/

Since Sept. 11, 2001, 32 Aggies have been killed in service to our country.

If you know of a former student who has died since Sept. 11, 2001, while serving our country and is not listed, email **AggieNetwork@AggieNetwork.com**.

What More Is Left To Do?

1st Lt. Jonathan Rozier '01 was killed July 19, 2003, in Baghdad, Iraq.

Captain Ernesto M. Blanco '98 was killed Dec. 28, 2003, in Qaryat Ash Shababi, Iraq.

1st Lt. Doyle M. Hufstedler III '01 was killed March 31, 2004, in Fallujah, Iraq.

Captain Sean Patrick Sims '94 was killed Nov. 13, 2004, in Fallujah, Iraq.

Captain Todd Tyler Christmas '00 was killed Nov. 29, 2004, in Operation Iraqi Freedom.

Captain Lyle Gordon '97 was killed Jan. 26, 2005, in Ar Rutbah, Iraq.

Sgt. William Meeuswen '03 was killed Nov. 23, 2005, in Baghdad, Iraq.

Chief Warrant Officer Richard Salter '85 was killed Dec. 26, 2005, in Iraq.

Major Matthew Worrell '94 was killed May 14, 2006, in Yousifiyah, Iraq.

1st Lt. Ryan Sanders '01 was killed June 5, 2006, in Baghdad, Iraq.

Captain Blake Russell '98 was killed July 22, 2006, in Baghdad, Iraq.

Sgt. 1st Class Merideth Howard '76 was killed Sept. 8, 2006, in Kabul, Afghanistan.

Lance Cpl Luke Yepsen '08 was killed Dec. 14, 2006, in Al Anbar Province, Iraq.

Captain Sean Edward Lyerly '98 was killed Jan. 20, 2007, in Iraq.

Specialist Daniel Gomez '08 was killed July 18, 2007, in Iraq.

Private First Class William Edwards '06 was killed Aug. 11, 2007, in Baghdad, Iraq.

2nd. Lt. Peter Burks '03 was killed Nov. 14, 2007, in Baghdad, Iraq.

1st Lt. Jeremy Ray '04 was killed Dec. 20, 2007, in Kanaan, Iraq.

Specialist Christopher West '04 was killed Feb. 4, 2008, in Muqdadiyah, Iraq.

1st Lt. Matthew R. Vandegrift '03 was killed April 21, 2008, in Basrah, Iraq.

1st Lt. Timothy W. Cunningham '04 was killed April 23, 2008, in Golden Hills, Iraq.

2nd Lt. Zachary R. Cook '08 died Jan. 12, 2009, in a training accident in College Station, Texas.

Lt. Col. Mark E Stratton '91 was killed May 26, 2009, in Panjshir Province, Afghanistan.

Staff Sgt. Christopher N. Staats '01 was killed Oct. 16, 2009, in Wardak Province, Afghanistan.

Lt. Col. David E. Cabrera '92 was killed on Oct. 29, 2011, in Kabul, Afghanistan.

Lt. Col. Todd J. Clark '94, a brigade-level adviser with the U.S. Army's 10th Mountain Division, was killed on June 8, 2013, in Afghanistan.

April 22 War Day 33

Robert 2327: *Sorry I haven't written sooner to get a letter in the mail. I never try to go more than a day without putting a letter in the mail for you. Easter was great. We had an Easter service in one of the hangars at the airport. The chaplain who gave the sermon was awesome. Very inspiring and I certainly felt God's presence there. Made me want to grab everyone that doesn't know Jesus and shake them and tell them they are crazy for not knowing Him. I have guaranteed blessings, protection, and a spot in eternity because I believe in His Salvation. How awesome.*

I got to send you an e-mail last night and read the Aggie posting. It was so sweet and thoughtful. Thank you so much for being such a wonderful wife. But I haven't gotten to communicate more in the past two days because after the Easter service we got told we were moving the next day and MAJ Kirk's replacement (LTC Miller) showed up. Seems like an okay guy, definitely no MAJ Kirk, but I'm partial because he has not only been my boss but a Christian brother-friend.

We packed up everything and left the little hangar we had made home. My little control box room was perfect and cozy, not to mention safe, but God wouldn't lead us into anything we couldn't handle. We are headed into Baghdad. Can't tell you where, but we are in the city now (not to discuss with others please). [This is a reference to our move into the City of Baghdad into the Olympic Stadium, right in the open between multiple highway inter-changes which later worked against us when we would often get shot at and never know where it was coming from]. Before we left, I went with MAJ Kirk to hear LTG William Wallace (5th Corps Commander – 3 Star General) speak to some medical folks. Ran into CPT Jeff Williams (Stephen F Austin buddy from 1st Medical Brigade) when they dropped LTC Miller off. Guess since the 1st Medical Brigade is here, he is putting his Fed Agencies applications on hold as well [Jeff and I both had the desire to leave the Army and become federal agents. In 2004 he was hired by the US Secret Service, and I was hired by the DEA. We lost track over time after I knew he ended up having a divorce and got re-married, sometime after I moved to Portland in 2008. He was a solid Lieutenant buddy and good to see him in Iraq].

Speaking of jobs and our life together, to even consider getting home early at all to ETS, I have to now submit a relief from active-duty request through this chain of command person to get orders. I'll just pray about it. God will bring me home to you when He is ready.

I drove on the way up here and I felt like I was in Houston or Dallas traffic. Iraqi people and cars were everywhere as we got close. Little nerve-wracking, but we are here and safe. Set up on a nice grass area nonetheless.

Getting sleepy. I **love** you so much. You are my world! I'll write more tomorrow.

April 23 War Day 32

Robert: *Just awoke to thoughts of you and how incredibly I miss you. If we are here too much longer, I'm going to go crazy without you.*

Don't think we have much of a mission anymore as we haven't seen casualties in several days. If things remain calm, it should probably stay that way. Occasionally we hear gunfire outside our perimeter, but that could be Iraqis celebrating by shooting their guns off. Who knows? Sounds similar to that in any American downtown city.

Certainly, would prefer this be our last stop and leave here sooner than later. I'm certainly looking into what it would take to get my Aug 23 ETS, but since a stop loss is in effect for deployed units, I have to get the relief from active duty approved at the personnel command level. Again, all in God's hands. Have to give it up to Him because it continues to worry and bother me.

*Last night I received nine letters: Four from you! One from Dad and Marie, one from Nicholas, one from Debbie Kirk (thanking me for being a friend to Dr. Kirk and for the "praising of God"), in the report of my accident, Sergio, and letters for my team from Marna's class. Trying to ensure I write everyone back who writes me, but I'm getting backed up. The first letter I always write is to my wonderful, sweet, beautiful, sexy, caring wife – Laura Payne! Sounds so nice to hear. I **love** all the wonderful praises of me and our relationship in your letters. I believe all of it in my heart as* well. I am getting close to running on empty because I haven't been around Laura in so long. Will need you 24/7 for many days when I return to bring me back to my loving Laura fill.

Our **love** and caring nature will complement us so well in our lives. How fortunate and blessed are we to have the **love** God has found for us to share? Praise God. "I know what I am planning for you… I have good plans for you, not plans to hurt you. I will give you hope and a good future" (Jeremiah 29:11). He has a wonderful future for us, we just must continue to pray for patience. I **love** you so much.

Laura: How are you doing today? I hope this letter finds you doing well. I'm doing okay. I miss you tremendously! Every day you just wonder when this time apart will end. It's like we're in limbo or paused and now we're just waiting for the time when our lives will come back together. Every day I wish for a letter to know what's going on in your life. I hope that you are beginning to receive my letters and packages. I'm so excited to possibly be able to talk with you this week. It will be the best feeling to hear your voice again.

What has happened here? Not too much difference. I'm still training for the marathon. I haven't been diligent with the weekly training, mainly just doing the long runs. It's not a good habit to have so I rejoined the Gold's Gym, but up here. Now, it will be easier to keep up during the week. It's not safe to run alone in our neighborhood. Some weirdos around here stare and come around the block again to see you.

The marathon is coming up soon. The fundraising is not going so well. I still need $1400. Neither of your parents sent any money, but Mawmaw did. But that's okay. (Please don't say anything).

God has not helped me with the distance I feel from her. I've asked for Him to **love** her through me. Do you think He might be telling me to cut ties with her? I'll just continue to pray for that situation.

Work is okay. We've been busy, and we just picked up another line this week. We trained on it yesterday. I've been to Plano twice this week, but I avoided it today. This morning I dropped off literature at five offices. My biggest victory will be the first surgery that I have with a surgeon Lanny has never done business with.

The living situation is okay. My family's dynamics suck. It makes for a stressful environment. Believe me, I'm ready to get out. My parents are unhappy, all they do is fight. I don't ever want to get to a point in our marriage. I know we have a relationship built on trust and respect, and we're friends. [I found reading this ironic as we approach our 20th wedding anniversary on Jan 3, 2023, and have been on the brink of separation or divorce several times and managed so many hardships. I have no judgment on anyone's marriage because it is such a difficult journey. As optimistic as we were during these letters, I don't think we had any idea what starting a marriage with war, managing a life moving around as a federal agent, dealing with infertility, and having four kids with no support structure, would truly be like…it took a toll for sure. I am just grateful to God we are still together today, and I love Laura with all my heart, so thankful we have endured these hardships and are still together. Re-reading these letters reminds me why I love her so].

It will be great to be able to move in with you. Angela says that it is like having a slumber party with your best friend every night. I'm sure it will be that way. I was thinking about how nice it would be to be in the same city, this was as I was sitting in traffic. Then I realized we'd still be driving an hour or more to see each other because of the traffic here. We don't have to live here, I promise. I'll go wherever God leads us. A job is a job, I can find one wherever we go, I just want to be with you, in **love,** and living our happy married life together. I miss you and think of you all the time. I **love** you.

April 24 War Day 32

Robert 1724: *I **love** you, I **love** you, I **love** you. I miss you, I miss you, I miss you, I **love** you, I **love** you, I **love** you. By the way, have I told you how much I **love** you and miss you?*

Things are fairly smooth. Took a trip into town yesterday to look at local clinics, that has been my most exciting/risky moment since the journey into Baghdad. [I remember this moment very clearly and frightening. Our new Commander, LTC (Dr) Miller, having just arrived wanted to go out to Baghdad and engage with local medical professionals in clinics. I think he intended to find a place where he could do surgery and move patients if needed. While we were in the clinic and he was talking with an Iraqi female doctor, a large number of media came inside with what seemed to be an Iraqi local official. They immediately came towards us because they saw US soldiers and surrounded us. I was the closest to LTC Miller with my M-16 and we were getting shoved and separated by the large crowd. SFC Smith was outside with the HMMWV but could still see us. We both knew we needed to get out of there immediately. LTC Miller wouldn't stop talking. Around the corner walked an Iraqi man in plain clothes with an AK-47 assault rifle in his hands. I immediately raised my M-16 and began giving commands to lay down his weapon. Due to the language barrier, he hesitated but he understood an M-16 pointed at him and a screaming US Army Captain. At that point, Iraqi Security Police ran over and told him to lower his weapon and gave me the sign that the plain clothes Iraqi were with him.

What More Is Left To Do?

I remember my finger on the trigger and off safe and came very close to pulling the trigger. I was scared and mad. I then moved to LTC Miller through the crowd, grabbed his arm, and shoved us through the crowd, past the cameras outside to SFC Smith. He looked at me and could see the anger on my face. All I said was "Let's go now Sir, this isn't safe anymore." I could sense LTC Miller's frustration with me, but I didn't care. He hadn't been in Iraq but a week and was assuming the unnecessary risk for his team that had been through war and just wanted to make it home alive. This was only the first of many issues that arose with our new Commander.]

We have pretty much been occupying a day. In our patio area, we have assembled soccer goalposts between our CBPS vehicles and the DRASHs [tents] we are sleeping in. We have draped a large canvas over the top with white sheets lining the sides with mosquito netting. The plain white sheet at the end serves as the movie screen as we have been watching a movie nightly. We have our showing around dark + for 30 min.

Today, MAJ Vinca, MAJ Lim, and I even had an afternoon matinee inside the CBPS, "Saving Silverman." We watched that one night on the couch. I watched it and you slept! I wish I was there to rent a movie, and have you fall asleep in my lap while I played with your hair. I even miss the little things, the intricacies that make you the woman I **love** more than life itself.

Also, spent some time today working on my request for active-duty release. Now, I have to wait on signatures before I can send it to personal command. By the time it is all done we'll probably be home! [Ironic to read this because I never submitted it, I just decided to go home with the team and ETS from active duty once I got back].

*Ohhh! Mail's here. I got a letter from Laura! Happy days are here again. Your letters are what I look forward to more than anything. I'm stopping to read it. It was sent on 9 Apr and today is 24 Apr. 15 days to make it. Great to hear you developed my pictures. I have a couple more rolls here. I haven't made it a habit of kissing lizards, I promise. As far as your mom, I am so sorry. I know it must be difficult. Please continue to pray for your mom and patience to live there. I certainly will do the same. Yes, she certainly has some resentment that stems from something. All you can do is pray for her. Talk to her with an open heart and **love** her unconditionally. As bad as she can get, continue to **love** her to death. Always strive to be the bigger person. Be the Christian! Jesus loved everyone, even those who didn't want to be loved.*

I am excited for you on your aerobics cert plans. I hope you can fit it into your schedule. I know it will always be great to have that to fall on. I miss lying in bed with you too and showering with you. Hell, I miss showering daily. Most importantly, Team Payne will be reunited in due time!!

2241: *Finished watching Charlie's Angels tonight and I thought of you when 'smack my bitch up' started playing in their fight scenes.*

*By the way, got to run tonight for the first time since Camp Pennsylvania. Had to borrow some shoes and run in my BDU pants because some Iraqi is running around in my PT gear and my $100 marathon running shoes! Oh well, praise the Lord I'm here. Verse to look at 1 Corinthians 2:9 is what God has in store for us. I **love** you so much. You are my everything.*

What More Is Left To Do?

April 25 War Day 36

Robert 2237: *What a blessing it was to hear your voice last night. I hope I didn't leave you sad but filled with love in your heart hearing from me. Just think about 10 years from now you'll probably tell me to stop yapping so much you're tired of my voice! Exciting to think we'll still have one another ten years from now. Where will we be in ten years? Whoa, what a thought. We'll have a family by then and we'll be in careers of some sort. You'll be old at the age of 37 and I'll still be young at age 36! You'll still be so beautiful. [Again, ironic as I re-read this because we struggled to have children and we had our first child via IVF when I was 33 and Laura was 34. But life-changing to finally have Avery in our life after such struggles, then later came Zach via IVF, Miles via IVF, and Ethan naturally when we were 40 and 41. Never underestimate God's will].*

Today was devoted to preparation and rehearsals for the chain of command tomorrow. COL Hightower is supposed to come to it. I'm the narrator.

Looks like Dr. Kirk will be out if everything goes according to plan. Wrote Debbie Kirk a letter thanking her for all her support and praising MAJ Kirk for his leadership and Christian friendship.

Got a nice package from my mom today and a letter from Sergio's mom. Sadly, no Laura letter but I'll be looking forward to one tomorrow hopefully. Tonight's movie was "The Living End" or something, it was the recent James Bond movie from recent. Didn't stay until the end because I wanted to write my beautiful wife. Today, we were told we can't run around the track. Guess the command doesn't think it is safe enough since we are here in Baghdad.

There are still very small pockets of resistance. Stupid Iraqis I suppose [although probably the start of the insurgency the US forces fought for over a decade]. Found the guy that came into the clinic the other day when LTC Miller and I were there, was some Iraqi money guy trying to claim power... not authorized by us. He had about 15 guys with suits and media everywhere. Certainly, nerve-wracking but thankfully we were fine. How can I fear when the Lord's angels are on my side? Well, time for bed. Wish you were here. I **love** you so much!

Laura: It's amazing to think we have now been apart for three months, three times as long as we have been apart before. I just can't believe it. It was so amazing to hear your voice yesterday. My heart was so overjoyed you were calling. The happiness I felt talking with you was so great. I haven't felt that way in a long time. The hardest part of the conversation is hanging up. I just don't want to let you go. I want to talk with you forever. God answered my prayer from the night before when I asked to hear your voice because I needed it to get through another week or two. Jessica Riker told me it gets easier, but I have found it to get harder. People do react differently to situations. She is very resilient. I admire that about her. [Jessica was married to one of my closest Army buddies from my time in 1st CAV, Randy. He deployed to the invasion as well with the 173rd Airborne and jumped into the war. Sadly, he and Jessica divorced several years after he came home from Iraq...many marriages are causalities of war. But he remarried and has a wonderful family, retiring in 2021 after 20 years of service. Randy Riker was a wonderful friend I will always think highly of from my time in active duty Army life].

This morning I went to a sports conditioning class at Gold's and got a good butt workout! Tonight, I have my free personal trainer visit at 6 p.m. I'm interested in the weights and getting a routine to slim and tone my hips, thighs, and butt. I've also started a 300 crunches/day workout. I want to work up to Britney Spears' 500 or 1,000/day! Ouch!

I had been down the past couple of days, but I can't explain how talking with you made a world of difference. Today has been so much brighter. I forgot to tell you that your mom says that she loves you and to please write your mama. That part was in caps, so I think she means it.

You know I have to say that I am so glad we agree about your homecoming. I would enjoy everybody being there, but I would want to be alone as soon as possible. Also, I want to be able to just hug you for a long time without interruption. We both know a lot of people will want to be there to welcome you home because they **love** you. I hope you don't have too much trouble working to get orders to leave. God will handle it, so all I can do is pray for a quick return so we can continue our never-ending vacation. I guess this time apart we can call "a long restroom break" in our vacation because you are in one area, and I'm in another. Just a little humor for you.

The stop-loss stuff is so incredibly vague. I read one document issuing a stop loss that made no sense to me. Hopefully, Bush will decide he doesn't need the FST there any longer and you can come home for your birthday. If we miss it though, I'll make it up to you, I promise! How about another trip for your birthday? Sounds awesome to me. The trip to Boston was so much fun and Disney was also fantastic! Wouldn't it be great to take off to Disney right now and relive the magical time we had?

I was looking at the wedding story app and they ask you about your relationship. I thought about our one-year anniversary celebration and what an unbelievable weekend and week that was. Thank you so much for giving me so much that week. I'm sure

*I've already said this, but I have to say it again. You just poured all of your heart into making that the most unbelievable time in our lives. You just made me feel so special and showed how dedicated you are to our relationship. I am so lucky to have you as my husband. Praise God for growing this into the **love** we share now. Thank you so much Robert for just being who you are, you have truly given me the world. You are the man I have always dreamed about, but thought could only exist in dreams. I know we are going to have the best life together. We are entering a new phase in life, and I am so excited.*

April 26 War Day 37

Robert: *Can I keep saying war day? I guess they haven't called a cease-fire yet. How is the media coverage now? Is the war with Iraq still the headlining story? My headlining story is 'I haven't seen Laura in 84 days!' That is 84 days longer than needed. I miss everything about you. Smelling you, touching you, hearing you, and feeling you. Today was Dr. Kirk's change of command and he is heading home within the next 48 hours, I think. Lucky for him, huh? He has certainly made the sacrifices, so he deserves it. It was a great change of command here in Baghdad. What a way to do it. How many guys can say they changed command in Baghdad? I was the narrator/emcee today. I think I sounded good. We served goodies from Saddam Hussein's silverware and linen! How appropriate, huh? Even a dozen or so Iraqis were doing manual labor right behind us during the ceremony. They are paying them $2 a day. Can you believe that? If they hire a professional like a doctor or engineer, it is only $5 a day, but to them, it is quite a bit. Wondered what was going through the Iraqis' minds when we* were saluting the flag while the National Anthem was being sung. A soldier from A10 3rd FSB sang it beautifully.

Anyway, everyone is sitting around in chill mode each day now waiting for what will happen next. Wish we were in our old location at the airport because I had my little hole. Found out Sergio's brother's old house is in Killeen so at least I have a place to stay while I clear FT Hood. Unless you are coming with me I'll put us up somewhere. I have to go to a meeting and be back soon.

Back from a meeting and have no significant changes. The buzz is certainly around redeployment, but no dates. Main point – I **love** you... nothing more I can say.

April 27 War Day 38

Laura: The weekend is over, another weekend without you. We did our 18-mile run yesterday, but I turned 17 miles to save my knee. It hurt bad enough last week that I couldn't walk. I did some research on the web and think I have iliotibial syndrome. Which is a tendon that starts at the hip and goes below the knee, it is a typical running injury where your knee aches on the outside and it is painful to run or walk. You have to do rest, ice, compression, elevate, and try to take it easier on your knee and there is a band you can put on your knee when you are running. I felt guilty for turning and walking painfully the last three miles. I just want to finish the marathon.

Last night, I tried to meet Heather and Paige, but I ended up saying hi and going home to sleep. I met them today in Dallas for lunch at Gloria's, and we laid out by the pool. It was another beautiful day. One of those top-down Jeep days. It made me think about how much I wanted to be riding with you to the park to play frisbee. I always **love** going to Zilker Park with you.

We got word that your new commander arrived. How was the ceremony? I could only imagine it was a sad time to see Mike step aside. Do you like the new commander? I pray your team will do well with the change. It sounds like you guys are just waiting for replacements to be able to come home. I hope so because the sooner the better. I miss you more than I can explain.

It's Monday now. On Monday mornings, I wake up at 4:30 a.m. to drive to Plano for our 6:30 a.m. meeting. The drive out there is fine, it's the drive that is difficult because I get sleepy. Scott is a rep on our team I went to surgery with today. They are afraid of Dr. Courtney (not really), but they like to bring me along because then the focus is off them. Dr. Courtney is the guy we had dinner with at Cool River. He remembers having dinner with us. Then we grabbed a bite for lunch, and I headed back to Ft Worth.

I bought a band for my knee to wear while running. Hopefully, it will help hold the iliotibial band steady. There is a group that meets on Tuesday and Thursday nights to run together. I'm thinking I might show up and try it. I want to run with you again. We haven't run together in about 5 months. I look forward to exercising together and being a healthy couple. I **love** how we share that. We'll be able to keep each other motivated to stay in shape.

Yesterday, Heather was talking about going to Europe. She said we should go, but I want to go with just you and me so we can be alone savoring the romance and passion in Europe. She is interested in backpacking so maybe we could get her and some others together for a trip to Big Bend.

I have to get some work done, but I'll talk to you again soon. I miss you with all my heart. I **love** you so much! Come home soon.

CHAPTER 20
OUR PURPOSE DRIVEN LIFE

April 29 War Day 40

Robert: *I just received two of your letters, made me so happy. One is dated the 3rd of April. Awesome to hear how equally excited you are about our life as I am. Even though I have no idea how things will work out and where we will be, I just feel it will all work out. God will provide for us as long as we "give it up" to him. No matter how difficult it may be, we'll have each other. How appropriate... I'm writing my letter to my only and Cranberries' "Dreaming My Dreams" came on my MP3 player [I know if my kids or grandkids were reading this they would ask what's an MP3 player...digital music files before everything was streamed over the internet]. What a wonderful memory of knowing I had fallen in **love** with you. I know without a doubt of God's blessing of our **love** and marriage having been separated from you. This relationship in my mind was never planned to go anywhere initially, but something attracted me to give it a chance. Then I thought, well I can't let it get too serious. Just have some fun because she is fun was what I thought. Then I began becoming closer and feeling so wanted and appreciated by you. Your patience was so wonderful. Before I knew it, I couldn't stand to not be around you,* talk to you, or go out with you. I can still remember the excited feeling I would get when your ring came on my phone (even when I couldn't answer). I remember thinking how wonderful it was to have someone putting as much into caring as much as I did. Not calling and talking at least once a day was not an option, we had to talk!

Then it happened... I knew I had fallen in **love** with you. It happened as it should, so naturally. Then our wonderful relationship evolved, and we loved one another so passionately, without question, unconditionally. I was soon realizing I would never find anyone else who could **love** like I do... except Laura. Then, the day in the shower as I was thinking and planning our year anniversary, it was obvious I wanted to plan things and do things sweet for you... forever. There is nothing more I want than to provide you with a lifetime of **love**. It wasn't a decision; it was an overwhelming feeling of what was right and what our hearts needed. I never expected to feel as I have with you.

I know our Savior and God have placed us together. He saw our hearts and caring nature deserved only each other. Laura, God has given you to me as my soulmate to **love** and care for. I never knew what I had said that day about soulmates. I didn't even consider the term, but being apart from you, I embrace the term and understand with my heart what it means. It is the overwhelming feeling of emptiness and incompleteness in my heart because you're not nearby. I miss you more than words can describe. God has made me who I am for many things. Although I do not know everything, He has planned for me, I know the gift of loving with a compassionate heart and loving with loyalty and unconditionally is something He has gifted me with. I have been placed in your life to give that to you. Laura, you are my precious angel and I only want to return to care for you and always **love** you like He intended me to.

Sorry to hear about your federal agency concern, but understand I'll apply, search for a job initially, and apply to grad schools. God will take care of the rest. He will take the lead as to the next step and what will happen. I have to surrender it all to Him because whatever I do will be for His glory. Always remember that you and our children will come first. Although, you'll have to understand the support I will need initially no matter what career I take on. I'll have to pay my dues. Just remember the understanding and patience we both need to pray for upon my return because of all the uncertainty. Only prayer and each other will lead us to our comfortable life together.

*Sorry, to hear your heart is not into your job, but that is maybe God's way of saying it is temporary. Only time will tell. Hang in there with the marathon training. I know you can do it. Physically it will be a piece of cake for you because you have been in shape for so long. You have to overcome the mental yourself. Let yourself know you can succeed. Good to know Scotty G will be there to visit with you. I doubt our timeline will get us back home in time, but I'll be thinking and praying for you. I wish I could share the experience with you. I'll make up for it by joining the team in training and doing a triathlon with you. We'll buy bikes together and I'll join your gym. We'll train together. Two things we will always support and drive each other to do – stay fit and **love** Christ. We will always hold each other accountable!*

The finances sound good. Found out from my end what we are entitled to. Here it is:

Save Pay $100 was $50
Hazard Fire Pay $225 was $150
Family Separation $150 was $100

The new amounts will be back paid through 1 Feb 03 except save pay which only started 31 Mar 03. Guess the defense money for the war helped us out! Also, no federal taxes (FITW) should be charged, only social security and Medicare. I should see my LES on this end. If there are any problems, I'll handle them. A finance team arrived yesterday. Feel free to invest, put money away, or pay on your vehicles as necessary. I trust you. Just realize we'll need some money to get us settled while I might not have a job, ensure we enjoy our honeymoon, and begin saving for (home, travel, etc.). Again, I trust you in all you do financially. It's just money. It's way down on the priority list after God, Laura, family, and friends.

Laura, I want you to continue to grow in your **faith** as well so please get this book and read it for me. Zondervan Publishing, A Purpose Driven Life, Rick Warren. It has been providing so much insight into my life, I want it for you as well. It has pointed out so many wonderful things about eternity and our relationship with Jesus. I know it is probably harder where you are at, but please try so we continue to grow together when I return. He has blessed us with such **love** to share we have to glorify and honor Him with everything we do. Some comforting words can come from Job 22:21 or Romans 6:17. I'll write a paragraph from the book that reached out to me (Pg 83/Ch 10).

<u>Surrender</u>

"If God is going to do His deepest work in you. It will begin with this. So give it all to God: <u>your past</u> regrets, your <u>present problems</u>, your <u>future ambitions</u>, your fears, dreams, weaknesses, habits, hurts, and hang-ups. Put Jesus Christ in the driver's seat of your life and take your hands off the steering wheel. Don't be afraid; nothing under His control can ever be out of control.

Mastered by Christ, <u>you</u> can handle <u>anything</u>. You will be like Paul (Philippians 4:13) "I am ready for anything and equal to anything through Him who infuses inner strength into me, that is, I am self-sufficient in Christ's sufficiency."

*Amen, huh? David can help you get this book because he sent it to me. I was getting worked up about the active-duty release and going home, then I read this chapter on Surrender. Gave it to God to work out in His timeline, not mine. I think of you always and **love** you so much.*

April 30 War Day 41

Robert: *So bored and tired of being here. The weather here has been beautiful. Getting a little warm. Wish I was with you driving around with my top down on my Jeep with the sun on our faces heading to Zilker Park. Such a nice thought, huh?*

Yesterday we had a nice break in things. We played softball in the Olympic soccer stadium next to us. Also, our new commander tried to teach us all some rugby, which was funny to watch, I'm sure. We played a softball game against Bravo Company but lost 14-12. We'll play again soon, I'm sure. Fortunately, things are quiet around here. Everyone occupies themselves with something. For example, I'm sitting in our DRASH tent and SSG Kufro is playing Gameboy, MAJ Vinca is reading a magazine, MAJ Beverly is on his computer, LTC Miller (new commander) is lying on a cot, and I'm writing a letter.

Earlier, I started back on my US Secret Service app. As soon as I'm finished, I'll mail it to you to finish typing and send it in for me. Of course, give them your cell number so if they call, you'll get it and you can tell them where I am. Hope I haven't missed the application turn-in period. Could you check and see if the ATF has openings? Probably easiest to call the local ATF if you can find the numbers. Wondering if I should investigate drug sales for this initial job. My background would help I would think. Southwest or American would be ideal so we can travel like crazy. Only time will tell I suppose.

If I was motivated, I would pull out the GRE book now. When I return, I must focus on that booger again. I'll probably have Aug, Sep, and Oct to take it. For the Jan apps. If I write a Princeton review, I bet I could get the course again if I say my course was confounded because of its proximity in time to my deployment. Worth a try.

So how is the job? Do you think the commission thing will pay off? Should I only look for jobs in Fort Worth/Dallas? So far, the accomplishments of today have been one question on the secret service and I took out our trash. Pretty crazy I tell you. Started reading the last "Left Behind" book I have, "Desecration." The one before, "The Mark" I was about ¾ through when it disappeared into the creek after my accident. It's Wednesday, almost 8 a.m. in Texas and I am wondering what you are doing right now. You're probably eating breakfast, getting ready to visit a hospital, or going to Plano, I suppose. I hope you have a wonderful day.

1945: Just finished working out and running 2½ miles. Nothing compared to the 13 miles I read about in today's letter. I'm so glad you feel even more in **love** with me. Didn't know it was possible to **love** me anymore, but I'll take all the **love** you have to give and then some. I hope my letters are conveying my feelings and emotions about how I feel about you. You are my world and I live to **love** you and God first and foremost.

As far as your running, it doesn't matter if you're the first in the group or last, just don't give up. I'm sorry to hear about the *anger and frustration in your house. Sadly, we both know why—God is not truly in their lives and is a priority. True happiness and comfort cannot be found without Him. Just try and let the Lord work through you to **love** them without reservation or judgment. You're their precious daughter and whether they show it or not you are their world, and they are so proud of you. They probably don't show it, but they **love** having you there. After I come home, they will never get the chance to take care of you again, so let them as much as you can because I know it comforts them to provide for you. Once I return, that becomes my sole responsibility as your husband, mandated by the Bible. Not to mention what my heart truly desires to do. Just stop and pray for your parents and hope Jesus can help your family and their hearts. I'll certainly do the same. Also, thank you for all the care packages! At this point, I have more than enough stuff, so please focus on the wonderful letters even more.*

May 1 War Day 42

Robert: *Tried to send an e-mail to you last night. I hope it reaches you. We had an 11-year-old boy come in last night with several gunshot wounds to his head. He died while with us. The father (or grandpa?) supposedly approached a military checkpoint in his car after curfew hours and wouldn't stop. After warning shots were fired, the car got shot. Sadly, the boy was hit and not the father. They found two AK-47s in his car. The father was here at the treatment area as the boy died wailing and crying. So sad. By far the saddest death I've seen out here. No one wins in a situation like this, and it is silly that anything should be happening like that this late in the conflict. I pray God will be with him. The father was detained as an EPW and taken away. You could tell* he knew it was his fault because he motioned to LTC Miller to get his 9mm to shoot himself in the head.

    Had another Bible study last night without Dr. Kirk. I am kind of getting the tone and leaving it for us (even though only two or three people come). Started to work on the purposeful life with one chapter per meeting. SPC Lundy has been coming and says he has fallen off track but knows of God's **love**. Good to know he is working through me to reach out to someone.

    In your last letter, you spoke of finding a church together. I can't wait. Going to our friends' churches is fine, but one we both feel comfortable at is most important. I look forward to it.

    2120: Just got a package from Michelle and you! Yours is awesome. You have given me more than I could ever use. Thank you for taking care of me. Today was a bland day. Just trying to work through the rumors as to what will happen to us. Let's just say I hope to celebrate the 4th of July with you. Maybe even my birthday. I have no definitive dates, though. Just know I **love** you with all my heart and miss you so much. I awake to thoughts of you and fall asleep thinking of you.

May 2 War Day 43

Laura: *Good morning, honey! It's 7:15 and I am up preparing for the day. There was a doctor's meeting that started at 7. Oops, I missed that. I am still tired from yesterday when my day started at 5:45 a.m. and ended at 7:30 p.m. My body is just like "whatever."*

    It looks like Mike is on his way home. Debbie just invited a bunch of people over for dessert at her house on 5/4. That is so great they will be reunited as a family soon, and they can continue with their life plans. I look forward to the day you call or write and say you're coming home. I won't be able to control my happiness that day.

Thank you for the e-mail this week. I really enjoyed receiving a personal message from you. It feels like I'm more special, though when I receive a personal e-mail. I do **love** the way you have shown how much I mean to you in your mass e-mails. I'm not sure if I should respond to your e-mails because I don't know if you'll be checking your mail again soon. Letters are better because you can keep them and re-read them.

I've been wondering what your mission as a team is now that combat has ceased. Where are you and what are you doing? Are you safe? These are just things I wonder about.

It's 5:45 p.m. now. Time has just flown by today. I can't believe how tired I am. I've decided I am going to turn my phone off and just watch a movie tonight. "Sweet Home Alabama" sounds like a good choice. I wish you could be here (well not exactly at my parent's house) lying on the couch with me. We could take turns giving each other massages and back scratches (your favorite!) I miss you so much! I would **love** so much to be able to talk to you tonight, it would make my entire weekend better.

Nothing planned for the weekend. I'm okay with that! It's been nonstop lately with people inviting me places. I appreciate it, feel obligated to do everything. You know how I like to stay in and relax sometimes. Always on the go is not my thing. I don't think people in general realize how far apart Dallas and the Fort Worth area are. It's 50 miles from our house to 75 in Dallas. I'm saying no more often or trying to get people to meet halfway. Save some hurt on the old Mustang. You would have laughed watching me try to put a 100 lb. crate into the back of my car. I started crying because I was frustrated and tired. It's funny after the fact.

Well, I'm going to take a shower and get ready to watch my movie. I hope you are doing well. I **love** you!

May 3 War Day 44

Robert: *Don't know about home, but it is getting hot in here! Starting to heat up here in Iraq. By next week 100°+. Time to get home to some AC!*

Played another game of softball in the Olympic Stadium and then worked out with little abs, pushups, and a two-mile run. Stepping up as the pitcher for our team is a very nice break from the realization we are still in the middle of Baghdad, Iraq.

Hope we can be settled in our church one day to play on a softball team together, that would be fun. Even though you don't think you're athletic I know you are.

Still no definitive word on home, but I think I can confidently say find out what dates are available for our wedding at the church and Bob Bullock in August, Sep, or Oct and tentatively book them now. Go ahead and lock it in, that way when I know for sure I'm on my way home, we just have to plan the details around that date. As far as I am concerned the sooner the better. If anyone gives you problems ensure they understand our story, I deployed and all. Certainly, will make them want to help us more and maybe cut us a deal. Money off is nothing we should turn away; we certainly deserve a break. I am pretty confident Aug, Sep, or Oct will be fine. The sooner the better because then the sooner we are on our honeymoon away from everyone and everything. I urge you to get an August or early September date because then we can do the wedding/honeymoon while I am on terminal leave and start working after I return.

Hope this isn't throwing too much on you with uncertainty looming, but hey, what's new right? God will help us as long as we give it to Him. I get so excited thinking about our wedding/honeymoon with God's blessing. Also, make sure Mac can make the date we set. Ideally, I get back mid-June, clear by July 4th weekend on terminal leave through August 26, and have our wedding in late August – early Sep (anniversary time??). Then go on our honeymoon and hopefully start working soon thereafter. If I have to start a job before, I'll do what I need to but would like a few months to spend all my time with you, search for a job, study GRE, and recover from all this crazy Army/war stuff. Hopefully, your job is flexible enough for us to take some small trips here and there to get away together. [That certainly did not quite work out according to this plan. Our wedding in Austin ended up being October 18, 2003.]

As far as the finding of a place to live, it will probably be the Jun-Jul timeframe. I would wait to sign any leases until I know a more definitive timeframe. No reason you can't start looking if you choose. Maybe Arlington (Grapevine)/Las Colinas area since midway for you between Ft Worth and Plano. How long do you think we should sign the lease for? Maybe three, six months, or a year? I would guess 6 months would be safe, but I'm not sure. As long as we don't have to live with your parents upon my return. No offense to your parents, but I have to be alone with you.

All I have thought about since I left was being with you! It will be so wonderful to live together sharing all our meals, waking up next to each other every day, showering together, going grocery shopping, buying stuff for us, *planning trips, handling problems and fears together, and working through everything as a team, finding a church, and continuing to grow in our* **faith** *as* one. *I have to have that as soon as I can exit the Army and get to Dallas.*

*If the Army does anything weird to try and hold onto me, they'll have one combat veteran go crazy. At least the FST knows when return I have to go, so they won't expect me to be around much! Got to **love** on Laura!*

What's happening here? Not much. Just trying to get answers on redeployment, order blood when needed, turn in OERs and awards, etc. Luckily, not doing surgeries on anyone. Late afternoon/evening, we play softball or work out. Our evenings consist of showers and a movie. Last night we watched "Chris Rock" thanks to you. It is good to laugh. Sucks because I have a damn fever blister. I hate them.

Hope I receive a letter today to see how things are going. Job, team in training, aerobics cert, living at home? I think of you often. You're always on my mind, in my heart, and part of my soul.

*I **love** you and miss you.*

CHAPTER 21
DEALING WITH UNCERTAINTY

May 4 War Day 45

Robert: *Another day in Baghdad, Iraq. It is surreal that I am sitting here in the middle of this city in an Olympic Center. As I was running around the track today, I thought about how strange it is how this all happened and what I have been through the past 90 days. Six months ago, I never really thought I would be writing you from Baghdad. Even as little as two years ago, I would never have imagined in a million years (ok… maybe in a million) I would be here writing my soulmate and beautiful wife, Laura, and aching in my heart like I never imagined because of our separation. Gosh, where was I two years ago… May 4, 2001? Still in 2-7 CAV GarryOwen gearing up for the Deployable Readiness Brigade (DRB) status, starting to fall in* **love** *with you, waiting on my FST job, having no expectations that in two years our country would be at war, I would be married to the most wonderful woman in the world, and I would be facing such an uncertain future about to leave the Army. God has led the path, and He will continue to. All in His glory. I praise Him you are with me forever now. I couldn't be more blessed. Went to church this morning and talked about as Christians we do not need to* worry. I thought of you and me and everything we have facing us. Please read **Matthew 6:25-34** with particular attention to verse 27, "Who of you by worrying can add a single hour to his life?" and verse 34, "Therefore do not worry about tomorrow, for tomorrow will worry about itself. Each day has enough trouble of its own." These are words I needed to hear from God. Comes at the right time, sometimes.

Another praise occurred today when we got word an American soldier had been shot in the head and was inbound. Immediately, I prayed for him. Upon arrival, he had been blessed by God because the bullet had lodged in the lower neck under the occipital lobe and he had full neurological processes intact and his vitals were fine. This guy was evacuated further to a neuro team [in Germany], but he will likely walk away from this war with a bullet in his head. Another praise be to God. [I'll never forget that moment that day as I was helping assess patients for evacuation and came across that young US Army soldier who talked to me as if nothing had happened, with a bullet in the back of his head. He had told me he and a few soldiers were pulling security in an open Iraqi market when a younger Iraqi boy walked behind him, pulled out a gun, and shot him from behind in the head. God had plans for the soldier to live on in his life and do great things...I hope].

Listening to "Strong Enough" (Sheryl Crow) right now. I know I'm strong enough to be your man now. I have no doubt or reservations whatsoever. You fill my heart and I do the same for you. This is so right because God has placed us together. This separation must have been placed in our life before our marriage to realize how truly important we will be to one another forever and that He put us together as soulmates to raise a Christian family for His glory.

Dealing with Uncertainty

After things calmed down, we got out of the heat by watching "Rookie", a Disney flick, in one of the CBPS' with the a/c on. The heat is getting pretty tough here.

Saw the first of the 1st Armored Division (1st AD) guys in the theater here to replace the 3rd Infantry Division (3ID). Our brigade's replacements are due toward the end of the month, but we aren't getting any definitive guidance from our higher Medical BDE. Even though it is the 21st century and we are the most technologically advanced Army in the world, we can't get through on our normal phones or cell phones. Have no idea why, but it sucks. Again, God's words settle my heart. CPT Sanders and CPT Felix are getting antsy about getting home to make their schools in June, but the Brigade Commander hasn't signed any school/ETS or retirement exceptions because the stop loss and stop movement policy still exists for deployed units. Supposedly it will be lifted on August 1, but they are waiting on the personal command US Army to put that out.

*Meanwhile, these two think I am not helping them and others (i.e. MAJ Kirk) are getting breaks. Man, I can't fix it for them. They are all worked up and I'm just as much affected and I'm not concerned. I am more affected because I don't have a job and I missed my wedding, but I have **faith** in Jesus, not sure if they turn to Him.*

The guys who have caused the most problems since deployed have been the nurses. They think the uniform standards don't apply to them, they meet, don't follow rules, etc. The surgeons have been really helpful, patient, and agreeable. MAJ Kuhns has been great, though. As long as we all get home safe is all that matters. MAJ Kirk should be making it home today.

I have to run 4 miles today (painfully) so I don't lag too far behind you when I get back. I am so sorry I won't be there for you *and your marathon like you were for me. You deserve better, I'm sorry, but I know you can do it and I'm proud of you. I've told everyone here about what you are doing, like the proud husband I am. I look forward to signing up for the next team in-training event together. Then we get to train together, sweat together, shower, rub each other down, and recover together. Continue training hard because, by the time you get this, you'll probably almost be leaving for your race. Don't give up. It's all in your mind. Do it for me and all the soldiers over here. 125 have lost their lives, honor them with your run. I **love** you and am so proud you're my wife, Laura Payne!*

Laura: *As the days go on, living with my family becomes even more frustrating. The competition, the fights, and the anger that lingers among everyone here are terrible. I often try to talk about it with my mom, telling her he needs help. But as you can guess, she takes it personally even after I put the disclaimer she is not to blame. I tried to explain to her you and I will have a certain way we want to raise our kids and she will need to follow our way of raising them. This stresses me out a lot and makes me appreciate even more the **love** we share. That respect we also have for one another is not found here.*

Last night I enjoyed spending time with Marna. She is such a great friend to talk with. She has an incredible heart. We went to a party that Todd A. invited everyone in Dallas to. Tubby and Liz, Todd and Crystal, Adam, Ben, Rina, and some other people were there. We had a great time just catching up with each other. I was in the perfect mood to just relax and have fun. I haven't felt that way since you left. It was such a good feeling to not be sad or tired yesterday. I also loved talking about you to everyone. My smile reaches from ear to ear when I talk about you and my heart and body are warmed all over. It's the greatest feeling to be in **love** with you Robert Daniel Payne. Now you are my husband with whom I am going to share my life. I am truly blessed to be married to you.

Yesterday was our thirteen-mile run, down from last week's 18 miler. My knee was killing me again, so I cut off two miles. It was frustrating to feel like I had the energy to run forever but have pain shooting through my knee. I'm going to make it through, honey. I'm going to finish the marathon for Garrett, for you, and me. I tried Gu for the first time yesterday. The Banana was gross and the chocolate was pretty tasty. They make a difference in your energy I could tell.

Next weekend, Heather and I are probably going to Austin. I want to run with the team. We hopefully will see JRyan and Brian. I'm not excited about this work week. It just means a lot of driving for me, though the job isn't bad.

All I care about is seeing you again. I know what you felt in your dream when you embraced me because I have felt the same way about kissing you in my dreams. It feels so incredibly real. Can't wait until it is real!

I've got to get some shut-eye. Tomorrow is Plano day and begins at 4:30 a.m. I'm so happy and comforted by the fact you can shower, do laundry, and relax more now. I'm looking forward to talking with you again. I miss your voice. I **love** you with all my heart. Please come back soon.

May 6 War Day 46

Robert: *Today was filled with watching movies. Two this afternoon and one tonight. Don't worry I was functional by working out. Very sad again because I didn't get a Laura letter. That is four days now. I hope you didn't stop writing as often. Got* several care packages from Justin and Mary. Gave away most of it because you have taken such good care of me with packages. I **love** your letters the most.

CPT Sanders and CPT Felix will be going home early. CPT Sanders around the 9th of May and CPT Felix around the 21st of May. Believe it or not, that was not good enough. Because the wait in Kuwait is so long, they went to the BDE S-1 to get out earlier. So ungrateful at the fact they are even getting home early for their school. Not sure about me, but I leave it to God. I submitted paperwork about my ETS but I'm not going to harp on it. I would prefer to come home with the team and finish my time in the Army the right way. Lord knows I want to see you today, but I've got to do what's right. If that means holding out a little longer to get back with the 126th, then so be it. I think there are good chances for the whole team to get back soon.

Sadly, I'm glad CPT Felix is getting away early. Her personality can be challenging to be around. Always in everyone else's business and thinks she is being put out by others. She makes comments about how lucky we are and that there are no guys around who would treat a woman like I do you. Kind of nice but in a weird way. One thing I would agree on is it would be hard to find a guy who **loves** you as I do! You're my one and only. I miss you so much. Please write soon.

Laura: I **love** you. What a great day it was when I received four letters from you. You have had so many experiences and I love hearing about everything going on in your life. These were your letters written during the first 21 days or so of the war. I can't believe you guys were in Saddam's palace. What a surreal experience to be in the home of such an evil dictator. I do want to tell you to be careful with things taken from the palace because the media has reported authorities are taking this seriously. Just an FYI. I need you to make it home and not be in jail. In one letter you mentioned we will have to get used to being with each other all the time. I have to tell you I disagree with that statement. I want you so bad right now I can't even imagine having to deal with anything like that. I understand you will have a lot to adjust to back home, but I am going to be sensitive to that and help you by being patient, understanding, and loving. You will have so much attention from me and more **love** than you will know what to do with. My heart is gushing with **love** for my dear sweet husband.

So, where are you living now? What have you been doing since we last talked? I pray you are safe. Life isn't different in Fort Worth. Still, the same working, working out, and missing you so much. I just got an e-mail about the speculation of your redeployment. Sounds like the colonel is working to get some answers. Would be so cool to see you in June!

Oh, I wanted to say that I think it is so cute when you fall asleep writing letters. I can tell when you do. I just imagine you falling asleep. You have always been good at that. How do you sleep sitting up? I know you must be so tired physically and emotionally. I hope you are now getting more rest.

I've got to go to sleep. I miss you!

May 7 War Day 47

Robert: *Sadly, another day goes by without a letter. Wish I could talk to you and find out how things are going. Every time I try and get on the internet someone is on or it's down. I pray my letters are reaching you. I find even in my letters to others I write so much about you. Man, if we were just dating, I would worry I'm smothering you with all my talk of how I feel about you. Luckily, you're my wife and I hope it all makes you glow in* **love***.*

Today there was another boring day. LTC Towery, our battalion commander gave me OER counseling. Even though I'm getting out he still gave me an <u>above</u>-center-of-mass rating. Told me my performance as an officer is in the top 5 percent of all officers and I should be promoted above my peers. Nice to get a pat on the back after you work so hard. Hope the federal agencies and jobs I search for ask to see my OERs because they all rave about me. Somehow, I fooled them!

When is Mike D. getting married? Will it conflict with ours? Not overly concerned because the only folks I want there are me, you, Mac, and most importantly God. I'm positive He'll show. Friends and family, I hope will come. Certainly, decided to wear the dress blues since the war pushed our wedding off thing. Your little combat veteran hubby.

One thing I did find out in my counseling today was as the most forward surgical team in combat in history to date. We were closer to gunfire, firefights, and artillery than we ever knew. Praise God for His protection through this… so far still have to make it home!

Saw my end-of-month pay for April $3000 pretty nice. Putting money back is certainly going to help us since I might be an unemployed broke cab driver. Be back – **faith** group time. Never mind, we'll meet tomorrow. Watched "Gladiator" tonight, what a great movie.

As days drag on, I think of you more and more and what it will be like to reunite with you. Time will stand still when I finally hold you again and everything will be right again the night you can fall asleep on my chest. I miss my beautiful princess and her little chick shirt. I long for that amazing feeling of safety and security when I lie with you. It feels as if everything is right when you're with me. I am so happy with you. I miss you and **love** you.

Laura: *Hey baby! I just wish I could ask you how you are doing! Today I was covering surgery and a James Brown song was on the CD. I started smiling because I could just imagine you dancing. I commented to this girl how much my husband would* **love** *this song. Things remind me of you all the time.*

For the past few days, I have been hoping for my phone to ring at 2:30 a.m. and it is you. It has already been 14 days since we last talked. You would think they would let you guys call once a week for morale purposes. It helps morale on both ends. It seems like they are having difficulties with phones there. I would give my leg to talk with you.

I would like to talk about the options we have when you get back. I wish we could talk live about it. I need to know what you are feeling about our situation. Do you need to stay in to find another job? Do you want to do a career in the military now? Do you want to take some time off and try living off my salary? There are so many questions. I will leave it in God's hands, but the most important thing to me is we live in the same city so we can finally be together. I'll do anything to be with you wherever!

Heather and I are heading to Austin this weekend. I'm going to do an 18 miler with the Austin team. We're staying at Brian and JRyan's, but JRyan will be in L.A. It will be a nice getaway from here.

Tonight, I went to another spin class. Great stuff! It's an endurance activity that keeps me in shape for running. I can't imagine how many calories you burn doing it because sweat just pours out of your body.

I can't wait until the day you call and tell me you're coming home. It will be a very exciting day! Not much else happening here just missing you daily. I'm going to sleep now to dream of you. I **love** *you!*

May 8 War Day 48

In their daily life, all are braver than they know.
- Henry David Thoreau

Laura: *I miss you. It has been two weeks since we last talked, and I miss your voice so much. Debbie sent over a clip of you saying you'd be home soon to me. Thank you for doing that. I loved seeing you and hearing you. It would be so wonderful to have you home soon.*

*Did you receive my homemade slide show? I hope you do soon. It was so much fun putting it together for you. Lots of great memories! We'll have to reinstate our adventurous life together. Traveling would be a great way to do that. We should pull out our off-the-beaten Path book and start taking little weekend trips to those great places. I **love** sharing those trips with you. Driving with you is fun and "special" things happen on the road. I've got to keep my man satisfied!*

Well, today I took it easy with work trying to catch up on things. Then, I went to my training session to work on my upper body. It was hard. My muscles will probably be sore on Saturday. There was an F3 tornado that hit Oklahoma tonight. Pretty scary. I can't imagine what those people went through.

Tomorrow it's off to Austin. I wish you were going to be there with me. We could go watch the sunset at Mt. Bonnell. How romantic! We have enjoyed our favorite spot so many times. I can remember so clearly sitting there before going to Hye, TX talking about how I'd like to take a vacation with you. That weekend and week were so incredibly perfect.

So how are things there? How's the team? What have you been doing? I can't wait to be able to hear how you are doing. It would be so wonderful to ask you about your day every day.

I miss you so much and can't wait to see you. I love you!

May 9 War Day 49

Robert: *Well, I finished the Secret Service stuff finally. I'll mail this letter same time as the packet. Hopefully, you can get this to them with no problems. What would be nice is if I arrived back before this packet did. But just in case I don't, I'll go ahead and mail it to you to type up, package, and send off. Thank you again.*

Got a reality check last night as I was brushing my teeth. Several shots were fired into our brigade support area from outside the stadium perimeter. Everyone quickly put on Kevlar and flak vests and grabbed weapons. In the end, it was someone from outside near a catwalk that overlooks our area firing a few shots at some guards near the tennis courts. Just something to remind us we're not in Kansas anymore. They sent out some roving patrols. [I clearly remember this evening that was the first of many evenings getting shot at because we were in the Olympic Stadium in the middle of the city of Baghdad. The frustrating part was never knowing where it was coming from the shoot back. Luckily no one took a shot that night]. *Who is so stupid of the Iraqi people to think they can still make any difference in all of this? I just pray we come home soon. We have so many different things flying around about our departure. Three different units and commands are involved, don't know if our vehicles will be loaded on a boat and we go on a plane. Or we load everything on a big USAF plane called a C-5 Galaxy. Only time will tell.*

Nothing else matters to me as much as returning home to my favorite person in the world. I can't wait to hold you and feel your body against mine. A song that makes me long for you to be near me...Body is a Wonderland by John Mayer. The acoustical song is in my mp3 files.

Just a song I thought connects us like "Come Away with Me.". These two songs are the songs I have listened to on this deployment to take me away to wonderful thoughts of you and me alone together. I listen to "Your Body is a Wonderland" and picture you and me at Ft Lodge in Spain again! [reference to 7F Lodge in College Station, TX which is one of our favorite getaway spots while dating].

We sent off CPT Sanders this morning at 5 a.m. to make her Baylor Medical Patient Administration Masters course starting 5 June in San Antonio at Fort Sam Houston. I told her to give you a call when she goes through Ft Worth before moving and tell you how much I miss you.

I guess the marathon is getting closer, huh? Hope all your training is going well. Again, I have **faith** in you. You'll do great! Trying to keep up my running a bit here, but it is easy to be lazy.

What do you think about our potential wedding dates coming up soon? Hopefully, August/Sep will work out. The sooner the better huh? The honeymoon will be so great, even if we head to Timbuktu. As long as I'm with you. Like my rhyme.

The places I want to eat upon my return: Wing Stop, Outback, Olive Garden (Pesto chicken), Texadelphia, Rudy's, and, of course, Z Tejas! If you book a wedding date don't forget Z Tejas for rehearsal dinner the night prior. I miss my life with you so much.

Dealing with Uncertainty

May 10 War Day 50

Robert: *Sitting out on the FST "patio" listening to tunes from my mp3 collection (thanks to you!) wondering what the hell is going to happen with us. It is a long story, but the 30th Med Brigade and 3rd Infantry Division all have a handle on us, but no one is deciding on what to do with us. Our new battalion higher when we get back is the 36th Med Evac Battalion and they have a boat to load their crap on 21 May, getting them home before the end of the month. They have space for us, but our new commander doesn't want to leave the FSB before they leave (which is the end of the month). Essentially, we are caught in the middle of the right hand not talking to the left hand. Sucks for us because we might sit here and watch a golden opportunity pass us by to get home earlier. Needless to say, not the way to win approval as the incoming commander.*

The concern is there is no surgical coverage close enough to Baghdad and no one is identified to cover our area. Guess I figure they'll fix it after we leave. Otherwise, why would they do anything if we're still here? Who knows? In God's time. Just know at this time our arrival home range is anywhere between 1 Jun – 30 Jun to give you some likely dates. Again, this is not confirmed so it is still secret and not worth getting anyone's hopes up. But I want you to have some semblance of what lies before us.

Upon my return, it will take 2-3 weeks to turn in paperwork to get released, physical, and turn in all equipment. We'll have to have patience because I'll have to be in Killeen as I clear out. I won't be able to be in Dallas until I'm on terminal leave, so I'm not sure what we can do to be together until my leave. I want to be with you 24/7 when I return and I'm not sure how we can work it. Please let me know what you think.

I know this isn't fun to think about going through after this separation, but we have to face the reality of our situation and uncertainty over the next 3-to 6 months. I wish I had answers, but only prayer and God's guidance will pull us through.

*The good news is there is an end in sight and I'll see you fairly soon. Being able to hold you again is more important to me than anything, look into your eyes, and tell you, "I **love** you." Everything else is mere details. I am certainly ready to get back since dumb Iraqis are still shooting sometimes. On the other day, a young soldier was killed by a sniper sadly enough (remember secret info) and his body came here before evacuation. This country will probably not be completely safe for quite a while.*

*There is some light at the end of the tunnel. If I have to shell out money on hotel nights for us to be together in Dallas/Waco/Killeen I'll do what it takes. Please talk to your boss about the challenges we will have initially and see what he recommends. I got three of your letters yesterday and my world is brighter. I **love** you.*

May 11 War Day 51

Robert: *Just received another letter. I miss you so much. I am so sorry to hear about your knee problem while running. If it makes you feel any better, the longer distances and the marathon, I had knee issues. Most of the time I just ran through it, but that's the "Army" in me. I need you to take care of that perfect body of yours. I'll ask Dr. Miller (my new boss) about it, maybe he'll have some advice. Only got up to about 5 miles so far. I can't believe 6 months ago I ran a marathon. Two months of no activity can take away from you for sure.*

Oh, and the Europe thing, you are right that is reserved for Robert and Laura Payne only. We should shoot for doing it this year. Start saving now and it will be no problem, I hope. The backpacking idea is awesome, you know I would **love** it. I so hope our marriage and life together are full of outdoor adventures and we go hiking, backpacking, and camping often. That time at Enchanted Rock is an exciting memory. I hope many memories like it come. Backpacking certainly requires a few more for safety. We could do it as two, but a handful of folks makes it safer and probably more interesting. Although group dynamics and individual personalities come out in that kind of environment. So, yes, I hope we can do something like it.

Hope my e-mail to you and my mom got off to you last night. Still trying to stir the pot on the redeployment behind the scenes. Hopefully, it will get us answers within the next 36 hours.

Today, Peppers and I started cleaning up ol' Laura 4. Stripped her down completely to start washing her down tomorrow. She is running pretty well now. Drove her to church today, which is only ½ mile from here. Try to keep my trips into the city of Baghdad to a minimum. The leaders recon through the city to this location and the trips to the medical facilities have been enough. The next trip I want to make is to an airport to get home to you!

The BDE HQ is trying to set up an internet café and phone center, but the internet is $3/hr. and phone is $1/per minute. The vendor is a local Iraqi, but I can't believe the Army will not pick up the tab. It has been very sad how difficult it has been to communicate back home, and we are supposedly one of the most technologically advanced militaries in the world. I miss your voice.

How long did you hang out with Paige and Heather? Did they come to Dallas? On these nice days, you should put the top down and drive the Jeep. It is yours now, too. Everything I have is for you.

Looked into our USAA account and saw $8000 plus. Awesome to see. About $5700 left on the Jeep. Outstanding! I assume the

Mustang is around the same. If I can make two financial recommendations: 1. Make one or two additional money payments to our car loans. 2. Disperse some of our savings into our mutual funds, specifically the income fund. Laura, I trust you, and please take these only as recommendations. You are at home, and I have trusted you and continue to trust any decisions you make on behalf of Team Payne!

2230: Just finished another **faith** group meeting with SGT Wilson and SPC Lundy. Lundy needs our prayers, honey. He is lost in his walk and focused on himself, but he freely admits it and wants to walk with God.

Today after services we passed the time sweating, then watching "Good Will Hunting" in the CBPS with a/c. We have started having many afternoon matinees to survive the heat. It is getting unbearable.

Got a package from Alan (CD from Hemant). Alan's letter was very thoughtful and funny. Sounds like Mike D's wedding is in July, so I guess ours should be the latter part of August or Sep. Maybe Labor Day weekend since people are off work? Again, I trust your decision. In summary, Europe, oh yeah, finances are cool, and I **love** you more than you'll ever know.

Laura: Today, I got an e-mail from you, and it made my day so special. Every time I hear from you my heart is filled with joy. Reading your thoughts often brings happy tears to my eyes.

It's so exciting to think you might be home in time for your birthday! I'm already starting to think of ideas for your birthday (the best day ever!).

I called your mom today to talk. She's doing great. She stayed home today in case you were able to call. When I got home from Austin I saw the e-mail, called her back to tell her you wrote, and forwarded it to their home e-mail to brighten her day. We are both *so anxious about your return. Speaking of your return, what are your expectations? I'm hoping to spend time with you alone on the first night. I think that a lot of people will come to see you get home. We could hang out for a bit (lunch, dinner, etc.), and then we head to a hotel in Killeen or one of our favorite out-of-town locations. That will probably be determined by time. Your mom and I talked about it, and she plans on being there when you come in, and then she wants us to be alone. Very cool! I just want you to have it the way you want it, but not have to plan it all out. Tell me your expectations and I'll make it happen.*

How do you think it will be returning home? I plan on being very patient and understanding. I don't feel like it will be awkward being around you, but the FRGs, say it will be for a while. I hope our open communication will help to alleviate those feelings. I think we should take some time (a week or more) and then start talking about future plans as Team Payne unless you feel comfortable talking sooner, Then I'm totally game. I've got to try and figure out our living stuff, though. I want to be with you, but I don't want to stay with my parents. Well, don't worry. We'll get it all figured out.

*I **love** you, Robert. I loved how you signed the e-mail with your best friend, soulmate, and husband. That is so awesome. You are all those things to me. I'm so excited God gave me the chance to fall in **love** with you. He is awesome. I'm so thankful God is so alive in our relationship. He has taken this opportunity to solidify our bond more tightly.*

This weekend I went to Austin. Heather and I stayed with Brian. We had a good time just hanging out. Friday night Heather and I went to dinner and then to Fados. We were in bed at midnight, and I got up at 5 a.m. I ran eighteen miles! I was feeling sluggish because of the humidity but I made it! Heather and I just hung out and then Sergio drove in. We went to PF Chang's and then to Fados where we ran into the Austin gang. They were out for Mike Bribb's birthday. Everyone asked about you and wanted to know when you would be home. It was great to see everyone, but it also made me sad because you should have been there. It would have been me and you hanging out in Austin. You are with me always honey no matter where I am.

Brian has a new girl, Julia. She's great as far as I could tell. He thinks that she is a cool girl, but is still a little reserved about saying he's dating her. Sergio is doing great. He's moving to Arizona in June. His family is in town right now, and his mom is too. He is down on himself about girls. He called himself a "lame ass" and said he was going to buy this shirt that says "Chicks hate me." I didn't know what to say. You want to help, but I don't know what to do. I would like to hook him up, but I don't know any girl to set him up with.

Honey, I miss you more than you know. I'm thinking about you every second of every day. I **love** you with all my heart.

May 12 War Day 52

Robert: *I just received your small package with discs and a long letter from the 25th of April. You are so wonderful to me. I never imagined how fulfilling this and of **love** could be. I have only fooled myself into thinking I knew what love was. It is here, away from you, in a foreign unsafe environment, that God has truly opened both our hearts to the ultimate capacity we have for unconditional, forever-existing love. Certainly, a **love** that could not exist in this capacity without both of our hearts with Jesus Christ.*

Dealing with Uncertainty

*I feel so blessed every day I wake up and think of you. It is a true testament to God's **faith** that when you give up things you truly see your purpose. Although you and I are about to face one of the most uncertain times in our lives, I do not fear... I do not worry. What matters more than anything in the world is the true **love** He has given us both to share. I know as long as we keep our hearts open to this wonderful love, glorify Him in all we do, and raise a Christian family, our lives will be blessed. I so look forward to figuring out our life together. It is like we have such an opportunity to look at a blank canvas and paint it together.*

In several months, around the time we get married, all the things I have known for years (the Army) will be behind me to start over with you. Luckily, God has given me you as my beautiful wife and soulmate. I know I can't do the things that will be coming into my life soon alone. I will need your support and opinions. I want to do whatever will be the best for you and our future children first and foremost. However, I also have the desire to do what God leads me to do in helping others. Above all, glorifying Him is first and everything will fall into place.

You know I've been thinking, if there was a way back to Austin, I wish we could find it. We were so comfortable there and had such a wonderful base (Lake Hills) to develop our spiritual life. I know it is a long shot but do give it some thought, please. Also, it puts us away from the proximity of others. Not that I want to ignore others, but you are my priority for my availability above others – always. I have given my hand to you as my wife, and you will always be in my plans.

I appreciate the CDs and truly look forward to looking at them. I appreciate the LESs to look at, too. Looks like the bucks are rolling in. Remember, the more we save, the more flexibility we have initially in our marriage. But it is money we will decide how we spend it together! Ahhhh, we get to do everything together now because you're my wife. That makes me feel so complete. Luckiest man alive I tell you. No other woman would write and express the wonderful things to me you do. We are made for each other that's why!

Hope the running is going better since the knee band. Chris Chase wore one during the Marine Corps Marathon. By the way, has Marna or anyone heard from him? It will be a great time when I get to see him, and we can share our war stories. Wonder if he'll stay in now?

I got the final word on the stop loss. Until I have been redeployed, I still fall under the stop loss and cannot be released. No worries because I wanted to come back with the team anyway. I just want to get back with enough to manage all the paperwork/phone call crap it will take to get out and use all 65 days of terminal leave. If not, I'll just have to cash in some days.

When does your commission title kick in? Are you ready for it? What do you think so far? Sounds like you are willing to drop-kick it if necessary. I'm game for whatever you want. As I have said before, and I'll say it again, whatever you want to do to be happy I'll support you. Is the aerobics thing still out there or is time getting the best of you? Well, off for some work right now.

May 13 War Day 53

Robert: *I got to talk to you today! It was so wonderful to hear your sweet voice. Sorry, it got cut off but at least we talked for a little while. Sorry to hear about the knee issue.*

Stop the presses, I just looked at the Corps orders on redeployment. Looks like the timeframe narrowed. The earliest return date is 1 June and the latest is on or about June 15. Not to worry,

Dealing with Uncertainty

June 1 is unlikely, so you plan on running that marathon and looking sexy!

Hopefully, my prayer of being home before my birthday may come true. Looks like a lot of details have to be worked out as to who is going to get us back. Oh well, time will tell. I'm going to stop and watch the CD you sent me.

You are the most amazing woman in the world! It took everything I had to hold back my tears as people walked by. I wanted to be completely alone when I looked at it, but I couldn't so I watched it anyway. Maj Lim saw it after I watched it for the fourth time. We both agreed that within a year you and I will meet up with him and his new wife for a trip somewhere. They had been planning a trip to Tahoe before the war as well. That would probably be an appropriate meet-up with another couple or couples. One stipulation – separate rooms!

Back to your CD. The best gift ever. What a blessed day – Talk to you and this awesome CD. Praise God. He knew I needed it. I liked so many of the photos. We are so happy in our pictures. I think I was starting to forget how amazingly beautiful you truly are. Your eyes, your hair, your smile, your shoulders, everything. You are my everything! Sorry, but the music wouldn't play. I opened Winamp and played 'Come Away with Me' as I looked through the show. I pray I get to hold you soon, I miss you so much. So many great memories from so many places. Guess we are going to start making new ones in Dallas with our wonderful life together. We'll travel, go out, cook at home, shop, shower together, ah… I'm so excited.

Tonight, I'm going to listen to Mac's sermon. Man, I wish we could get back to Austin somehow. Again, thank you for your CD. It made my world. My **love** for you is never-ending.

Laura: *Today I was woken up in the best way, with a call from you. Hearing your voice makes me so incredibly happy. I wish we could have talked longer, but I know the phones aren't great. I felt like I had so much more to talk with you about, but it was like I didn't know where to start. I could have talked the whole time just about how much I miss you.*

It is crazy you guys are just having to sit there and wait. Maybe they'll decide soon they don't need the FST anymore because the medical company can handle the surgeries now. You would think without combat your mission is complete. I'm thinking you'll be home within the next few weeks by the way everyone is talking. I really can't wait. I just want to touch you and kiss and hug you. Then, I just want to talk with you for a long time. I'm so happy to hear you don't think it will be awkward to be together at first. My heart just wants you here so much I don't feel I will need to adjust to you. Also, memories of you are so vivid I feel you are with me always.

I'm writing you while I'm standing outside of an OR waiting for the neurosurgeon to finish his position of surgery. It's a great time to sneak in a letter to my husband. For the wedding, I'll start looking into available dates. How exciting! Our wedding may not be far away. You know I was thinking I would like to ask Heather to be a bridesmaid. Randy and Jessica probably won't be able to come so there would be room. She has been a great friend, and I am so glad to be back in touch with her. What do you think about asking her?

I miss you so much, Robert. You are my world. I know you want to make me the happiest woman, I have to tell you just being married to you makes me the happiest woman in the world. I'm also the luckiest woman to have a man who is thoughtful, caring, romantic, sexy, handsome, funny, charismatic, understanding, *and patient, and I could continue with so many attributes you possess. Your mom told my dad when we visited I have the most romantic man. She is so right. I **love** that our relationship is filled with romance and passion.*

I am glad you received my CD and hope you get to see it soon. It is filled with happy memories, but it makes me tear up, too. Just think, we have so many more memories to make. We are going to have such a wonderful life together, honey.

This weekend is Christopher's graduation. Also, the FST families are getting together on the same night. To be honest, I feel obligated to go to the graduation, but I want to go to the FST thing. I've missed every FST thing. What do I do? I'll let you know what I decide. Decisions are hard for me to make, but I find God facing me with more and more decisions to make. I think He's trying to show me to just let Him decide.

*Now, it's the next day. The surgery went okay. I didn't remember how to use this one instrument that has been updated, but I have the old version. I called Lanny and he helped, but they ended up not needing the instrument. I'm getting ready for work listening to my Happy Halloween CD. I **love** every CD you have made for me.*

*I have to go to work, honey. But I will write when I get home this afternoon. I miss you! I **love** you with all of my heart. Come home soon.*

15 War Day 55

Robert: *Wish I could say things are going well here, but as the heat goes up, the morale goes down. Crazy correlation, isn't it? I went back to the airport this morning to drop off CPT Felix so* *she could make it her school. Feel bad, but everyone is glad she is gone. It will be much less painful to redeploy without her.*

Listened to Mac's sermon on war yesterday morning. Pretty unique biblical perspective, but I certainly agree. He has quite a gift for conveying the Word of God. I wanted to write a letter to him, but I couldn't find the church address in all my Lake Hills papers. Then, it got me to realize no one from the church had contacted me since I'd been here. Have they contacted you? I think that is kind of strange. I have heard from all kinds of folks, but not from our Christian brothers and sisters at Lake Hills. Maybe I'm overreacting, but I think it would be nice to hear from our church family.

Yes, we continue to sit and wait. This wait is miserable. I miss you so bad. It would be different if we were occupied but we're not. We did an Iraqi surgery two nights ago, but it wasn't something that could have gone on to the combat support hospital that's close. Our forward support battalion commander, LTC Lowery, is trying to get us a plane like the one we came in on out of Baghdad instead of Kuwait. He has looked out for us and if he can get us a C-5 plane from Baghdad, he is the greatest man alive. They (he) said he wants an invite to the wedding if he gets us home soon. If he can see me home to you, can I send one to him and the FSB officers I have served with? Also, do you still think it would be cool to have a saber arch if I can find 10 sabers, we could get the soldiers to do it. I think it would be kind of cool. Just think about it.

I have an Aggie bud 1LT Jason Robert '99, who comes around and hangs out with me some. We have been trying to get me, him, and a guy named Matthew Broderick '98 together since Muster. I want to take a picture with my A&M flag next to a big Saddam Hussein picture in the stadium. I should be in the stadium working

Dealing with Uncertainty

out, but I smoked myself with some running of the stairs last night. Trying to get in a little shape to keep up with you.

Guess what? Today is my four-year mark in the Army so you should see a raise in my base pay by the May 1 end of the month. By the way thanks for the LESs.

You know I was thinking about where we'll live, etc. and I don't know if you should get us an apartment with a 3- or 6-month lease before I return or wait until I'm back. Guess we'll decide as I get closer to leaving. I hate to have to move on your own again, but do we want to already have a place we can go once I get back? Then that is something we don't have to worry about. Not worried, God and time will work it out. No reason to get anything until we know for certain I'm coming home. No certainties right now.

We got a filler nurse in for CPT Sanders from the closest CSH, his name is CPT Holchek, and is a nice guy. Believe it or not, he is from Monroe, LA. Not too far from ol' Shreveport. Back in my traveling days to Shongaloo, we would sometimes go to Monroe for some reason or another. I just know it's close. Sadly though he is attached to us, but when we leave we have to take him back. That will suck to watch us pack to go home and then go back to wait with his unit.

Today's afternoon matinee was "Grand Canyon," an older movie with Steve Martin, and then "Were We Soldiers" which I didn't finish because I was hungry, and it wasn't lifting my spirits at all. I realized while watching it that when I saw it for the first time with you I wondered what it would feel like to leave his wife for combat. Over a year later, I'm watching it again and I know personally what it feels like. I never want that feeling again like the one in my heart the night you drove away after our time in the chapel.

We watched the 2nd Chris Rock tonight and now I'm preparing for bed, but it is so freaking hot. Difficult to sleep. Seems like the gunfire around the area is increasing. Today, we had someone shoot inside our area again. I think we shot 1 or 4 of them. Kind of nerve-racking, but all you can do is pray and be situationally aware, not to worry because His **love** will continue to protect us. Hopefully, we'll get some word in the next few days on our departure. Can't be soon enough.

My beautiful, amazing wife I miss you so much. Our **love** keeps me motivated because I know I get to come back to my life with you.

May 17 War Day 57

Robert: *It's about 1245 in the afternoon and it is really hot. Sitting around in PT and sandals because it is so hot. Not to mention a small heat rash on my thigh near my crotch. Sorry, you probably don't want to hear that.*

Still in the waiting game. An order (the one I talked about before) that came from V Corps to the Medical Command to the 1st Medical Brigade. 1st Medical Brigade is sitting on it waiting to get COL Hightower's guidance. We should hear something within 48 hours. Meanwhile, LTC Towery from the FSB is trying to get us a plane out of Baghdad Intl Airport. Essentially, we don't know jack crap! There is lots of talk about redeployment, but no decisions are being made. Sadly, there are rumors of 3rd ID not getting to go home early. There are some evil rumors about 3 more months. I pray these aren't true because I don't want to even consider getting caught up in it. Lord, it is time for me to come home to you!

The flies here are horrible. You can't even eat a meal without having to swat them away. Ahhh… you can tell my patience level is less and I am complaining more. I think it will increase and decrease respectively. We are doing nothing every day and sitting here in case something happens. No reason to leave a 20-man surgical team… just in case. That is what Medical Evacuation choppers and Combat Support Hospitals are for.

Today's afternoon matinee and naptime were "The Fast and The Furious" and "Star Wars II." Yesterday afternoon was "Chasing Amy," which reminded me of you because that guy has similar features and she is almost as pretty. Well no she isn't close, but the falling in **love** and passion reminded me of you. Then I thought of you again as we watched "Panic Room" which we saw together. Oh, what am I saying; Everything reminds me of you. I think of you so much. I miss you more than I ever thought possible. Every day I wake up just thinking of the day when we will have our life together. Well, time to eat dinner.

2039: Dinner was okay. Chicken breasts, rice, and stovetop. The only problem I have is dinner is at 6 p.m. and I workout/run at 7:30 p.m. Doing it any earlier is too hot. I end up burping the whole time I run, but I keep on keeping on. We sent off our latest FRG newsletter which mainly has notes from us. I have a few lines from me to you.

We got a replacement ICU nurse from 28th CSH out of Ft Bragg, NC and his name is CPT Keuhns. Ran with him last night and he is a nice guy just like CPT Holcek from Monroe, LA. Both of them will get the Combat Medic Badge and 3D ID Combat Badge because they have come out here and got attached to us [although they were not with us since the war started, no one made any issues of them getting the Combat Medic Badge that I can remember]. Today, we tried to clean the inside of the DRASH as much as possible, but it is hard when everything seems dirty.

CPT Holcek is studying for the GRE, which is what I should be doing. I just can't get motivated in this heat. I almost have all the last Left Behind series done. Wish I could say more, but it is getting tough to be here. Laura, I miss you so much. I only pray God allows me to hold you soon. I **love** you.

May 19 War Day 59

Robert: *Had quite an interesting experience yesterday. Instead of going to the 9 a.m. Protestant service we (MAJ Beverly, SGT Wilson, SPC Garcia, CPT Holchek) went to the 1 p.m. Gospel service, Whoa! That was different and certainly typified well in the movies and TV. Very powerful though. The singing and clapping you can't avoid getting into it. The strangest part was the use of anointed oil and the touching of foreheads, etc. Folks lying on the floor and one girl running around certainly kept it interesting. All in all, they are praising the same true God – Jesus Christ so all is good! Man, it was a long service, though.*

Last night brought about some excitement. We were told intelligence reports the BSA we set up here at the Olympic Center was to be attacked by a small band of 20-30 Saddam Faydeem Baa'th Party members. We were awakened at 3 a.m. and stood guard until 6 a.m. just in case. God's protection was with us, and nothing happened. Let's pray it continues to be that way. [I remember that morning and how unsettling it felt to be up taking shifts armed and walking the wall, not being able to truly see what was outside the perimeter. Thankfully we were not attacked but the fear was real].

Dealing with Uncertainty

*We sat around this morning and created a Five Most Influential Bands/Musicians of All Time vote list. I voted for Beatles, Elvis, Led Zeppelin, Run DMC, and Michael Jackson although I might change Led Zeppelin to Bob Marley. Ahhhh… I went ahead and did it. Jah Rastafria Bob Marley! Wish I could hold you on the couch and share Bob Marley with you as I did so long ago. Isn't it awesome to have those memories of us falling in **love**? It all started with green St. Paddy Day cookies. Otherwise, I would have never thought, "Man, this girl is thoughtful" and Sergio wouldn't have told me to keep going out and talking to you.*

Since that day, I would have never imagined what our relationship would have amounted, to. You're my wife. My wonderful, amazing, thoughtful, sexy, beautiful soulmate for the rest of my life. Coming home will be like coming home with the best Christmas gift ever! My life with you! I can't wait another day as I pray to the Lord daily to reunite us. I also pray our initial transition between me clearing the Army in Killeen and you working in Dallas will work out. I pray there is some way we can be together, but I don't want you to have to sacrifice your new job. I wish I could tell you how long it will take me to clear the Army, but I can't because of all the bureaucratic b.s. I will encounter. God will see us through it.

A few guys from the 1st Armored Division are here (taking over for 3D ID) and they said they have an FST with them which is a good thing. There is no need for more than one FST in an area. So that is a positive note.

I haven't even asked but have you found a church you like in the area? Have you been getting the chance to go? Maybe see if your parents would like to go with you. Certainly, couldn't hurt. We'll find one together wherever we live. That was something that I enjoy about how our relationship developed, through our continued walk with our **faith** and membership at Lake Hills. Do you even think they know we are gone? Again, I'm a little disappointed I haven't heard anything from them. Where's my supportive church community when I need to know they are there? Although I know they are praying, I'm sure.

Well, it is about 11:30 a.m. and getting hot! Finish later as I have to go over to the stadium to pick up some blood from a Medical Evacuation chopper.

1708: Went to the stadium and the blood was supposed to arrive at 1245 I was getting ready to leave after sweating my butt off at 1:45 p.m. when it finally arrived. Then back to the tent, jumped back into shorts and a t-shirt, and the CBPS to watch the last part of "Men in Black II" and "Goldmember." Now, I'm back outside on our patio area just sweating. Got a letter from Mawmaw and Dad but none from you. It has been almost five days with no letters from you. I'm sure you're writing it's just the mail system. Makes me sad, though. 100 letters from other people do not compare to one letter from you.

As these days drag on, it is getting more and more miserable. I think I'm going to have to say something to LTC Miller because everyone is getting the impression he doesn't care when we get home. His actions are reflective of it, but I don't think it's intentional. As a courtesy, I should probably let him know he is losing a lot of people's respect from the get-go. Something I'll continue to pray about. We just all want to get home to our families. I just want to get home to start mine with you. Hopefully, we'll be in a position within two years to start having kids. I do want time with just you, but I know as I grow to **love** you more and more every day, I'll want our kids. I get so excited thinking of what an amazingly loving and caring mother you will be. Our kids will be so lucky.

*I wish I could tell you things are going well here, and I'll see you so soon, but I can't. It is beginning to suck bad sitting around all day doing nothing in this horrible heat. [By this point it was well into 110 degrees each day]. No one making any clear decision on redeployment leaving us in the existence of ambiguity and vagueness. It is harder to get out of bed each day, but it starts getting so hot you must. Then, the wonderful breakfast (not really). Sorry to keep complaining, just miss you so much. I think of you always. I will **love** you forever.*

Laura: *I was hoping to not find myself writing another letter because you were making your way back home. COL Towery told us to stop writing on 15 May and then last night changed his mind to 24 May. It seems unfair and uneconomical to have sent three of your people home and not all of you. I understand people have school to attend, etc., but I bet everyone on your team has something major they would like to be home for. For example, SGT Smith has two graduations happening: one college and one high school. I'll stop complaining because I am overall thankful those three have made it home and you guys are safe.*

Another early Monday morning. It has been somewhat of a waste of time and gas money to go to Plano every Monday morning. The meetings are repetitive. I'm going to suggest someone take minutes at each meeting, and I'll come over every other Monday or something. I leave at 5:30 a.m. and am never home before 10 p.m.

This weekend I went to MAJ Kuhn's home to make a welcome home banner. There were only four of us there, but I enjoyed their company. It's great to hear Lynn has told his wife how much he appreciates her and has made her feel special. Have you guys been talking with him? I'm sure the environment makes you reflect and appreciate even more what you have back home. Did you know

COL Bruckhart's son is a freshman at A&M. Mrs. Bruckhart told me he's home for the summer and ready to be a sophomore.

I hope you get to come home soon, honey. I miss you so much! I can't imagine what it will feel like the first time I see you. My emotions will go crazy with happiness, excitement, anxiety, etc. I just want to hug you, look at you, and kiss you as long as I can before everyone else gets ahold of you. I've talked with both of your parents, and they both plan on being there to see you back. I'm working on some plans but will wait to make them final until I understand better how Ft Hood will work on your return. Ft Stewart has sent us the stuff on how their return will work but no info specific to the FST.

I've got to get back to work. I **love** you, Robert. I can't wait to see you.

May 21 War Day 61

Robert: *I finally got one of your letters after about five days of not getting one. The last one was dated 27 Apr and the one I got yesterday was 7 May. I hope letters aren't getting lost. That is one of the things I look forward to more than anything is letters from you! I hope you are getting mine promptly. The day before yesterday I was getting sad without you, so I re-read all your letters. You are so loving, and I can just feel your passion, commitment, and praise in your words. How did I get so lucky to find you and not kick me to the curb? I guess we both know it was in God's plan we found each other, dated, never quit, fell in **love**, and now are married.*

Yesterday, we watched "Monster's Ball," "Black Knight," and "The Heist" last night. We are running out of DVDs to watch so we have to search for folks to borrow them from.

Dealing with Uncertainty

Inside I'm thinking about how lucky I am to have you. I **love** the feeling. I have been fortunate enough to feel that way many times about you and me. Of course, I don't say, "Oh, Laura and I do that… etc.…" but I think it.

It's now 10:00 a.m. and the heat is already kicking our butts. Had to strip down to a PT Shirt and shorts with sandals just to make it. Sounds like your fitness level is truly at its peak. Guess it helps Robert isn't in the way and you can completely focus on working out. But aren't I a good distraction? I know you'll do great at your marathon. I just wish I could be there for you like you were for me. You deserve so much more and I'm truly sorry. You know I want to be there for you more than anything in the world. You know how important it is to me to always be there for things like that. You are an amazing woman who has always been there for me. I do not doubt in my mind it will never be any different for me and our children. You know how important it is because your parents were always there for you. Know I will be there, too. As soon as I can get back from this war!

Sounds like things are still on track for our return in June sometime, but certainly still vague and ambiguous. Hopefully, we can celebrate my birthday together. That would make it the best birthday ever! I don't want anything else in the world except being with you on my birthday. We can go wherever you want, doesn't matter to me as long as I'm with you. It would be fun to get away. Pack little clothing, though, we won't need it much. Unless we are going to sacrifice until our wedding. Yeah right! There is no way I would make it unless, of course, you wanted that.

I wish I could talk to you, but unfortunately, the phone lines have been restricted for some reason. I'm resourceful, though, so I'll find a way somehow. Please understand I want to talk to you so badly, but it's not my fault. I think it is sad on the Army's part *they can't do better. If MAJ Vinca hadn't jacked up our phone, we wouldn't have this problem. I know he didn't do it on purpose, but what a bad mistake. He has singlehandedly kept every member of the team from talking to their family weekly. [Due to the Groundhog Day-like living, we collectively agreed to shift to using the Iridium cell phone each day. Our new Commander supported it and I kept the sign-up list. One night when it was MAJ Vinca's turn he wasn't entering the correct code and rather than wake me or SFC Smith, who knew the access code, he entered one too many times essentially making the Iridium cell phone inoperable. It ended as our only way to call home at that time. Trust me, he was so mad at himself and apologetic. He even tried to see if he could buy one online and have it shipped to us in the theater but that wouldn't work. We eventually got access to another contractor DynCorp's team's satellite phones to make calls home].*

As to the questions you wish we could talk about, I'm not sure I have the answers. I have two options: #1 is getting back and staying in Killeen for the 1-3 weeks it will take to clear the Army and go on terminal leave, thus allowing me to get to Dallas and be completely free of the Army to begin all our plans of job search, apartment finder, wedding, honeymoon, etc. #2 is get back almost immediately, go on leave to approach the items mentioned above and about 2 weeks before my ETS date in Aug go back to Killeen to clear from the Army. Or a crazy #3 option is to let me get back and clear the Army while we plan a month or to journey to Europe or Australia.

Once I go on terminal leave, we just go. Take some of our savings and make a memory of a lifetime together. Of course, we wouldn't get a place to live until we got back, and you would probably have to quit your job, but when we return, we find a place to live, get married, and find jobs together. Of course, it's crazy but *if you're willing I would do it in a second because we would never forget it. Although logic would keep us grounded and stable for a little while and do it later. No matter what, I will have a few days upon return to devote to you before initiating an option. Pray and think about the options and we'll decide together before my return. Just know my priorities upon return are spending time with you, Army clearing, spending time with you, FED Agency follow-up, lots of time with you, finding a job, dinners with you, planning a wedding/honeymoon, showers with you, finding a place to live, eating at our favorite places, finding a church, more time with you, and family/friend visits. As you can see you are the priority. Spending time with you will be somehow inhibited by the proximity of Dallas and Killeen (while I'm clearing) and I'm not sure how to fix it. Maybe option 3 is the best answer and you just quit, I get out of the Army, I pick you up in Dallas, we run away somewhere for a while, and come back and completely start over together?! Just think about it because we have the extra money, we only have a few bills, no rent to pay. It is crazy enough to maybe work. God will lead us, that is one thing I know for sure. Hope this reaches you soon to get you thinking. I miss you so much, it hurts more and more every day. I **love** you, my beautiful angel.*

May 21 War Day 61

Laura: *It's Thursday before the Memorial Weekend, and I wish you were here. I'm just sitting here watching Fox News. Not much happening here. My mom and I went to Target today to shop for your birthday package. I figured I should send it now just in case you are there on your b-day. I will continue to pray for your return before then.*

This weekend Marna, Alyson, and I are hosting a fundraising dinner because I need $943. Thank you for mentioning my marathon in the Mom's Day e-mail. I sent reminders to your mom, your dad, and David. I'm confident I'll raise the money as long as I can get an extension for the end of June. Saturday Heather and I are going to Austin to hang out with JRyan, Brian, and Mike H. JRyan is taking us out on the boat. I want you there rubbing sunblock all over my body.

You know, I keep hoping for your call or e-mail or something. I just miss you so much and want to talk with you more than anything. I've been praying to hear your voice. Especially since last week when we talked the phone just cut out on us. That is the worst!

Next weekend is the race, June 1. It would have been awesome if you were back for it. I'll need your prayer support because of my knee. I've taken it easy on running the past 2 weeks and focused on cycling class and weight training for endurance. I ran 2 for 20 min and the knee felt better. I've come to terms with it will hurt during the race, but I will endure the pain and finish what I started.

Just got back from running around for work. It's busy on the roads already because of Memorial Weekend and because a woman is playing at the Colonial golf tourney. Not very exciting but history is in the making.

Well, honey, I've got to get ready for dinner. I hope you are doing well. I'm thinking of you always. I **love** you.

May 22 War Day 62

Laura: *Good morning! I'm feeling a little sad today. Last night, I went to our reunion briefing at Ft. Hood. Sylvia (SFC Smith's spouse) told us you would hopefully be home in July. We were* *all getting excited about your return and now we have to deflate some hope. In your letters, it sounds like your mission is complete, but I guess the Army doesn't think so. Maybe if they knew what you were doing every day, they'd change their minds. Every day I look forward to a letter, e-mail, or phone call, and every day I am more disappointed that communication is unable to be more constant. I pray you guys have a phone soon. I'm looking forward to talking with you about all of these things in person one day soon. The most important will always be at least we're together. I **love** you, Robert.*

May 23 War Day 63

Robert: We are still being told 1st Armored Division will be here at the end of May to relieve the 1st BCT/3D ID (who we support) during the first week of June. Therefore, allowing us to head south for redeployment the second or third week of June put us home mid or late June. Hopefully, before the 25th we can celebrate my 27th birthday together!

The 1st Armored Division Brigade replacing us is supposed to be bringing the 628th FST from Germany with them. This is key because we need replacements to go. Again, nothing is on paper or definitive, so we just continue to pray it works out this way. I am ready, so incredibly ready to get back home to you. I miss you more than I ever thought I could. I am so tired of this heat, the flies, waking up sweating, the food, mosquitos, carrying a water can to flush the toilet, walking ½ mile to the shower, hearing gunshots in the distance, watching three movies a day just to pass time, and on and on. Now, I feel better. I thank God every day for all those little things He does provide for us all which includes His protection, and what He has provided me waiting at home.

Last night, we had a little more excitement in the BSA. Somebody fired shots into our area around 11:30 p.m. and the guards on the wall by the tennis courts fired back. Everyone knew when they fired back because they fired automatic weapons, and it was loud. We all put on helmets, Kevlar, and loaded weapons to stand by our vehicles. Everything ended up okay and nobody got hurt. Tired of being around this city.

Tomorrow, I might break up the monotony by going on a convoy with the chaplain to some orphanages to deliver goods. Thought it might be an interesting experience. Granted it will change up my normal day of wakeup – hygiene – meeting – breakfast – sitting – lunch – afternoon matinee – sitting – dinner – workout/run – movie – shower – bed. That is about the extent of every day here. Since MAJ Kirk left on April 29th, we have only had 2 or 3 cases and those weren't critical.

Last night, they were washing out an Iraqi's blown-up foot when the shooting started. It interrupted our movie night. Earlier in the evening, we played a tiring game of ultimate frisbee with the 1st Brigade staff and the 3D FSB officers. Yes, your man did well, but the 3D FSB officers lost twice. Oh well, it was fun. Anything to pass the time. [Ironically by this point we were becoming so complacent with the amount of shooting into our perimeter that often instead of running to our security posts with our weapons, we would just pause the movie we were watching, see if the shooting stopped, and if it did, we would unpause the movie and just keep watching it. Not proud to admit but I guess that was getting comfortable with war].

I hope family life is better. Just take **faith** that there is a light at the end of the tunnel if everything goes according to plan. Then I will be there to save you and whisk you away! Just continue to pray and we will be home soon.

Sounds like your job is starting to keep you busy. Do you enjoy the autonomy and flexible hours, or has it not come to that yet? When would you start the full commission? Or do you even want to keep doing this? Do you like the idea of leaving the job, running away with me to another country for a while, and then coming back and starting over with me? (Option #3!!) We could start over in Austin if you wanted. We'll have time to discuss it and figure things out as I get closer to heading home. The uncertainty and open future are getting me excited because it's with you and I have 100 percent **faith** *God is in control. How could we lose when He will make our paths straight?*

I know I need to focus more on His word. SGT Wilson and SPC Lundy recently kept pushing off our **faith** *group meetings, so we haven't met in a while. I can't force people to meet for the Lord. I attest to the fact other Christians help in holding one another accountable to God. That is what is so great about our relationship based on Christ. It will be the key to our marriage being wonderful forever. Well, off to an XO meeting.*

3:05 p.m.: I received a letter today from you dated April 17. This mail system is messed up. You seemed frustrated with life and the thought of me being here for 6-8+ weeks. Well, take the frustration and know I'm right there with you. I'm sure you can tell from my past few letters this sitting around sweating is killing us. We are so ready to leave.

Took the time today to make you a CD like I used to. Not telling you how long it will take to get to you, but hopefully, the mail will reach you promptly. I'll mail it shortly after I mail this letter. The one thing I have to look forward to each day when I wake up is it is one day closer to you coming home to my life with you.

Working with LTC Miller is a bit more challenging than MAJ Kirk. He is not a bad guy, but it is apparent a single 40+-old guy wants things his way, and when he is the commander, you can't argue. For the past few weeks, the team has become frustrated with our redeployment (or lack thereof), and they feel he doesn't have any concerns about getting us home. He goes to the local clinics in Baghdad near here to do surgeries, so it looks like he is here for his agenda. As I have been stirring the pot to get us home, I finally had it and pulled together a meeting of me, LTC Miller, MAJ Kuhns, and SFC Smith. I pretty much laid it on the line, asked him his intentions, and told him about the rumors. I recommended he communicate with us more and it is better now. Always good to confront the issue head-on.

Hang in there and never forget I am always thinking of you. I **love** you.

Laura: I hope this card doesn't find you in the desert on your big day. But if it does, Happy Birthday, honey! I wish so much I could be there with you. Well, this box is just a little something to make your day brighter, your real birthday present is waiting at home. We'll have a birthday celebration when you come home. I can't wait for that day! My mom included the football and a movie for your birthday! The bucket and rake are just a little to make you laugh. I wish that we were on the beach building sandcastles together. I hope the fans will help out at least a little. I truly miss you with all my heart. It gets harder to not talk with you more often. But someday soon we'll be reunited and be able to take trips to our favorite B&Bs, work out together, have dinner together, and so many more things. I've started (want you, need you, **love** you) working on the wedding dates and it looks like Aug 2 or 9 might work, but we will need to change the cake (happy birthday) or photo because they aren't available. Anyway, we can talk about it later. I **love** you, honey. Happy Birthday! I miss you!

Dealing with Uncertainty

Chapters 17 – 20 Personal Observations

This time period was truly about intestinal fortitude and reliance on faith and love to get by. It was also very introspective to assess what is a Purpose Driven Life. The wild journey to Baghdad and taking the city was over and we had survived but then the real work had to begin. That required establishing our FST with the Medical Company and facilitating the wartime mission in a way much different than being at the front of the fight with 1st Brigade, 3ID. Rest assured having survived the vehicle rollover and getting settled at BIAP in a hardened aircraft hanger was somewhat comforting, but when we were alerted we had to move further into the city of Baghdad at the Olympic Stadium, that sense of safety and comfort ended quickly. Our surgeries lessened because most causalities arrived requiring non-surgical treatment or deceased. The saddest moment I will ever forget is the sound of the father's moans and yells as he reached his young son who had been shot in the head after they crossed a military checkpoint and didn't stop. MP's held him back as the child died in the arms of one of our surgeons just a few inches away from me. Nothing in your ROTC and field exercises prepares you for something like that and how you process it from a humanity standpoint.

To compound the stress and anxiety of the war was missing my new wife even more recognizing the risk we had endured moving into Baghdad and seeing firsthand many injured and dead Iraqis and soldiers. All things you cannot unsee and whether you like it or not leave a lasting effect on you. I was starting to also contemplate when and if our deployment ended and what would I do with my new life since I was planning to separate from the active-duty Army. Laura was also facilitating a new job in medical device sales and dealing with the stress of living back home and maintaining the normalcy of friendships while missing me. The letters to one another helped us both tremendously in those times, not only to know what was going on in one another's lives but also to connect us to the passionate love we had since we had just married.

Needless to say, our FST, 3rd FSB, and 3D ID were exhausted from fighting the war. Getting home was on everyone's mind as the lull between the warfighting and the future insurgency existed. The days became very long and very hot. Although we had hot meals and hot showers, it was still pretty miserable conditions, and sometimes with no work, the days felt like Groundhog Day. We would pass the time reading and watching movies, often waiting on mail from our family and friends much like I assume our fellow veterans of prior wars had done. We did not have ready internet access and once our Iridium cell phone was locked, our connectivity to home was minimal to none. The other thing that had gotten us through the war and the languishing days was each other, the soldier to your left and right, knowing you were there enduring it together. That is only something soldiers who have deployed into combat will ever understand. Although I maintain very little contact with the members of the 3rd FSB and 126th FST, I will never forget them and our experience together.

CHAPTER 22
Transforming Our Minds

May 24 War Day 64

Robert: *Just read a great chapter in "The Purpose Driven Life" called How We Grow (Ch. 23)* **Romans 12:2**, *"Let God transform you inwardly by a complete change of your mind. Then you will be able to know the will of God – what is good and is pleasing to Him and is perfect." Certainly, a clear way to understand how our life can become Christlike. How we think and approach things is something we can continually help one another do. It gives me such a feeling of peace, comfort, and security being here 1000's of miles away to know, without a doubt I have you to share my life with. What a blessed feeling to know I will always have you to rely on and be supported by. Of course, you'll get the same from me. I can't explain how much it fills my heart to know I am your husband. To know I can completely devote every part of who I am to love you, support you, and fulfill your life. I feel so complete like I've never known. It is so clear God made me truly love you. All our life experiences, regardless of good or bad, have brought us to this point for us to come together as one. In summary, I* **love** *you with all my heart and pray for the day to come when I can return and begin my devotion to you and our life together.*

What's happening today? This morning I tried to call home again, but the lines are all jacked up from 1st AD coming to take over. I wish I could hear your voice. Then I made sure someone was going on the orphanage run, I didn't go with them mainly because I have to focus on when the handoff to 1st AD should start happening, within the week so hopefully everything will start falling into place as planned.

Taking a little MRE – Chicken with cavatelli lunch break and square away files. I miss so much talking to you every day. Just hearing the little things about your life. What made you happy today, what did you eat for dinner, what did you do this weekend, and what movies you watched?

This afternoon I think we are going to watch the "Lord of the Rings", which is the one movie I can recall in which I fell asleep on you while we were watching it, not vice versa. I even miss you falling asleep during the movies we rented. So many times you have done that, you've never known, but I just sit and look at how beautiful you are while I touch your face and hair. I do miss that.

Got to talk to an NCO today, SFC Jones, who grew up in Houston and went to Prairie View A&M. It's always good to talk about Texas cities and College Station folks who have been there. I look forward to heading back to Ol' College Station with you for A&M games, Reville 5-0, or 7-F!! Hopefully, we can make a few games this season. Alan and a handful of folks went in on season tickets so at least there are more opportunities to get tickets and sit with friends if someone doesn't go. Maybe by next season we will be settled enough to get season tickets? Wouldn't that be something? No, not the season ticket but "settled enough" makes you wonder where Mr. and Mrs. Payne will be on 24 May 2004. All I know is I'll be happy no matter what because I know we'll be together!

Now we have been authorized the 3D Infantry Division patch to wear on our left shoulder as a combat patch and also the combat medic badge, which is just the EFMB I already have with a combat wreath around it. We will also be authorized a bunch of ribbons and the combat award. Might even get a Bronze Star for Meritorious Service. MAJ Kirk put me in for one. It would probably be a plus in the federal agency apps, job apps, and grad school apps. It is all just cloth. I would rip off any award, ribbon, or badge to be back home with you. I guess if David finds me a good reserve unit, I'll get to report in with all my combat hooah stuff. The only problem with the Combat Medic Badge (CMB) is when you wear it you can't tell if you earned the Expert Field Medical Badge (EFMB) or not. There should be something to designate both. Oh well. [Earning a combat patch and the CMB was a great honor. Until much later in my career I realized the importance of seeing others who had your same combat patch or CMB and how you knew you were connected without saying a word to each other. I earned the EFMB in 2000 at Fort Hood which was a two-week test of medical and soldier skills that was grueling and tough. I don't see a lot of EFMBs these days and even fewer CMBs are awarded for providing medical care under direct fire in combat operations. I have always ensured I have one uniform with the EFMB and one with the CMB, but wear the CMB on my dress blues].

*Still miss you more than ever. I pray this time next month I'll be holding my beautiful angel. I **love** you.*

May 25 War Day 65

Robert: *Just finished up a small package for you with a CD and a poem. Something to let you know even though we can't talk or see each other I'm still loving you as much as the day I left.*

Our Chemical Biological Protective Shelter System (CBPS) is having problems, so our afternoon matinee is on hold. Luckily, I get to sit here and sweat my butt off because it is so much fun! Went to church this morning and there was maybe 1/3 of what is normally there. Strangely enough, the topic preached on was not forgetting to honor God and continue your spiritual journey after adversity. If we turn to Him only in times of extreme fear and need, aren't we using God? Anyway, the folks who needed to hear it were not there. I still try to get closer to God, but sometimes it is hard when I get frustrated, tired, etc. The spiritual journey towards a Christlike life is a long one that takes our whole life, but we can help each other. What we do have control over and both present act upon is serving others and building our character. Hope by now you have been able to get "The Purpose Driven Life" book. If not, we'll go through it together when I get home.

Man, it is so hot. Want to know how hot it is? Right now I am in a brown T-shirt, red umbros shorts, with a fan. My camelback hot water! Ahhhhh… we're going to go crazy in this heat. We fought the war, won it, ended it, and got left here to bake in the summer heat of Iraq. Thanks, US Army and US Gov't!! I'm done with this hooah Army. It can kiss my booty. Okay, I've got it off my chest.

Right now, I'm listening to my "coming home mix to you." 'Rapture' is playing, and I wish I was partying at a club with you dancing like we used to. It has been a while since we have truly gotten to dance together. Like at the good ol' Amazon days or the night at the Red Jacket. Certainly, on the to-do list when we get back. People need to take us out and not vice versa, right? I miss my party buddy.

The last few months before we left were stressful and hard to always have fun out because of friends, circumstances, etc. Just know our party life now is not just about Laura or Robert, it is all about Laura and Robert <u>Payne</u> enjoying their life together. If our friends want to be an asset for fun great, if they choose to be a hindrance, forget them. We don't need anyone else for a good time, just Mr. and Mrs. Payne. Just think of our weekend getaways, Boston, Disneyworld, Austin, too many to name where we have played together without the help of anyone else.

I hope when I get home you won't get tired of my 'one time… in Iraq' type stories. I'm sure they won't all come at once but unfold over time and through a picture.

1623: Yeah! Just got a letter from you dated May 13, the last day I called. Your beautiful words touch my heart so much. I just want to cry I miss you so incredibly. I hope my poem explains in some small way how I feel being away from you. I am so glad just being married to me makes you feel like the luckiest woman in the world because now I can sit back and do nothing! Only kidding I want to do so much for you, with you, and in you.

No, I don't feel our reuniting will be awkward at all. The only strange obstacle will be adjusting to having something I've wanted more than anything else in my life, which is you. I have never felt this way and experienced the feelings I have had since being separated from you. I knew I loved you more than anything and wanted to spend my life with you, but the feelings I have come to understand and comprehend are almost spiritual in a sense. I think many go through life not ever having or experiencing true **love** with that one person God intends for them. Not sure if it is because it is God's intention or if people don't allow themselves to open up emotionally, physically, and spiritually with one other person. We have all of those levels in such a way I now know God intended for us to spend our lives together. I pray I will never forget for a second what we both have come to understand with this separation. I hear people make jokes about marriage and their spouses, but I don't think they ever came to know this feeling we share and embrace it as God's gift.

Oh, Heather at the wedding... yeah! Whatever you want. She seems to have been supportive in all of this and I appreciate that. Not sure about the others.

Sorry to hear about the FST thing coinciding with the graduation. Your resolution to give it to God is so true. I know it is hard sometimes, but we both have to learn to do this for our marriage and family. We have a lot of decisions ahead of us and the one true key is to find what He wants for us as man and wife.

Sounds like work is keeping you busy. I hope you're enjoying it. I am anxious to see where God will lead us with everything when we get back. Do you think He wants you to stay in that job, stay in Dallas? Are you still thinking about the aerobics instructor? Probably something to consider again after you are victorious at the marathon. In about six days you will be tackling 26.2 miles and by the time you get this, you will have accomplished a great task. No matter what you finish or how you do it, I have to tell you I am so proud of you. I have told everyone here about what you are doing and the team in training. I remember times when running was difficult and you would get angry. Look at you now on your own you trained for a marathon and finished. All for a great cause, too.

I **love** you for everything you are and everything that drives you to do what you have done with this marathon. I look forward to sharing the next challenge with you, as Team Payne! I miss you incredibly and I hope you enjoy this poem and CD. I **love** you.

Away From You...

*Away from you so long
I am certainly not the same*

*I can't smile quite as much
And I can't laugh quite as hard*

*Away from you each day
I only enjoy waking up in the morning*

*Because for the first few moments
I forget that we are apart*

*Away from you, I have realized so much
About the true gift God has given us*

An unconditional **love** *everlasting
That will never fail, falter, or fade*

*Away from you, my heart aches so
Because of the way only you can fill it with* **love**

*An emptiness in me exists like
I have never felt before in my life*

*Away from you, I have come to understand
The definition of the word 'soulmate'*

Phantom Fast

Something before I had never known
Until I was apart from you for so long

Away from you, I can only look to the future
Because the present is nothing without you

I awake and fall to sleep
Praying He will bring us together soon

Away from you, I comprehend God's true intent
Of loving you as Christ loves the church

And through your letters and words, I know you
***Love** me as the church loves Christ*

Away from you, we have been so blessed
To see God's intent for our life

To show the world what He can do
*When you pray and find your one true **love***

Away from you, my perspective is so clear
Of what truly matters in life

*The **love** God has sent through you*
And our amazing family and friends

Away from you, I am never left alone
Because my memories of us get me by

Even though I miss you more each day

In my heart, you have never left,
So I am never without you

Away from you Laura, my wife…
*I still **love** you more than you will ever know*

To Our Future Life,
*I **Love** You, Laura*
Robert Payne
Deployed – May 25, 2003
Baghdad, Iraq

CHAPTER 23
GOD'S TIMING

May 27 War Day 67

Robert: *Still waiting to see the whites of their eyes… the new FST! Not here yet, so, of course, we are. Got an a/c unit for our tent yesterday, but no way to power it right now. Needless to say, sleeping when it is 90°+ is difficult. Our OR CBPS is having problems. So, the afternoon movie was moved to the ICU CBPS.*

Yesterday, we watched "American Beauty," which is a poignant movie on the facade of the American family and how appearances are perceived. I think most American families have their problems, just of varying degrees. Just look at our own families. Fortunately, they both **love** *us both. Doesn't every family have a hint of dysfunction in it? Let's try and avoid it with ours. I believe it is attainable with positive* **love**, *communication, and Christian beliefs. The end of the movie is cool because it addresses the view of eternity without the Christian overtone.*

The evening movie was "High Fidelity" with John Cusack and his relationship with Laura! Ours is much better because we never broke up. It had a funny guy in it named Jack Black. The guy from "Shallow Hal." Today's selections will be "From

Glory," "Knockaround Guys," and "Rounders" (with your favorite Edward Norton).

It is crazy I just wrote so much about movies, but there is not much else to our lives here. Since we have been at war, we have had to take a pill every day called Doxycycline. Not to worry, the FDA-approved drug to combat the effects of biological agents, but the main purpose is the prevention of Malaria. I will have to take it for 30 days upon return. What sucks is it makes you even more susceptible to the sun so now I have my second fever blister in two months. I hate the darn things! Back from trying to get our a/c unit running for our DRASH sleep area.

In this letter, I have included my second letter to the family. Mom/Joal, Mawmaw/Marvin/Nanny, David/Karin, Dad/Marie, and Uncle Bobby/Joani. You're special because you get almost daily personal letters. Only my favorite person in the world gets them. I'm thinking about a letter to all our friends who have written me. I'm pretty sure I have written back to everyone who has written me, but a nice follow-up letter would be nice. Some folks haven't written at all, which saddens me a bit. Oh well. The guys have sent some great letters that have been supportive and funny. I hope they have been checking up on you and helping you with anything you need.

Have I told you how much I miss you? Each day seems longer and longer. We have a running joke about the number of hours until dinner because then it is another meal closer to being done. I hope and pray it is soon because I don't think I can sweat anymore. Lord, please get us home!

1905: This afternoon consisted of taking a nap on the floor of the CBPS, watching "Knockaround Guys" (mafia movie), then it was dinner time! Only 23 hours to go until tomorrow's dinner. Our **faith** group hasn't met for a while. Not sure if I should push the issue. I have asked Sgt Wilson, and SPC Lundy when they would like to meet, but they never settle on a time. Kind of feel like they will come to me when they want to.

Sitting on my bunk now with the a/c running in our tent. Certainly, cooler in here but not great. It should help at night though. Probably the hardest thing is sleeping when it is hot.

We are going to have so much fun in our marriage I can't wait! It's like looking forward to a summer trip or special birthday party when you were a kid feeling. Never forget it and we'll always be on a vacation together for life now. It is so amazing to see God's work when I think back to the night, I met you and told you my theory on **love**. Would you have ever thought I would have been talking about spending my life vacation with you? It is so awesome to see how He answered our prayers for us. I am just so anxious to continue my vacation with you.

We haven't received any mail in two days now. What is sad is that the 1st Brigade Commander put out to slow down mail because of the redeployment plans and now the soldiers have to go back and say, "Sorry honey, don't stop sending mail because I won't be home like I said I would." Not sure what I can tell you, but our chances of being home in June are good as soon as the new FST gets here. Only time (and God) will tell. I just think it is so sad a senior leader doesn't see this as wrong to leave the division that won the war here to sit in this heat and deal with the stability and peacekeeping stuff. It is just wrong when there are other units here to do the job. If I even had an idea of staying in a little bit longer sitting around has killed it without a doubt. This life is not right for me because it has kept me from you for 118 days now. I miss you so much.

May 29 War Day 69

Robert: *Well, on the 4th month day of being away I broke down and had to find a way to call you. I miss you so much! I am so glad I got to hear your voice and about your life. Better yet, a Laura letter was waiting when I got backdated just before Memorial Day. Sounds from our conversation you had fun. Sorry, I couldn't be there; you know I wish I had been. I wish I could have talked to you for hours, but sorry I had to get off abruptly because of a guy who had gotten shot in the leg. Had to call in a Medical Evacuation with an iridium phone. I'll have to find a way to call you after you come back from the marathon. Again, I am so very proud of you. Wish I could have been by your side.*

From our conversation, I gather living at home is still difficult. Hang in there honey, only a few more months (or less) hopefully. Think of all the money we are saving for us to go on a great trip, down payment on a house, wedding, etc. Remember to provide Christian **love** *to them. Sounds as if the money situation is going okay. After May we should have at least $10,000 saved. Awesome you are paying off our little debts as well. Will be great to only have car payments and car insurance to pay on. Just think, we are beginning our marriage with no debt as we planned! Sounds like the friends' circle is moving along like they normally do.*

Your job is moving along, but understandable to not be as motivated as you could be because of our separation, or is it because you just don't like it that much? Well, keep in mind the options I spoke of because option #3 means you can walk away, and we can both start over wherever we like… maybe Austin? Just start thinking because before I arrive, we'll need to decide so I know how to approach the Army thing. Our future is so wide open, we can do whatever we want (as long as we have some money put back!).

Wish I hadn't complained so to you, but it is getting tough to be here just sitting in case the soldiers of this area need a surgical assist. Although I found out after I talked to you there are two other FSTs in a 10-mile radius of us. That is crazy! The brigade we support might move and we have to wait and see. I just have to remind myself this is all in His purpose!

Got a visit from COL Hightower, finally. Good to see him, but he didn't say what we wanted to hear which was when are we going home?! 3D ID was to release us from our mission until he and the 1st MED BDE could do anything. Since we don't have Dr. Kirk to fight the fight and we have LTC Miller who hasn't been through everything with us, we are in a tight spot. I am truly happy for Dr. Kirk to be at home with his family, but I've got to wonder if things would be different now if he were still here. I will say if the stop loss is lifted and I can get out of here, I will without hesitation. I wanted to do the right thing and come back with these guys, but I have got to take care of you and me if I can.

The friend's support has been overwhelming, huh? That is what I had hoped for. Just tell them you need time to relax, or you just don't feel like hanging out. They'll understand. If I were you, I would probably stay in my room all the time staring at pictures of me, too! Nice thought to know you would be safe there and no guy could hit on you or stare at you. I'm not there to be the jealous husband. I know you only have the hots for one guy—Robert, 'the stud muffin, super sexy' Payne!

Sleeping in the same tent with eight other guys is getting old quickly! I had to tell one of our specialists not to pee in a bottle in the tent. Last week, I told one soldier to go and take a shower! Can you believe that? Need to be back in your bed, taking showers with you soon. Glad I got to hear your beautiful voice today. I miss you so much. I **love** you more than you'll ever know.

Laura: These are the things you requested in your e-mail today. I apologize for not putting additional items in here, but I promise to send another package when I get back from San Diego. Hopefully, you have already received your b-day package with the fan and other fun stuff I sent last week. I am missing you! I **love** you.

It's so wonderful to wake up to your voice. I miss you, honey. We had a good conversation this morning. I miss just being able to talk with you. I wish I could ask about your day and share your happiness, problems, etc. with you. I won't take it for granted after this time apart. Thank you so much for calling me. It means the world to me how you find a way to call. I just look forward to talking with you every day again, I miss it so much.

Today is pretty much a wasted day because I'm getting ready to leave for San Diego. It would have been so fun to explore San Diego together. I'll be thinking of you while I'm there. Thank you so much for telling me you are proud of me. I **love** how supportive you are of me. You really inspired me with your dedication and determination. You also have always believed in me even when I didn't believe in myself. I want to change the habit of giving up on myself.

I'm so glad you told me about our three options. I've been wondering about it. I like the Europe option a lot, but I want to investigate the job thing more. This job is challenging, but I'm not sure how much I enjoy it. The pressure in the OR bothers me occasionally, and some doctors are not very nice in surgery. It's no reason to quit, though. I'm just not into it because the thing I care about most is being with you and living our life together. Probably not the way to be, but I am so in **love** with you. Anyway, I'll start looking into more jobs to see what's out there. Then, I'll think about our options. We won't live here, especially if I can help it.

Well, I have to get some more work done. I'll write later. I miss you so much. I **love** you!

Hey, hot stuff! I **love** you. Well, I already wrote today but wanted to write you again to express my **love**. I agree it has been a great day because you called, e-mailed, and I got a letter! Your words are so comforting. I am going to get the book you have been reading. It sounds like a very good read. I've still been working on "Assassins," but I hope to get a lot of reading done this weekend on the plane. After I finish that book, I'll start your book. I'm so excited about how amazingly strong your **faith** in Jesus has become. I'm looking forward to learning from you and striving to make our relationship Christ-centered.

I am so sorry you are not busy. That must make it harder to keep morale up. I wish someone would bring you back home so we can hop on a plane to Europe.

Tonight, my dad and I figured out race day and how it will go. I'm glad they will be there. I am looking somewhat forward to race day. Hope I can remain calm amongst the crowd. We're only used to running with twenty people or so. I plan on walking at least through the water stations to conserve some energy.

I've got to get some sleep because tomorrow's an early rise. I wish you were sleeping next to me. You're in my dreams. I **love** you!

From San Diego: Here's a pic of San Diego, so you can share it with me. The marathon went well. It took me 5:47:10 to finish, but I did it. I wish you were there, but I thought of you and finished for you! We didn't do anything except sleep and drink lots of water afterward.

I was so happy to hear your voice before the race. It gave me motivation. Oh, and my knee was pain-free! Praise God! Know

*I am thinking of you always. I miss you more than you know. I hope you have an amazingly blessed day! I **love** you!*

May 31 War Day 71

Robert: *I wish I knew where to begin. Things here seem like they are going from bad to worse. Not only has the 3rd ID been extended for a while, but our replacement FST showed up without a general surgeon, so they are not complete. We have still passed on information to set them up for success. They are the 628th FST, which is a reserve FST, with most of its members from Texas. The XO is a CPT from outside the Houston/Galveston area. Older guy with five kids. Certainly, it was a long haul for them as they were assembled and alerted in Feb. Then, sent to sit at a military base in NJ for weeks. Finally, months later they are here, and they claim as a reserve FST they are supposed to go back in 90 days. Doubt it will happen, though.*

We thought the obstacle to overcome would be getting them a general surgeon until the Med Ops guys of 3rd ID started talking about making us go support the 2nd Brigade. Well, here's the lowdown. We have been here with the 1st Brigade the whole way and the only reason they want us to cover the 2nd Brigade is because the 555 FST up and left them weeks ago and now are loading their stuff to redeploy. They want us to pack up and cover down on guys we don't know because someone allowed 555 FST to leave when their mission wasn't complete. If we get sucked into it, we are only taking steps backward from leaving here. Plus, we have a huge case among the Corps FSTs (126th, 555th, and 745th) that all came out here; we are the furthest forward deployed and the 745th and 555th will be home before us. 745th is from Ft Bliss, TX. When I get home, if I ever see anyone from 555th I'm going to smack them for screwing somebody. Even if we don't cover the 2nd Brigade, someone will get screwed and likely some other FST. Can you imagine the morale if we have to tell the team we have to move again for another mission that wasn't ours because they went home? Someone would get shot. In summary, no clear end sight because things are extremely vague and ambiguous. Our commander, LTC Miller, doesn't seem to help the situation. The way he talks to others you would think he went to war with us and has been with the FST for years. He doesn't communicate well and certainly keeps me and SFC Smith uninformed like he should, even after my conversation with him about communication. He hasn't changed. When we addressed some senior Colonels on our experiences as an FST in combat and the chain of command from the 628th, you would wonder why anybody from the team was there as he dominated the conversation with his 'infinite wisdom.'

Occasionally, he shows a good side, but professionally he is digging a hole with the team. Ahhhhhh… much better now since I have vented. Kind of like after work at home except these problems are keeping me from you and our life together. The only thing I can do is continue to pray. Sadly, I don't think I'll be home for my birthday. Guess we'll make it up later. Certainly, to overcome this emptiness and frustration my **faith** is needed, as your support and **love**.

Read an awesome verse perfect for you and me as best friends, and best Christian friends at that. I type it and include it in this letter. Got to go pee… much better. Getting to talk to you yesterday was so good. Sad you are not receiving my letters more regularly. I have never gone more than one day since I left without writing you. I pray they reach you soon.

Started working on getting a microchip to fix our iridium cell phone so I can call you at least once a week. The way it was *intended before Dr. Vinca broke it was 10 min call once a week which would be better than now. Not sure if you are running the marathon today or tomorrow, but I wish I could have been there. I'm very proud of you for following through. Hope the days afterward didn't hurt too bad. I wish I could have been there to return the massage rub down you gave me after mine. I promise if the stop-loss is lifted, I will come back sooner if I can, but it's all in God's time I suppose. He has a reason for keeping us here. It is just hard to see sometimes.*

*One positive is sleeping at night is much better with the a/c unit blowing through the DRASH. Not perfect but better than waking up several times a night sweating. Like the new notebook paper? Never thought I would use up the yellow pads. By the way, have I told you how incredibly crazy in **love** I am with you? Just making sure. Well, the commander has been sorting through this mess and we're having a meeting… be back.*

1930: The meeting wasn't so bad. LTC Miller wasn't there so I gave them all the info I had. Then he came in and stated there were many uncertainties but assured us the chain of command knows our sacrifice and will work in our favor to get us home. The only person I know working in our favor at this point is God, and we're on His timeline. No sense in worrying about it at all. In the grand scheme of things, this will be nothing as far as time goes. The only problem is separation from you.

By the time you get this, it will have been a few months since you started working. What do you think now? Close to commissions yet? Or does option #3 for us look more and more appealing – quitting your job, running off to Europe with me, and both starting over? From sitting here, it sounds super exciting, it just isn't as practical as we should be. Then again, when will we ever get a chance in our life to not be practical? After careers and children are launched, all we can do is be practical. The thought of option #3 is becoming more appealing by the day. No decisions to make until we have more time to talk. I just can't think of anything better than being somewhere romantic, having fun with only you, with no worries, and completely alone to be bothered by no one!

*We have so many options in front of us it's amazing. Even if we need a little time to decide, we could rent out one of those extended-stay places for a month or something. We could pay Owen some rent money and live at his place and leave on the weekends when he comes home. He is working in Orlando for the next 9 to 12 months. He has invited us out to stay with him. The only perk of being here into the early part of June and July would be the continued incentive pay. $5000 a month is pretty nice, huh? Something I could get used to – not deployed to Iraq, though. Not much more to say other than how much I miss you and **love** you!*

CHAPTER 24
Walking the Steady and Patient Road

June 2 War Day 73

Robert: *Hope my phone call in the middle of the night didn't tire you for your marathon. I'm sure you did fine but are certainly sore and hurting today! You'll be surprised how quickly your body will recover; except I had the wonderful hands of Laura on me. Certainly, owe you a massage. A small gleam of hope today, the stop loss was supposedly lifted. Hopefully, there will be some guidance within the next few days on those who can head back. The sooner the better! Man does this pen suck. Kind of want to hold off a day or two on the stop loss questions to see if LTC Miller even asks or inquires for me. See if my commander is looking out for me at all. I wish I had more to say in this letter, but there isn't much happening as you can probably guess from my phone calls.*

The only direction we have been given is that the brigade of the 1st AD that was supposed to switch out with our 3D ID brigade is now here and operational. They are less than ¾ of a mile across the street set up in a police academy that is abandoned. Some of their units are coming into our Olympic Stadium but we agreed in a meeting yesterday with their battalion commander to leave their medical assets in place, including the FST. The whole notion of switching us over to another brigade was handled by a phone call from LTC Towery (our FSB commander) to LTC McHugh (1st Med BDE 5-3) and he expressed his positivity in his relationship with us. He is a great commander to have worked with through this war. He certainly looked out for all of us.

The problem, though, is using the excuse of our having to stay in place because the other FST has no general surgeons. Well, that is another roadblock because we have to wait for the other FST to be backfilled by a general surgeon until we can start asking about heading home again. Not sure how long that will take. But we have more of a chance to get home before our FSB, which is probably August or Sep. Have you heard from Debbie or Mike Kirk since they got back? Wonder if he is out of the Army yet. Taking a break for lunch now.

1256: *A little bean and rice burrito MRE for lunch. Had to track down some salsa, though because the dang MRE came with peanut butter. What to do with the rest of the afternoon? Probably a movie. Been trying to be consistent with having quiet time each morning after breaking where I'll read a chapter from The "Purpose Driven Life" and then follow up on the verse from the chapter overview. Today's chapter was about the steady and patient road we must walk to become Christlike. Molding us as God-honoring Christians takes time and He understands us. Our walk with **faith** is not something to be rushed. That is good since I feel I struggle in some way every day, but hopefully am growing closer than before.*

Excited to think about the opportunity to hold each other accountable in our marriage. It will only make it stronger for us both. We certainly have to be able to have a certain relationship in our Christian walk before bringing our first child into the world, which I have no doubt we will. Can you imagine? The thought of our children and our family is so exciting to me. Just think within the next three years we probably will be a mom and dad together. [Sadly, I had no idea the fertility struggles we would have, and it was seven years and multiple treatments and IVF before we had Avery]. It fills my heart with so much **love** knowing you'll be the mother to my children. Your heart is so big and caring I know already our kids will be loved so much by their mother. I promise I will never forget you come before anyone else, including our children. If I ever forget, you can smack me. Initially, when we first start having kids, it will be hard to remember, but I think we'll manage fine. One of the more important issues we can e-search and talk about together will be the discipline of our kids. You hold 'em and I'll beat 'em… that kind of thing (just kidding).

I put the Master G and Josie pic on my laptop [from one of the funniest Halloween parties we ever went to in Houston in 2002]. So, what if everybody sees it? Only means they can see how lucky I am to have such a sexy wife. You were so hot that night! Anxious to get back and see her again. Starting to get pretty hot up in here. Might go throw on some shorts and sandals here shortly.

What physical event do you want to tackle next with team in training? Hope I can join in easily and we can do it together. The only problem is fundraising will probably be difficult for both of us because of the same resources. We'll just have to work harder and maybe throw parties. Hope you have been receiving my mail. I miss you so much. I **love** you.

June 3 War Day 74

Laura: *I may have already sent you this card, but I **love** it so I'm sending it again. It's two days after the marathon, and my* legs are starting to recover. It's so surreal to think I completed my first marathon. I hope to keep up the long-distance running and tackle another marathon at a faster pace. Today is the first day back to normal diet and exercise. We decided we all needed to cut back on the amount we were eating during training. It won't be too hard because you aren't training hard like before. Anyway, I talked with Lanny today. Spinal Concepts was bought by Abbott Labs yesterday for 170 million. You and I (Team Payne) will be receiving approx. 9,000+ dollars for the stock we purchased at @$1600. It's a true blessing. The trips we want to take should be no problem now. Everyone keeps their jobs and things will operate as normal, but we now have cash flow. This does not change my view on opening up to new opportunities. I prayed this morning and read some scripture relevant to jobs and doing God's work. He knows it is weighing on my heart right now. Maybe this money is God's way of showing us He will provide for us if we go to Europe and begin our lives with a fresh start. There's no doubt in my mind He will.

As for the wedding stuff, I'm going to call the vendors and put them on hold again indefinitely. I want to wait for (I made a wish and you came true) the call from you telling me you're coming home for sure. It's because of the uncertainty of concrete redeployment dates. I jumped the gun and got too excited. I know 3ID has a new mission, so I'll pray for your safety. I'm not sure what you'll be doing, but please be safe. I **love** you with all my heart.

June 4 War Day 75

Laura: Hey sweetheart. I'm taking a bath right now which has become a nightly ritual to just be alone and relax in the warm water. It would be a lot better if I could share it with Robert Payne. Our bath would include candles and bubbles, unlike this one.

Today, I went to Plano for "on a whim" training with Lanny and the other new girls. We discussed Lanny's expectations of us and the tools we need to run our business. It was good, but we were there from 10-4:30 with a 1 ½ lunch and made it through three flipchart sheets and one product. We got off track because Lanny enjoys talking. He is a wonderful person with a good heart. It's hard for me to remain patient and attentive when things get sidetracked, though. That is the challenge I must overcome somehow. I was thinking about a letter I received yesterday, and I want to tell you I am so proud of you for taking the lead in your Bible study. It makes me smile and so happy. You have grown leaps and bounds in your walk with Christ and leading the study has made you even stronger. One day, we can lead a study at our house together either with friends or through the church. Leading a study is a goal of mine because I want to become strong and confident in God's Word. It is going to be so exciting to share our **faith** again. You are so strong, and I will be looking to you to help me reach the next level.

Did a little exercise at the gym today to get back on the horse after the marathon. My body feels good, but I'm taking it slow until next week when I'll begin lifting weights again. Hopefully, you got my card telling you about Spinal Concepts being bought by Abbott Labs. We'll be getting a check for $9,000 plus in a few weeks. We need to go to Europe when you come home. I'm going to talk with Lanny soon about our idea to feel him out. Then, I'll know better what to do about the job. How romantic! Europe! [We took that Europe trip in 2003 and was one of the best trips of our lives. We had extra money and didn't have to rough it in hostels. We had the Europass and traversed Germany, Austria,

Switzerland, and Italy. We met up with MAJ Lim and Lisa Lim in Venice, Italy, and hung out together. We even took a gondola ride together! The greatest part of the trip was our time in Cinque Terra, Italy along the Mediterranean coast. Trip of a lifetime before Laura and I began our life together!]

Patrick called this week, so we talked tonight. Sounds like his life is challenging. It was good to talk with him, though. Just need to stay calm and let things work themselves out. I've got to go to sleep. My dreams will be filled with you. I love you, honey.

June 5 War Day 76

Robert: *Got a letter from you yesterday dated 19 May and read your e-mail about your marathon accomplishment. I can't tell you how proud I am. I remember a girl who once told me she could never run a marathon and wanted to quit on long runs with me sometimes. Now, that same girl just finished a marathon and is talking about the next one she'll run with her husband! That cool girl is none other than Laura Payne, my hot wife. Of course, I'll run one with you. I think the Disney marathon in Jan would be awesome. We can recreate our engagement week. I'll certainly investigate Team in Training as well.*

Things here are not much different. Losing my desire and motivation to do anything. Haven't worked out in two days, don't play sports, and no reading because I finished the last "Left Behind" book I even have. Most of the day is spent sweating, something I have become proficient at because it is so hot. Sadly, we had to give the Proxima projector back to the battalion TOC because theirs blew up today. No more big-screen movies. Very sad! An omen to send us home?! LTC Towery said he doesn't see the need for us any longer and will brief the Brigade Commander this weekend. Hopefully, we can get some redeployment answers flowing. The best case scenario is home by the end of June and the worst case is probably mid-July. Better than we thought. Although the Brigade Commander could say he needs us for another mission, I pray that will not occur. Each day is getting a little bit harder to wake up. What is sad about all of this is the war and all our accomplishments seem such a distant memory. This idleness and monotony have completely overshadowed what we did here for our country. It was like we got left here and the Army and gov't. forgot about us. What we have done since we have been sitting here in Baghdad, Olympic Stadium, and the war we were in feel like two distinct memories. Dr. Kirk had it just right to get home when he did. Wonder if he got to ETS still because the stop-loss came out today and looks like my date is officially moved to Dec 20. He got reassigned to the hospital, so I'm sure it was easy then because he wasn't in a deployed unit afterward. I'm still going to do everything in my power to get out on time.

*I wish I had more to say, but things are really slow here. Luckily, I will get to e-mail and talk to you more frequently because of the civilian guys near, or at least that is the plan. We came up with a solution to our movie problem. We found a 20- or 25-inch computer monitor and hooked the DVD laptop through it. It is no movie projection theater, but good enough until we head home. Wanted to say thanks for working on a banner for us, but it isn't necessary because if everyone is like me, the only thing I'll be focused on is your beautiful face and eyes that I missed so much. Wish I could program myself to have wonderful dreams about you tonight. Miss you more every day. I **love** you with all my heart.*

June 6 War Day 77

Laura: *Good morning my sweet husband. I really don't feel like working today, but I have to and then stand in surgery with a very slow surgeon. I pray everything goes well. My attitude needs to change before I go, so my surgeon doesn't see me like this.*

Oh, I wanted to ask about your progress with your ETS date. I'll do whatever we need to do just to be with you, even move back to Killeen or Austin. I just want to be with you, honey. I've got to go to work. I'll talk to you soon. Have a wonderful day.

CHAPTER 25
COMMITMENT, PASSION, LOVE

June 8 War Day 79

Robert: *Sitting inside the DRASH trying to stay cool because it's got to be at least 110° heat index. A/C kind of works but not when it is really hot. Still sitting here sweating. Including a chapter from "The Purpose Driven Life" for you. It came at a time when the adversity and difficulty of being here were too much. Having to be away from you when our mission here is over and almost non-existent.*

LTC Miller made a reference today about having the available people from our team for surgery and I threw out my comment, "Oh we have the available people, it's called the 628th FST across the street!" Many chuckles from everyone around. Today we are waiting for LTC Towery to brief COL Grimsley on letting us go, so we hope it has word today or tomorrow. I haven't been letting LTC Miller's inability to communicate effectively and lack of evident motivation to get us home stop me from talking to the chain of command, making phone calls, and keeping the team informed. I think this week is crunch time and I'll do everything in my power to get answers on when we can redeploy.

MAJ Beverly's wife, Ronnie, just had a baby last night. Amen to them! Healthy eight-pound baby girl. Man, if I was stuck here and you were having our child, I don't know what I would do. Getting out of the Army should prevent it from ever happening. Need to get back home so we can practice for when we want to start making babies. Lots of practice to make up for, huh? Our bodies will go crazy when they make contact for the first time. Looking forward to our moment.

Everything will be exciting as we start over because it's like getting a second chance to make something perfect as a marriage knowing what we know from dating, our **faith**, and from this separation. What a blessing! I sat down and read through many of your letters today because I was missing you. Thank you so much for all you have written to me. It has made such a difference to me and my morale. You have been so wonderfully supportive and understanding. Hope I have been the same way through my letters. Our letters will be so neat to read through 10 or 20 years from now. They are so full of commitment, passion, and **love**. We can never allow ourselves to let go of it. Just like holding each other accountable to our **faith**, we have to hold each other accountable to our marriage and its focus on commitment, passion, sex, dating, listening, planning, and loving. I think we have a huge advantage at the beginning of our marriage most people don't. Realizing the importance of these emotions and faithfulness to one another because of this separation will make things so good for us as we start to grow together. Well, time for a little lunch.

8 p.m.: Just received the news that 3rd ID is releasing us! Now, there is light at the end of the tunnel. I think the best-case scenario is being home by the end of June and the worst-case the first or second week of July. The point is we should be home soon. It still

has to be run through the 1st Med Brigade and COL Hightower to get redeployment orders cut.

9 Jun 1100: Holy geez it is hot out here. It was wonderful to talk to you last night for as long as I did. What wonderful news about Spinal Concepts being bought out and the stock options money. What about all your friend's jobs? Do they still get to work there? The extra money will certainly come in handy. Hope we have quite a bit put back from all my extra deployment pay. By the way, my four-year mark hit last month boosting my pay by an extra $170 a month! If we manage our months right, we can have our first year of marriage debt-free, travel some, and save enough for a down payment on a home! What a blessing it would be.

Not much else to do here except wait for orders to head back. Fear still exists for the 1st Med BDE to screw us over, but I sincerely hope not since they should take care of us because we belong to them. My patience is running very thin.

I'm sure the weekend in Houston with everyone was a good time. I wish I could have shared it with you. I've missed a lot of stuff with you, huh? I'm so sorry. I **love** you.

June 11 War Day 82

Robert: *Received the package yesterday with my shoes and toiletries. Perfect timing as I had run out of clean 'n clear the day before. You are the greatest! We got word from the Med BDE they are briefing their higher Med BDE this weekend and we should get a final answer to our fate. Several things could occur: 1- we all go home, 2–they take a few personnel from us to fill holes with the other FSTs and send back the rest, or 3- give us a whole other mission elsewhere. I think they will get us home because we have been here since Feb and fought the war. If they don't, it is our people* from FT Hood screwing us over. I have been doing everything within my power to expedite this. Yesterday I even called the 1st Med BDE, got the S-3 (LTC McHugh) on the phone, and had SFC Smith go get LTC Miller and make him talk to him. [Small Army world moment in 2015 when I showed up to a new Army Reserve job at the Office of the Surgeon General in Falls Church, VA. I was assigned to the Medical Command Operations Center and reported to my boss...none other than COL McHugh, who I had known from Ft Hood and Iraq. It took me almost 10 minutes to make him understand I was not an active-duty officer any longer because I was in the Army Reserve. It was cool because I worked in that job and was able to attend his retirement ceremony. COL McHugh was an awesome guy and an excellent Army officer].

I can't sit idle and do nothing, but I'm sure you know that about me. Here's the flipside to all of this. Since we should know something by June 15. I went ahead and submitted my ETS exception to the policy packet to leave the country on June 20. Even if something happens to the team, hopefully, I can still get back and try to get out in August or sometime sooner than Dec. My branch manager, MAJ Alexander, knows I extended so I could come to war and that should count for something.

All in all, light is still at the end of the tunnel and it is always in God's hands. Got a call from my mom yesterday. Think she was really glad to hear from me. Although she had many great things to say and talk about, when I brought up the wedding, she referred to the cost! Alluding to the fact we could use some of our money being saved for it. I understand we will pitch in some, but we need our money for our life. The least they could do is handle their part of the wedding stuff. It's not like they haven't had five or six months to put any money back since I've been deployed! Got to go... heading to the Elka Hotel and Saddam Palace. Will get to e-mail and maybe a phone call to wake you up!

[For some reason I did not write about it in my letters, but this was the contract hotel for our DynCorp civilian friends we made. They had a team of medics who had come to our FST to see where the closest surgeons were. They offered us to come to their hotel to use their open satellite internet and cell phones. MAJ Lim was the leader in this effort, and we made several trips to the hotel until... on our last few trips there we hit a car traversing through the city but had to keep moving. Someone approached our convoy angrily and I had to raise my weapon to them to back off. After we were at the hotel a few times one day we were all typing happily, enjoying our hot Iraqi tea when we got shot at! Essentially it was a drive-by attack on the hotel and the contract Iraqi Security teams returned fire with their AK47s. We scrambled to the windows with our M16s but by that point, the insurgents had driven away. The windows were riddled with bullet holes, and we were all shaken. Luckily, everyone was okay. Ironically, for SPC Vasquez, it was the only day she felt comfortable joining us. I remember she was on the phone with her grandmother, whom she had not talked to since before the war began, and after she started the conversation, she had to tell her "Grandma, I gotta go, we are getting shot at" and then hung up. Luckily, she was able to contact her and tell her she was okay, but it was a funny war story for sure. Needless to say, we had to promise the DynCorp contractors we would not come back to the hotel again and bring undue attention because of our vehicles and uniforms. I think the DynCorp contractors ended up having to find another location after that shooting. Oops!].

2044: Got to talk to you for 30 minutes this afternoon and send you a beat greet! Showed Dr. Lim how to send one to his wife. It is a warm memory to think back to when we used to send them to each other so often. Sorry, since we talked today most of what I told you on the phone was in this letter.

Most of the afternoon was spent playing Yahtzee. Going to watch "American Outlaws" for tonight's movie.

2330: Pretty entertaining to talk about Jessie James. Didn't work out or run today. Haven't been too consistent because the heat just drains you during the day. Mostly work out every other day. Running in my shoes was great, thank you! About to sleep into another day. Can't wait to see you again. I **love** you.

CHAPTER 26
WHAT WILL OUR LIFE LOOK LIKE?

June 12 War Day 83

Robert: *Not much to say about things going on here but had to take the time to write since I received three Laura letters today, dated May 4, 11, and 29 each letter expressed so much* **love** *to me. Your pure, unconditional, loving heart shows through to me in all your words. I feel just as you do how God has blessed me so much with you in my life. I didn't think I could find someone who could* **love** *me as much as I could, but God is so great He gave me someone who* **loves** *me more than I could have ever hoped for. Your heart for me makes me* **love** *you more and more every day. I just have to praise God every day for you. I could not have ever done this deployment and remained sane without you. You are my perfect angel to spend all the time here on earth with me until we meet again in eternity. As long as we praise Jesus for our salvation,* **love** *Him, serve Him, and praise Him to others; we can one day spend eternity together! Perfect eternity. We have so much to look forward to; marriage, children, grandkids, traveling, careers, buying a home, buying cars, planning, growing old together, and then eternity with Christ.*

*Haven't asked if you got "The Purpose Driven Life" book yet? I am almost finished with it. What a wonderful book. Makes me think more about my Christian life and the improvements I need to make. Something we can certainly work on together; is accountability partners. Who is better than your best friend? About to eat some lunch. I finally broke down and am about to eat an Iraqi marinated beef wrap. Everyone else on the team has been eating them for the past two weeks and no one has died, so I hope it is safe. If not, you know I **love** you! Saj Al Reef is the name of the sandwich guy in case I die later. It was pretty good.*

Now I am sitting on our patio with our surgeons, MAJ Kuhns, and SFC Smith... just sweating. About every 10 minutes I think the heat is brought up in a conversation. It is averaging 115°-120° a day. I thought Texas was hot.

I checked on my 'release from active duty' memo I had to get scanned and e-mail to 1st Med BDE along with two forms needing the commander's signature. Well, I got it all done and e-mailed it to the 1st Med BDE S1, MAJ Cook, and he wrote back saying the scan has a small portion of LTC Miller signature cut so I need to fix it. Can you believe it? Do they know where I am? Anyway, working on getting it fixed. No word on my early release of June 20th. If they did release me, it would be unfortunate to get back on 29 or 30 June because if I am still here on 1 July, we get all the entitlements. Won't turn it down.

So many uncertainties here and at home for us. The only thing to do is pray and have patience for His purpose. Easier said than done sometimes. Again, thank you for everything you are and for the man you make me. I miss you so much.

Laura: *Thoughts of you make my world so bright. You make me feel so loved even from miles away. You have written so many letters filled with such **love** and passion. It will be such a magical*

What Will Our Life Look Like?

*day when we are reunited and can share our physical connection again. It has been so much fun to see us fall in **love** in another way, through letters. I feel like we have made the best of the situation. Hopefully, you have felt the tremendous amount of **love** I have for you through my letters. I went to Killeen today. I miss that town. It was always our place we could go to and be completely alone and just relax. But it was a sad day because I went to Sergio's grandfather's funeral. I am so glad I could be there for Sergio. His mom loved getting a letter from you and she gave me a big, warm hug.*

*So, are you home yet? No… that sucks! I miss you. I **love** how you said you miss my smile. makes me feel so good. Robert, I will always have it for you. I remember the poem you wrote at Christmas about my missing smile. It hit home and just kind of confirmed how I had been feeling. I didn't like not being happy because you didn't deserve the effect it had on us. Never fear because you made it all better. You gave me the best present ever. You for a lifetime! Robert, I **love** how you want to take care of me and you proved once again you are committed to making me happy. I want to make you happy always and forever. You are such an amazing man. I can't believe how lucky I am to have you. Thank you for just being you… loving, compassionate, romantic, understanding, patient, intelligent, caring, respectful, adventurous, sexy, and the list goes on. I'm looking forward to hearing your voice again soon (I hope)! My heart aches without you. I miss you so much! I **love** you!*

Laura's Card: *This is just a little card to say I love you. I am so thankful to God for you. You have made my world so much brighter over the past two years. You **love** life so much which has been an inspiration to me. I **love** how you have such strong friendships and a close relationship with your family. God blessed you with such an amazingly kind spirit. You have allowed me to open* up and be the person I always knew I could be. You taught me three little words can make all the difference to someone. I miss so many things about you already. Your laugh, your smile, your voice, your chest (where my head fits perfectly), your arms (for those big hugs), your touch… I just miss you! **Love** you. Please be safe and come home soon! We have a wonderful life ahead of us, and a beautiful family to make. I **love** you honey with every piece of my heart! I wish you were here!

Laura: This card is funny. Anyway, I'm not even sure you'll get this card, but I'm sending it anyway. I've been praying every day for your team to get good news saying you're coming home, and you can fly out of Iraq. You deserve it after all you have endured the past five months. The thought you may be home in a few weeks makes me so happy. I feel as though I didn't express my excitement to you on the phone. It felt like I shouldn't because I didn't want to feel sad like I did before when they changed their minds. I am soooo excited and am relying on God to make it happen.

In the letter I received today, you mentioned getting away for a weekend when you get back. Don't worry many friends understand we need to be alone and not to smother us because we've been apart so long. I'm planning to have a welcome home party where they can see you without us having to travel all over Texas or be swarmed with visitors. Many people **love** you though, so we'll need to decide what you want, and we'll stick by it. I think people should come to see us, but that's just an opinion.

Went to dinner last night with Mike D, Todd, Owen, Rina, and Jen. We had a good time. Rina has planned my bachelorette party for July 25-27 [We ended up doing joint bachelor and bachelorette parties in New Orleans and it was awesome. We had two nights separate and then combined the parties the last night where I finally found Laura singing karaoke in the Cat's Meow!].

It sounds so awesome; she has done a lot of planning. I told her you wanted to put in some special requests for the lingerie shower. Rina suggested I register somewhere like Frederick's. Do you want to help me, or would you rather my lingerie be a surprise? Not much else happening, just missing you, Robert. I can't wait for Team Payne to be reunited. I love you!

June 15 War Day 86

Robert: *Still here. Still hot. Still boring. Still sucks. Been trying to burn your CDs but my laptop sucks. Still praying for an end in sight. Been trying to work on my release and my ETS date. I know it will work out. I miss you so much it hurts. You are everything to me and I can't wait to get home and give you the world. I **love** you.*

CHAPTER 27
HEADING HOME

June 16 War Day 87

Robert: *Just received a letter from 4 Jun, which took only 12 days! Still no definitive answers on returning, but hopefully the FST will get released or Friday my ETS date will get me home. I read in your letter about your excitement growing in our **faith** together and I certainly want it for us both. I would **love** to first take our steps together by going through "The Purpose Driven Life." I think it puts some great perspective and guidance to the development of our walk with Christ. Have you found any churches you like in Fort Worth/Dallas? Have you been going? Makes me wonder if Lake Hills is important enough to make going back to Austin an even stronger consideration. Want to get into a consistent Bible group and some type of ministry. Eventually, I want to work towards having our own Bible study group and going on mission trips together. That would be great.*

Sounds like you like the Europe idea. I know I like it too, or maybe Australia? Something to keep in consideration. The only limitation would be having a place to stay until we would take off. Don't let me forget about asking Owen about his place during the week. If we wanted to do this, we would have to begin planning as soon as we decided, and I would go on leave right away. We could do our apartment shopping before we leave and set the move-in date for when we get back.

Nice to know Patrick called. He hasn't written, though. Funny how we always got along so well since our personalities are so different. Guess childhood friendships can work through it, though. Well, about to work out for a bit. Been doing abs, pushups, pullups, and running about every one to two days. Haven't run more than four miles so you'll probably kick my butt when I return.

2153: Laura… we just got released! We are heading home. I wish I could scream to you right now. COL Hightower told us to redeploy with the 3rd FSB. Have no idea if it means we'll end up in Savannah, GA, or not but who cares, it is the United States and not this craphole! What happens now is we will head back south to Kuwait with one of the companies from 3rd FSB to Camp Pennsylvania, where we were initially. No, telling you how long we'll be there, but I'm guessing a few weeks. I'll be home in July sometime.

I feel better because now I will get to redeploy with the FST and not on my own. Guess I had always envisioned marching into the gym back at Hood, in uniform, with the FST. On my own would be me in civilian clothes like Sergio came back. I want my last real Army memory coming home back to you with the guys I went to war with. Sadly, though, we will have to give back CPT Holcek and CPT Kuhens (the borrowed guys) to their combat support hospital. Wish we could take them home with us as they are stellar guys. Rob Holcek and I have become pretty good buds. We have been running together and share a common bond of Louisiana and playing Yahtzee. Please pray for both and their families. Today, Rob and I ran only two miles, and were smoked! I have never been so exhausted after two miles, but then we looked at the thermometer and it was 100° at 8 p.m! We didn't even notice because it is 120° during the day. [I remember that late evening I woke up in my sleep and had to run extremely fast to pick up the water cans we used to flush the porcelain toilets we had access to at the Olympic Stadium. Because the water system was not back online, we realized we could flush the toilets with a lot of water, so we used water cans. I was clearly dealing with heat exhaustion, which was causing my explosive heat-related diarrhea! It is comical thinking back to when I had to dress, grab water cans, and run across the field to the toilets near our DRASH. Almost as if it were a prediction of the future of the Army Combat Fitness test carrying water cans!]

Looking forward to the bearable Texas heat! Things we must do are spend alone time initially, eat at all my favorite restaurants, ride around with the top down to the park, go drinking and dancing all night in Austin, and float the river with all our friends. Would **love** a weekend at some point in the summer with everyone camping and floating. [We had an amazing weekend when I returned where many close friends came together in San Marcos, TX for us to all float the Comal River together and enjoy great food and drinks]. Do not think even for one second you are not a priority. You and our time together supersede everything else. Laura, you are my wife, my best friend, my soulmate, and nothing comes before you except God. It excites me to no end to realize I get to provide and care for you forever! It makes me smile just thinking about it. Listening to some rave music now. Also, makes me want to go to a club and dance with you like at Red Jacket or like we have in New Orleans! We danced so well together. Guess that is where the spark initiated itself, huh? I'll never forget you telling me you had never danced with anyone like we did before at the Amazon (Austin, TX).

Had a good talk with MAJ Lim today about him and Lisa. He shares similar excitement about getting back to his new wife. Although initially, it was a bit rough because in April her ex-husband committed suicide over his failing life and losing her. Whoa! That is quite a lot to deal with on your own. Sounds like things are okay with everything now.

Just found out that LTC Miller would like me to go down early to Kuwait with a small group to find us a place to sleep, where we go, etc. I'm game. Just hope it isn't a waste of time. There is certainly a little more light at the end of the tunnel now. Continue to pray and hopefully, you will be seeing me soon after receiving this letter. I miss you and **love** you.

June 21 War Day 92

Robert: Sitting here for the second day in Camp NY, Kuwait. Feel much more at ease and out of harm's way. Got here with an advance party early to find us a tent and start working on redeployment issues. I was in an HMMWV with the Bco 1SG and five other HMMWVs with the Command SGM leading the pack. Which we found maybe wasn't the best idea as he went the wrong way twice, one time almost taking us into Al Nasiriyah… a city not kind to soldiers, even now. We turned around and went the right way. We also needed to stop to find a tire for the flat the SGM had. No one brought a spare, so we had to go find one. Turned out to be a good break for lunch and a nap in the shade, since we had left at 2 a.m. By 5 p.m. the next day, we had finally made it to Camp New York.

As soon as we hit the Kuwait border, the sandstorms began. Boy, I did not miss that. It was also about 10° hotter so the wind was slapping me in the face. It was so painful. Almost two miles *away another vehicle had a flat, while we were towing a broken-down one. Once we finally got here, we moved into a few tents and waited until the next morning to move folks around. My main concern was to get just one tent for us, and I succeeded. Then, as I went to eat dinner, I saw a III Corps Patch on a soldier (from Ft Hood) and asked them what they were doing there. She told me they ran the Soldier Personnel Center which hooked me up with a POC who got us in today once the team arrived, not to mention the use of a phone to contact the III Corps Redeployment Ops Center to ask questions.*

Also, the two lawyers next to me struck up a conversation and I got to use the internet and e-mail you to let you know I'm safe. Was getting worried last night about the team because they were supposed to arrive in the evening. I didn't see them until noon today because their convoy stopped to sleep. So, I had this whole twenty-man tent to myself. Had some awesome thoughts of you and me together here. I can't wait to touch your beautiful, soft, sweet-smelling, hot body.

We have a lot to figure out with our lives, huh? **Proverbs 3:5-6** *says, "Lean not on your own understanding, love God with all your heart and in all ways acknowledge Him, and He will make your paths straight."* [**Insight:** *A right path is a righteous path...going the right way and not my way...the wrong way. When I acknowledge Him in all things, He is my focus...I am focusing not on the problem but on the Problem Solver!"*] *I think that is right. My first memorized verse. I think staying in Dallas, continuing working, finding a place, and maybe Australia or Europe for the honeymoon after the wedding. You could quit before the wedding if necessary. It would be kind of like continuing with our plans before. It will be interesting to see where and what we are doing 6 months from now. If we made a grand trip like that for* our honeymoon, we have two things in our favor: 1. Saving more money and 2. Planning more appropriately. No matter where we go or what we do, we have to go somewhere and stay in one place the first week to enjoy just being together.

As for now, I have to work on getting us home! Hopefully... the ideal situation... is leaving on 1 July because then we get the incentive pay and make it home on the 4th of July! Wouldn't that be cool? Guess time will tell. I love you so much and miss you.

June 25 War Day 96

Robert: Wanted to take the time to write you a letter even though I can't mail it. Today is my birthday and I am in Kuwait. I am certainly sad to turn twenty-seven without you here with me. I know you would have something really special planned because you are so loving and wonderful to me. I have the most wonderful birthday gift I have ever had, my beautiful wife Laura at home waiting for me. You weren't my wife this time last year, so you're my wonderful birthday gift today! Guess we might be able to celebrate a joint birthday by the time I get home. I pray I am home by your birthday. Something is messed up if not. But again, only take one day at a time here. I just put my **faith** in His patience for a purpose and remain optimistic you'll be back in my arms in July sometime.

This morning, we started the first cleaning process with our DRASH tents. Had to wake up at 5 a.m. just so it was cool enough. It was fun to play and clean around the water. I am more relaxed and myself around everyone. Guess I know when I get back, I won't be working with any of these folks so I can let up on my professionalism a bit. Also, the imminent war threat doesn't exist any longer, so just trying to make the best of things and if I can make people smile while doing it, then so be it. Guess it is God's gift to me. Maybe being a comedian to the Christian community is what I can do to share my gift. Guess I would have to get better at writing material, etc. If I could combine making people laugh and smile with praising God, I think I would **love** it.

I heard MAJ Kirk and his family made it off to Kentucky this week. Guess we'll have to visit them one day when we visit Jason G. LTC Miller continues to be something else. He certainly is not Dr. Kirk. LTC Miller tends to think he has all the answers, yet he has never been, nor does he continue to be as proactive as he needs to be to get us home. That doesn't stop me from handling things myself. Get this… when the FST finally got to Kuwait, he met a civilian friend of his who used to be in the Army with him. Well, the first night we were here, he stayed in Kuwait City with him in his hotel, showed up the next morning with his Chili's doggie bag from his dinner the night before, and made us late for an appointment at another camp to discuss redeployment. Then, after he tries to talk over me and MAJ Kuhns. When we were talking to team movement contacts, he would interrupt us. Later that evening, he expressed when we are in a room with him, he wants to be the only one talking to others, unless he or they address us for info he doesn't know. Can you believe the arrogance? He doesn't know the first thing about command, and looking out for his soldiers, but what is bad is that he thinks he does.

Since this is the only time, I'll have to work with him and he'll be signing off on all my leave, I won't stir the pot with him. I have already made my opinion known to him on how he needs to communicate better with the team. I told him one day how even the little info on redeployment we have, the team needs to hear it. I recommended a team meeting, but he said it wasn't necessary since there wasn't anything new. I disagreed and told him to keep the confidence of his soldiers, they needed to hear it from him as the commander. He said (to me and SFC Smith) "You guys pass it around." Then, when I (or SFC Smith) talk in front of the team, he interrupts. Ahhh... I have vented.

Time for some lunch now. I miss you so much, wish we could share my birthday. **Love** you.

June 27 War Day 98

Robert: Things here are certainly progressing each day, very little to do with the commander's help, yours truly, and MAJ Kuhns. I would say we are at 50 percent solution to get home now. We finally decided on a sea redeployment of all our equipment rather than waiting on the approval for a C-5 to carry everything. We will be called down to a port to load our vehicles on a boat with a big container for all our crap. I had to go find us one of the containers because LTC Miller left it in the hands of the 3rd FSB and they were dragging their feet. At this point, waiting is not an option. I found a unit from Ft Carson getting rid of some. I let LTC Miller go ask their Commander for it even though she was a Captain like me. You have to make him feel like he is contributing in some way. Tomorrow, we are loading our stuff and by Monday we'll be pretty much ready and wait to be called to Camp Doha or Arifjan to load the boat and wait to get on a plane. My vision of seeing your beautiful face is going to happen within the month. Hopefully, by the time you read this letter. It would be cool if I were right next to you as you're reading this letter.

It has been so good to talk with you on the phone out here for longer periods. Rob Lim brought up Lisa and you talking, so I gave him your cell number to pass on. Plus, if you guys get to know each other a bit, it could make a little vacation to Tahoe later in the year more fun with all of us knowing one another. Maybe it will work out. I have to go drop off a parts request.

2103: Just got back from another lengthy dinner. Most of the meals I have been eating here at Camp NY take about 1 to 2 hours because we just sit there talking and eating ice cream.

Got to talk with you for almost 40 minutes tonight which makes me so happy. I like the fact we are talking consistently so we can be familiar with each other's lives once I get back. Plus, it is just wonderful to hear your voice. Just talking to you and thinking about you makes me feel like I did when we first fell in **love**. It is like getting to re-experience falling in **love** all over again but having the good fortune to know you're already in **love** and I know the outcome. It's just so neat to have such an indescribable feeling of completeness and comfort only a soulmate can provide. The kind of feeling God intended me to experience.

I got you a DCU hat made in honor of Team Payne that will serve as a good float the river or ride with the top down in the Jeep hat. It'll match my DCU beanie hat I have to wear every day out here, except yours outranks mine.

Tomorrow, we pack all our stuff in a container, and on Sunday this big machine will come to pick it up and move it to an area for movement coordinated by yours truly. We have hit a small speedbump, but we are going to call an LTC guy we met on the way down here who is in charge of the entire redeployment operations cell at night. Time to pull out the connections and see what that gets us. He flew into Kuwait with us on the way down because he knew MAJ Kuhns. Hopefully, home will be in sight soon because I miss you so. I **love** you. [I think fondly of my time working the re-deployment with MAJ Bill Kuhns as the Unit Movement Officer. When we would hit road bumps or have time time to kill, we would end up having a coffee together at the 'Green Bean' coffee shack at Camp Doha. If it had not been for MAJ Kuhn's efforts, the 126th FST would have not been redeployed when it did from the war. MAJ Bill Kuhns was an amazing man, and I am so proud to have called him my friend during Iraqi Freedom].

July 6 War Day 106

Robert: Sorry it has been a while since I have written, but since the end of June I have been busy with redeployment stuff, Plus, I have had the good fortune to e-mail and call you fairly regularly. It has been so wonderful to hear your voice and laughter. By the time you are reading this, God should have me back in your life for you to grab, hold, hug, kiss, and **love** on.

We were in Camp NY the last few days trying to get some sort of resolution on everything. Even headed up to Camp Virginia again to get run around in circles. Finally, this one Major after being told our saga several times, and getting many of our persistent calls, recommended we go back to Camp Doha and begin pushing it ourselves. With patience and optimism, MAJ Kuhns and I set out a day earlier than the team to begin coordination to find a place to live.

I was able to talk to you last when I called the first night in Doha. The first two days were so painful and frustrating. Either we were dealing with civilians or Army folks in starched uniforms who had been in Doha the whole war. Most of them did not share the same concern about getting home as we did. I never lost my temper with anyone, but I did express my displeasure with the service and attention a few times because they had not been to the actual war.

In one office we visited today, we had to schedule some movement equipment, but they did the wrong thing on the paperwork.

Then they gave me a customer satisfaction form after they were an hour late moving something for us. Someone even called me back over the issue and my complaint claiming I was a bit rude to his employees. I explained I was and had good reason. Switch the roles and maybe they would understand. I'll raise my voice, get rude, or kick somebody if it means getting home to you!

All our equipment and vehicles were taken to the port today. We have nothing to do now except load a plane. The problem now is getting confirmed on one. Thought I might make it back for Mike D's wedding, but not likely. Even if I come back before, it might be the tenth, but I would want to be away from everyone and alone with you. I think about you so much. It is so surreal to me to know seeing you soon is a reality. We have some big decisions in front of us, but let God lead as you have said.

*With little time to relax, I have been eating or watching movies. They have a small movie theater and café place which plays movies. There is a nice gym I haven't used! The night before last saw Arnold Schwarzenegger and took a pic with him and a group of folks. Can be viewed on www.uso.org (I think). As I sleep to thoughts of you tonight, I pray I'm next to you within the week (by 12 Jul)!! Miss you and **love** you.*

July 13 War Day 113

Robert: *Within the next 24 hours I will be home safely, back in your life as before. I purchased this card days ago intending to write my last letter to you from this deployment. The letters I have written over the last 6 months will serve as a great diary of my experience before, during, and after combat, but more importantly, a true testament to God's hand in our life and the amazing **love** we share. At this moment, I am sitting in Frankfurt,*

Germany, after the first leg of our flight home. When you read this, I will be home with you. We will have shared moments we will never forget as we have reunited after the tough separation. God was with us throughout this and certainly showed us a **love** we both possess even stronger than I ever imagined. We have a lot in front of us to sort through and plan. We will never have to make decisions alone and all our experiences will be shared. I can't begin to explain how comforting it is to my heart. This separation has even further proved to me what an amazing woman you are and how truly blessed I am to call you my wife. If I haven't said enough, thank you for everything you did while I was away. It was a difficult time and you handled everything so well. There are no words to express my gratitude for your unconditional support, (and missing you!) loving (and numerous) letters, packages, and handling of all the life issues I left behind with you. You truly are a strong woman who made these past six months bearable for me. I could not have made it through this without you.

By now, we have gotten to be alone and away from others (hopefully at 7F Lodge as I planned). I have missed holding you, kissing you, and making **love** to you more than anything in my life. Without physical contact with you, I feel quite empty. Now we have the opportunity to re-experience many things all over again knowing what we already know. There is so much to look forward to with our wedding, new home, honeymoon, new careers, and ultimately raising our children together. You will be such an amazing mother. I know without a doubt God intended for us to share our lives and raise a family.

As silly as you may think I am, I have fully realized what you being my true soulmate means. No one could ever fill the emptiness I felt being away from you while I was out here. I can tell you since it is all over now, but those times in which I wondered if I *was going to come home, my **faith** in God and the fact I had the opportunity to meet, fall in **love**, and marry my soulmate comforted me in such a way, I had little fear of death. I already believe I have been allowed to have you in my life most people never get in their relationships.*

*Now I begin the closing in a long series of letters that have probably expressed every emotion I possess and my unconditional **love** for you. Hopefully, this experience will always make me realize how fortunate and truly blessed I am by giving me such a wonderful and beautiful wife, great friends, a loving family, and the opportunity to live in the greatest country in the world. We are all so lucky.*

*Also, learning the full strength of God's power and control in our lives is something I will continue to use to strengthen our family. "Patience for His Purpose" will be a common theme for Team Payne through the wonderful times and the tough ones. In short, I **love** you more than anything. Thank You, God, for bringing me back to you!*

Chapters 21-26 Personal Observations

At some point, I knew the journey was over and I had survived. I don't remember when that was but as I re-read these letters, I think it was somewhere around the time I crossed back into Kuwait. As I reexamine my experience about love, faith, and war, I realize it was truly a moment in time guided by God's hand. And for some, many never came home, and I trust that was God's will as well, because how else can I or any other veteran rationalize why I came home, and my other brothers and sisters of service did not?

One commonality of these letters is intense heat. Yes, I pray I never endure the type of heat I experienced in Iraq and Kuwait. At times it was like sticking your head in a microwave and throwing sand at your face. It all started at the Olympic Stadium where the heat was so intense, we felt like frogs in boiling water, not even noticing that 100 degrees were extreme. Ironically, the next place I lived after I re-deployed and Laura and my life began was Tucson, AZ. If there was a location on earth like the heat of Iraq and Kuwait it would be Tucson, AZ! The other biggest challenge of this time was monotony and waiting for re-deployment orders. It was quite a challenge because we had been operating at such an extreme tempo to prep to deploy, train while in Kuwait, get to Baghdad, and then the tempo slowed to a crawl halfway through the deployment. The uncertainty of when and if we would go home was very difficult to process. That is why I felt for so many after me whose deployments were for over a year. But because ours involved a war, what ultimately was only 6 months, felt like 6 years. Also, my deepest empathy went out to the 1st Armored Division that followed us because they were left in the theater for almost 18 months while the insurgency started.

It was a comforting feeling for me Laura had Team in Training and the marathon to train for while I was away. A marathon is quite a lengthy endeavor and was ideal for someone back at home managing the stress of their husband away at war who may never come home. I was so proud of her accomplishment and what she was able to do in completing her first marathon. Endurance events like races and triathlons became a part of our marriage together...until the kids came along and then our life changed forever.

Closing Thoughts

On January 3rd, 2023, as I write this Laura and I celebrated our 20th wedding anniversary. We have four amazing blessings from God…ages 13, 10, 7, and 4. I have been in the Army for 24 years and served as a Special Agent for 19 years between the DEA and FBI. But it has all come at a cost. Beginning a marriage with war is not ideal. There were many unrealized repercussions from war, but I am thankful to God we are still together. We have and continue to have tough times, but the passion described in these letters translates to perseverance and dedication to God's will through His ordained marriage. Rest assured, as I read these letters, I have failed many times in honoring this commitment to love God and Laura above anything and it makes me sad. I can often be the very best Army Reserve Colonel and FBI Executive but stumble again and again as the best husband and father. Life is hard and marriage can be even harder. Adding children, although wonderful and the best thing in life, makes the marriage even more stressful and tough as you drift from one another. To endure, to sustain, and to love requires a never-quit mentality and faith.

In my opinion, had we not had our faith, we may not still be together to this day having survived war, infertility, demanding careers, and limited family support as we have moved around the US. Yet, that is the beauty of His will and grace that he can sustain us through the challenges and obstacles of life. Although this compilation of letters, with context, is for our children, their children, and their children to know us. There is an unedited version of all the letters should it ever be handed down throughout our family. This compilation of our letters portrays the story of how to sustain marriage and love, and how one must make an active decision daily to love God and their spouse, all the while knowing it will never be perfect and as passionate as it was when it starts, like in these letters. This story is an amazing reminder to never forget the foundation of faith the marriage was built upon and the tremendous love and passion that started it all. For these reasons, I love Laura will all my heart, so thankful for her, and how our marriage and life together began within a **Story of Love, War & Faith.**

Final Words

We wanted to encourage you and other veterans with Scriptures and Insights that you can declare, write down in a journal, and simply remember when you are in one of life's **war**s that requires all the **love** and **faith** you can muster. Remember that when you pray, God will supply all the **love**, **faith**, hope, courage, compassion, and boldness you will need to endure.

Trust what God is saying to you…

LOVE

"So **love** the Lord God
with all your passion and prayer and intelligence
and energy....'
Love others as well as you **love** yourself."
(Mark 1:30-31 MSG)

WAR

"And everyone assembled here will know that the Lord rescues
his people,
but not with a sword and spear.
This is the Lord's battle,
and he will give you[victory over our enemies] to us!"
(1 Samuel 17:27 MSG)

FAITH

" For I know the plans I have for you," declares the Lord,
"plans to prosper you and not to harm you,
plans to give you hope and a future.
Then you will call upon me and come and pray to me,
and I will listen to you.
You will seek me and find me when you seek me with all
your heart."
(Jeremiah 29:11-14 NIV)

phantomfast2003@gmail.com

John 15:13

**In their memory
3rd Infantry Division's Killed in Action
2003 Iraqi Freedom Invasion**

Capt. James F. Adamouski

Capt. Tristan N. Aitken

Spc. Edward J. Anguiano

Pfc. Wilfred D. Bellard

Staff Sgt. Stevon A. Booker

Spc. Matthew G. Boule

Sgt. Henry L. Brown

Staff Sgt. George E. Buggs

Pfc. Michael R. Creighton-Weldon

Spc. Daniel F. Cunningham Jr.

Cpl. Michael E. Curtin

Staff 1st Class Wilbert Davis

1st Sgt. Joe J. Garza

Chief Warrant Officer Erik A. Halvorsen

Staff Sgt. Terry W. Hemingway

Staff Sgt. Lincoln D. Hollinsaid

Pfc. Gregory P. Huxley Jr.

Chief Warrant Officer Scott Jamar

Pvt. Devon D. Jones

1st Lt. Jeffrey J. Kaylor

Capt. Edward J. Korn

Sgt. 1st Class John W. Marshall

Pfc. Jason M. Meyer

Pfc. Anthony S. Miller

Spc. George A. Mitchell

Sgt. Michael F. Pedersen

Pvt. Kelley S. Prewitt

Spc. Gregory P. Sanders

Pfc. Diego F. Rincon

Final Words

Chief Warrant Officer Eric A. Smith

Sgt. 1st Class Paul R. Smith

Sgt. Roderic Solomon

Staff Sgt. Robert A. Stever

Sgt. Eugene Williams

Captain Robert D. Payne
United States Army
Operation Iraqi Freedom 2003

Phantom FaST

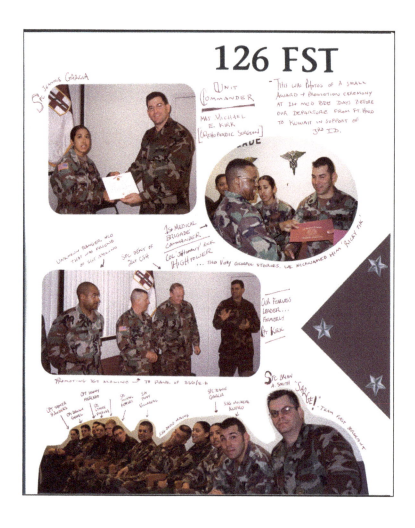

Final Words

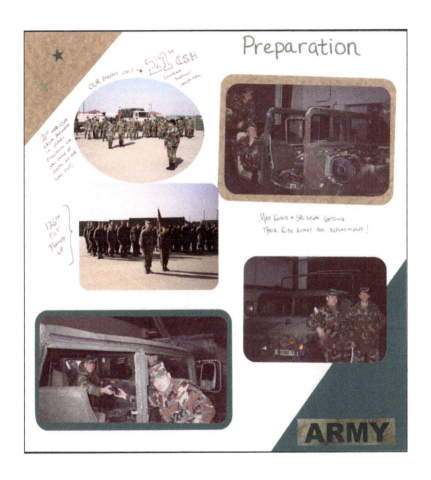

Phantom Fast

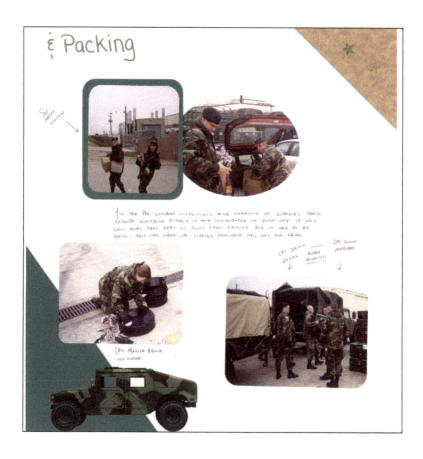

Phantom Fast

Final Words

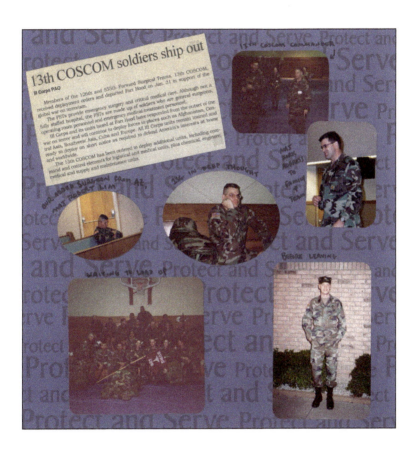

Phantom Fast

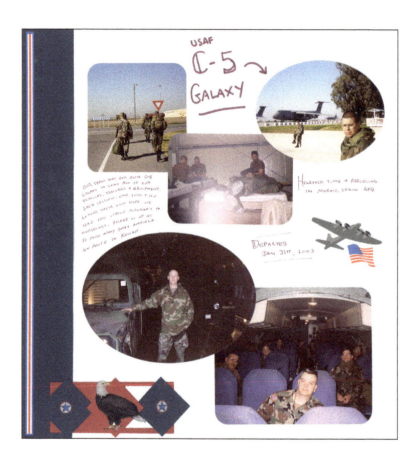

Final Words

Phantom FaST

Final Words

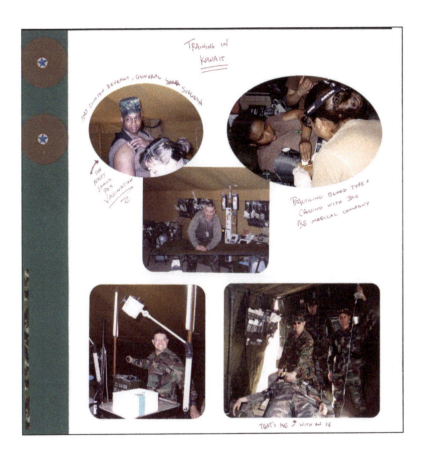

Phantom Fast

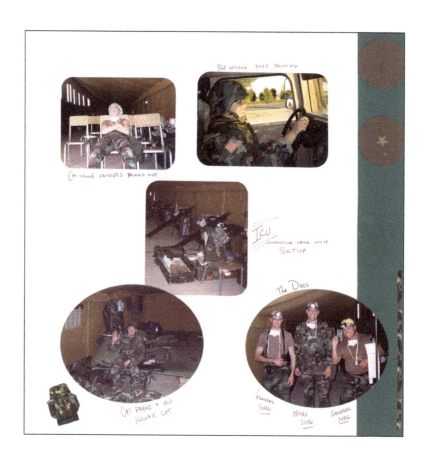

Final Words

Phantom Fast

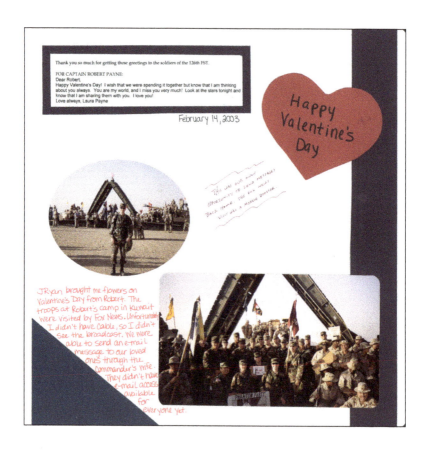

Final Words

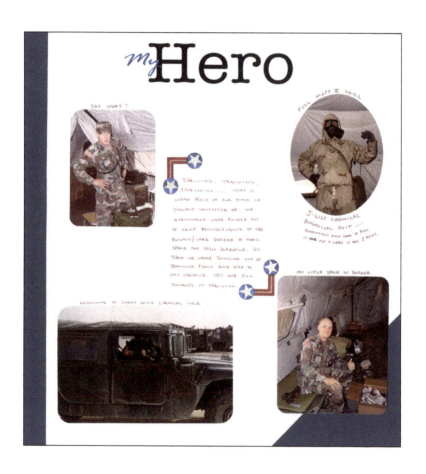

Final Words

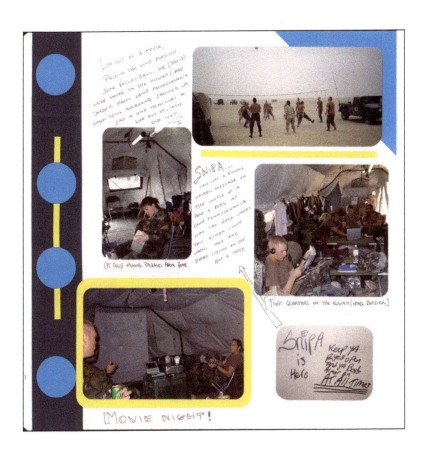

287

Phantom Fast

Final Words

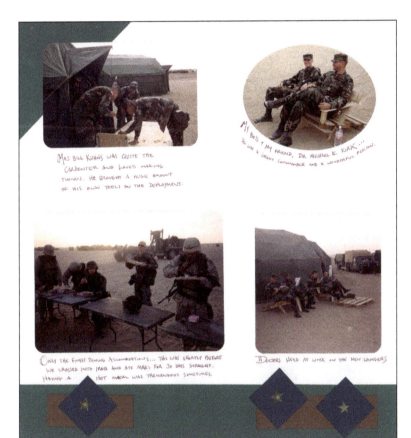

Phantom Fast

Final Words

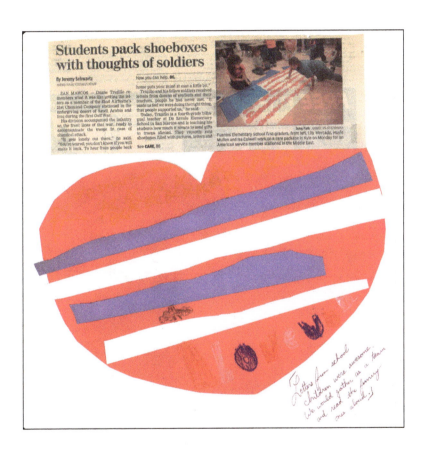

Letters from school children were awesome. We would gather as a team and read the funny ones aloud. :)

Phantom Fast

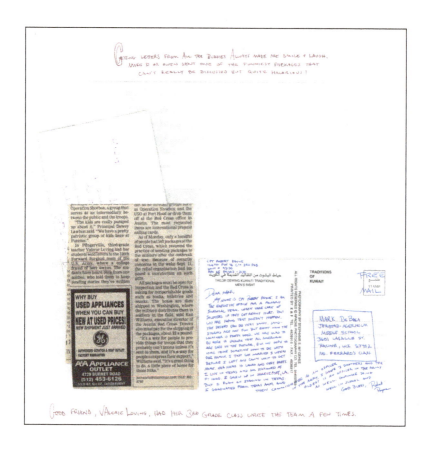

Final Words

SUPPORT FROM HOME MADE ALL THE DIFFERENCE...

Texas Aggie Corps of Cadets Association

6 MAY 03

Howdy!

Hope all is well on the front lines of democracy and freedom! I am sitting at home today recovering from a nasty bought of strep throat. I still can't believe that I came down with it. Karin and Alex had it first. I think it is the first time I have had strep throat in nearly 23 years. I thought I had developed an immunity to it because of all of our strep illnesses during childhood. I guess I have some protection because my throat never really gets that sore like it does for everyone else. Still, this one packed a nasty punch. Felt like shooting myself. My legs were aching terribly. Feel better now. I think the antibiotics are kicking in.

Just finished with a rough few weeks. We had a major 4th Region Command Inspection on 30 APR. We came out pretty good considering our severe manpower shortages. Just wish I had not put in some seriously long hours in CI prep. I am in the doghouse with Karin. This was followed by our Joint Awards Ceremony and Joint Military Ball with the Air Force ROTC. Took my record APFT on Monday – yep, I made a 274 (no laughing). Maxed everything but the run. Old age and laziness is getting to me. Anyway, all of this was packed into one "hell" week. Now I am sick to top it off. Please pray for me and my sanity.

We went home for Easter. Had a good visit. Would you believe Joel was reading the 40 days of Purpose book? Karin and I had a chance to talk to him about it. Hopefully, God is working on him. Now Dad on the other hand, I worry about. Looks as if GE will offer him an early retirement sometime this summer. He is staring the prospect of retirement in the face. Strangely enough, despite all of groaning over the

Phantom FaST

My driver throughout Iraqi Freedom, SPC Michael Peppers, whose wife was also Laura. We dubbed our vehicle appropriately "Laura 4" because we were PDT 4.

The anesthesia set up for the operating room.

The EMT or ICU recovery set up.

Practicing IV's on OU Savage. SPC Lundy doing the stick was an OR tech so didn't normally do IV's.

Final Words

Phantom Fast

Final Words

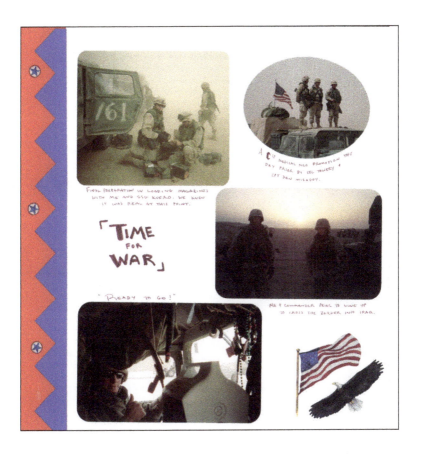

Phantom Fast

• We knew the order was coming the day prior but I actually heard the details on BBC radio.

Final Words

Phantom Fast

Final Words

Phantom FaST

Final Words

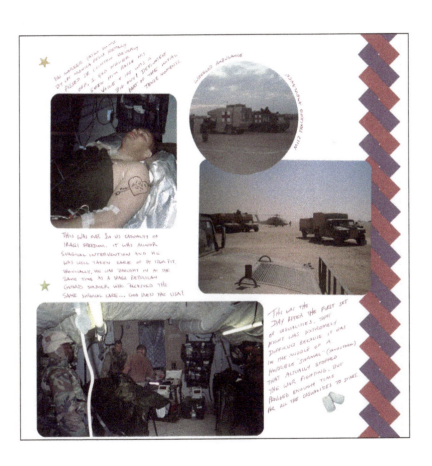

303

Phantom Fast

Final Words

Phantom Fast

Final Words

Phantom FaST

Final Words

Phantom Fast

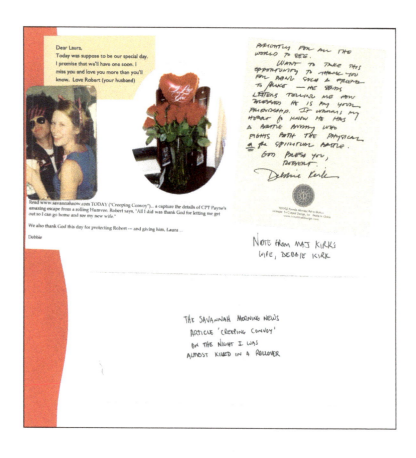